A
FULL
PLATE

Anna Kirkpatrick

Fulton Books, Inc.
Meadville, PA

Published by Fulton Books 2020

Whereas many of the names have been changed and some particulars altered out of respect and sensitivity to individuals involved, the events are genuine. This narrative is for enjoyment only and accuracy is reshaped by recollection, with all unconscious omissions and distortions. My regards to the former owners of the Trail's End (formerly the Ponderosa), who loved the business as much as Bill and me.

ISBN 978-1-64654-417-2 (paperback)
ISBN 978-1-64654-942-9 (hardcover)
ISBN 978-1-64654-418-9 (digital)

Printed in the United States of America

*This is dedicated to my four amazing grandchildren,
Drexler, Dawson, Kyle, and Mattison.
I love you more than you will ever know. Fill
your hearts with joy, love, and kindness.*

Acknowledgments

I wish to thank my sister Marilyn Rich (a.k.a. Tootie) for the countless hours spent in editing. And if not for her persistence in convincing me to share these Ponderosa stories in a book, they would have remained latent. Marilyn's unremitting energy with encouragement and superb writing skills helped to create *A Full Plate*. I thank Tootie, a published author herself, from the bottom of my heart.

Sincere thanks to my devoted husband, Bill, for his support and patience. And a wholehearted thanks to my two amazing children for their strong will and loving nature, plus blessing me with four beautiful grandchildren.

Gratitude to Kerri Simonson for my author photo. Many thanks to Kari Greer Photography for the book cover design, Cal Newman for his artistic Idaho map, and to published author Terry Shaffer for his help in moving this book forward. My appreciation to John Rich for his inspiration at the early stage of my writing endeavor. Regards to Cheryl Van De Grift-Edison and Burny Wells (another published author) for their assistance. I must thank my siblings for all their motivation and love throughout the years. Warm gratitude to my employees, neighbors at Lower Banks, and our loyal customers of the Ponderosa. Your friendship was heartfelt.

A shout-out to Costco Wholesale for making the cherry pie on the book's cover.

IN LOVING MEMORY OF MARILYN
"TOOTIE" RICH
1954–2016

*"Since your passing, it's as if I've been throwing rocks
into the river nonstop. But it doesn't matter how many,
or how far or how hard I throw the rocks,
the anguish of your demise continues to torment me."*

One does not need a prestigious title to
perform a significant role.

—Mary Jane and Robert Smith

Go ahead. Be your own boss and make your dreams come true! Location, location, location—this Idaho restaurant and motel has that covered. Nestled among the Ponderosa pines and sandwiched between a scenic river and a busy highway, it's a sure moneymaker. But remember, business is seasonal. Your kids can help, and the value of their experience will last them a lifetime—even though their interest may fizzle in a week. At 5:00 a.m., just roll up your sleeves and put on a pair of comfortable shoes, and you should be back in the sack by midnight. But that's not a promise.

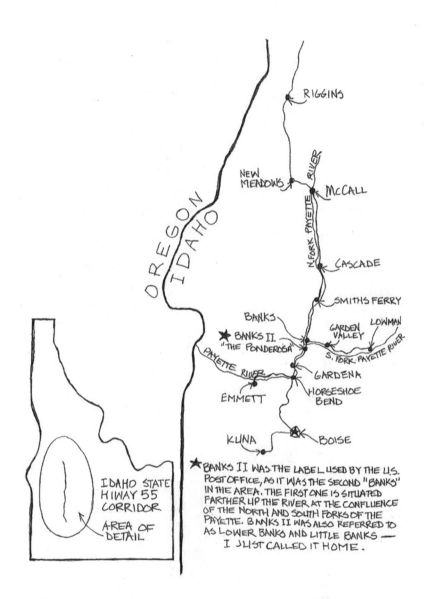

RIGGINS

NEW MEADOWS

McCALL

N. FORK PAYETTE RIVER

CASCADE

SMITHS FERRY

BANKS

★ BANKS II
"THE PONDEROSA"

GARDEN VALLEY

LOWMAN

S. FORK PAYETTE RIVER

PAYETTE RIVER

GARDENA

EMMETT

HORSESHOE BEND

KUNA

BOISE

OREGON   IDAHO

IDAHO STATE HIWAY 55 CORRIDOR

AREA OF DETAIL

★ BANKS II WAS THE LABEL USED BY THE U.S. POST OFFICE, AS IT WAS THE SECOND "BANKS" IN THE AREA. THE FIRST ONE IS SITUATED FARTHER UP THE RIVER AT THE CONFLUENCE OF THE NORTH AND SOUTH FORKS OF THE PAYETTE. BANKS II WAS ALSO REFERRED TO AS LOWER BANKS AND LITTLE BANKS — I JUST CALLED IT HOME.

Prologue

The siren's echo, sharp-edged and poignant, pierced Marie like a dagger. Sirens always rattled her, and this one, its close proximity upsetting the quiet Sunday afternoon, was no exception. As she stood alone on the sidewalk, fumbling with her snarled key chain while trying to unlock the front door of the Kuna Sav-On, exasperation took over. When the door swung open, she quickly stepped inside to escape both the noisy disturbance and Idaho's sweltering July sun. When she turned to relock the door, her purse strap slid from her shoulder and nudged a tall rack of hair accessories, almost toppling it. Relieved she wouldn't have to waste time reorganizing hair barrettes and bobby pins, Marie sighed gratefully and moved to the back of the store.

On Sundays, her drugstore was closed, but today she had stopped by after church to collect some unfinished paperwork; once again a simple day off evaded Marie. The Sav-On, established in the early 1950s, was hunkered in the heart of Kuna, Idaho, and over the past four years, Marie and her husband, Sherman, had owned and operated this flourishing business. The store included a liquor section featuring hundreds of colorful bottles of bourbon, gin, scotch, vodka, and liqueurs. Although the sales from alcohol provided a steady income, this merchandise was no friend to Sherm, Marie, or their eight children. Marie knew a limitless supply of booze mixed with an alcoholic husband didn't generate a happy hour.

Marie filled a glass with tap water, dropped in an ice cube, and paused while it crackled. After taking a sip, she absently placed the chilled glass against her temple and licked her lips. Her short salt-

and-peppery curls accentuated her large brown eyes and gave her complexion its radiance. She resembled a woman much younger than her forty-five years except for the gauntness in her cheeks and dark hollows under her eyes. Nonetheless, Marie radiated classic beauty and remarkable vivacity.

Marie glanced around at the sturdy shelves stocked with the customary drug store paraphernalia, enjoying the rare tranquility of her closed shop. As she walked down the last aisle, out of habit, she faced up shampoo bottles and deodorant and mentally noted that additional Q-tips and baby wipes should be reordered. The dull hum of the compressor that powered the ice cream freezer interrupted the quiet, and she smiled as she recalled an incident two weeks prior when her youngest sister, Phillis, was visiting. On that day, the Sav-On had had a rush at the coffee counter, when a customer ordered a chocolate milkshake. Marie, busy at the cash register, couldn't immediately fulfill his request. Phillis, however, who had watched her make several milkshakes, wanted to help.

"You're busy. I'll make the milkshake for you, Marie," Phillis said with the confidence of a skilled Baskin-Robbins employee. Phillis scooped hard chocolate ice cream into a stainless-steel container, added a splash of milk, and clipped the tall cup onto an antique Hamilton Beach mixer. Mistakenly, she assumed everything to be secured and proudly switched on the machine.

Marie glanced over her shoulder in time to see the spinning blade scrape the lip of the cup and fling it to the floor with a loud clank. Stunned and immobile, she stared at the sticky brown froth splattered from floor to ceiling. She wanted to cry, but when she noticed the wide-eyed patrons sitting at the counter and also Phillis's face, flushed with embarrassment, Marie held back her tears. Everyone went silent and waited for Marie's reaction.

"Whoops!" Marie said, bending to pick up the now-empty container. When Marie came up, she laughed loudly, and within seconds, happy tears began to roll down her and her sister's high cheekbones. The two sisters had the kind of laughter that swept through every person in their presence. Even under pressure, Marie maintained composure, which made her the heartbeat of the Sav-On and created a special place for her patrons.

A second siren jarred Marie's senses and brought her back to the present. To Marie, this one sounded different—extra shrill and a hundred times more personal. The store's plate-glass window framed an ample view of Kuna's main street, and Marie watched as an ambulance zipped by at top speed. No one ever enjoys the sound of a siren, especially in a small farming town like Kuna, where people know their neighbors. With unexplained urgency, Marie grabbed the stack of paperwork she needed and rushed to the front door. Later, Marie couldn't recall locking the heavy door plastered with colorful flyers. As she left, the CLOSED sign slapped the door and then peacefully dangled, cockeyed from its hook.

Chapter One

THE VISIT

TEN YEARS LATER

After an eight-hour drive, I pulled onto the crunchy gravel of a narrow driveway. My newly paid-off Chevy Hatchback, streaked with mud, sported a freshly chipped windshield, compliments of a clueless truck driver. I stared at the mobile home in front of me and took in a deep breath. A single light bulb with its welcome glow protruded from the weathered metal siding and saved the structure from looking doomed. I sat mesmerized for a few seconds before the trailer's door flew open. My body, as fatigued as the "welcome" mat on the front stoop, was instantly energized by the sight of the tall, wiry man and his shaggy white poodle standing in the open doorway. The jumpy pesky dog barked excitedly, but that didn't rattle my father one iota. Several windows lit up in nearby homes—the neighbors weren't as oblivious to the disturbance. My dad reached down as if to discipline his overzealous pooch, Tuffy, but instead rewarded her by tenderly patting the top of her head. He grinned broadly. His thin white hair, flattened in the back, stood up on the top like a rooster's comb—an indication he'd dozed off sitting in his recliner awaiting my arrival.

I left my car, raced up the steps, and hugged my dad for the first time in nearly two years. Dad returned the hug, practically cracking my ribs. Slipping his bare feet into a pair of worn-out leather slippers, he stepped off the porch to help unload my car. We noticed the engine's warmth appealed to his old cat, Chester Boy, who hunched close to the front tire. I stooped over to pet the cat's thick winter coat and wisecracked, "Dad, February in Idaho is too cold even for Ol' Chester."

Suitcases in hand and steps synchronized, Dad and I returned to the home he had moved into soon after my mother, Marie, lost her battle with breast cancer. The two-bedroom, single-wide trailer was affordable and easy to maintain and had plenty of space for an unpretentious man and his four-legged companions.

My intention for this trip was twofold: after quitting my job—in which I helped a friend sell reconditioned appliances—I wanted to chill out and also spend time with my father. Two years prior to that, while living in Rainier, Oregon, my husband, Bill, and I had owned and operated a mom-and-pop convenience store, gas pumps included. "The Lindberg Grocery and Gas" was a quaint relic of a business with oiled wood floors, poor fluorescent lighting, and a cash register with a pull-down handle. After enjoying our customers (some more than others) for ten years, we sold the business to a young couple eager to take over the long hours and seven-days-a-week commitment. Our two adolescent children, Mike and Lisa, a part of the endeavor, shared our enthusiasm for the change.

Tuffy, snuggled up in Dad's recliner, was finally silent, but the night was not. Dad's clean but cluttered kitchen was filled with laughter and exhilaration. I recalled what Bill had said to me before I set out on my journey earlier that morning: "Tell Sherm hello and ask him if there are any businesses for sale around Boise." Bill, bored of daytime television, was eager to start another self-employment adventure. Since the sale of the Lindberg Grocery, Bill had worked part-time installing hardwood floors, and on Saturday nights, he'd pour beer at the local tavern. The backbreaking work and minimal pay weren't the worst parts—he didn't enjoy working for others and dreamed of being his own boss again.

As soon as there was a pause in our conversation, I blurted out Bill's question—and instantly regretted it. "Dad, do you happen to know of a business for sale around here?" I quickly added the important words, "Bill wants to know." Dad stared at me, and as usual, I could read him clearly. He was easy to understand. When I was growing up, he wouldn't have to say a word to my seven siblings or me—we had only to look at his expression to know if we were in trouble or had pleased him. Just past midnight on this early Sunday morning, Dad leaned against the kitchen sink, his left eyebrow lifted, and his skinny lips curled into a slight smile. Although my question delighted him, he appeared perplexed by my desire to return to Idaho after leaving sixteen years earlier. I was as surprised as he was. Me? Living in Idaho again? Evidently, exhaustion from my long drive and being emotionally overnostalgic had annihilated my common sense. But it was too late to recant because Dad had me right where he wanted me—back in Idaho where I grew up. His eyes danced and his smile grew as he took my question and ran with it. He purposefully darted to the kitchen table where he hoarded daily newspapers for occasions such as this.

Dad grabbed the top paper from the stack and beelined to the classifieds as quickly and intentionally as a grade-schooler departs the classroom when the bell signals summer break. At this point, I wanted to go to bed and dream about being on vacation, but instead, I watched Dad, bursting with adrenaline, scrolling his index finger down the *Business for Sale* column. Ample opportunities were listed—apparently, not too many people want to buy themselves a job. If I had wanted to operate a tavern or buy a franchise, I could have been in business before daylight. Other than that, prospects were limited. I saw in the dwindling possibilities an opportunity to hit the sack and start an entirely new conversation in the morning, but Dad, unready to give up on his newly revived hope of my return to Idaho, kept reading.

"What about this?" Dad asked, pointing at a caption in bold print. Listed as a **Foreclosure**, the ad he read aloud intrigued me— foreclosure could mean *cheap*. The business description was vague; however, it wasn't the actual business that had us both prancing around the kitchen at one o'clock in the morning—it was the location! Dad said he had a good hunch about the locality, but we'd have to wait several hours to confirm it. This was fine with me because it was time for bed. Careful not to wake the sleeping dog, I tiptoed down the hallway, entered the guest room, plopped onto a mattress as hard as granite, yanked the thin blanket and dusty bedspread up to my chin for warmth, and smiled contentedly. I would be spending time with my dad.

The smell of Maxwell House brewing and the sound of a barking dog had me out of bed in a single motion. The overnight snow flurries had left behind an inch of white powder, and it was still spitting snowflakes. I dressed with urgency—we had a Realtor to contact! After drinking a pot of coffee and speculating about the foreclosure, I decided it was an acceptable time of day to dial the phone number listed in the *Idaho Statesman*. At eight o'clock on Sunday morning, I shouldn't have been surprised when an answering machine picked up. Right before the cutoff tone beeped, I repeated my name and Dad's phone number. After waiting thirty minutes without a callback, Dad and I became antsy and decided to investigate on our own. Dad, convinced he knew the precise business, said for the tenth time, "I'm pretty sure it's the old Ponderosa!"

With boisterous Tuffy onboard and our to-go cups filled with needless coffee, we traveled out of Boise northbound on Idaho Highway 55. We talked nonstop as we drove the familiar route through Horseshoe Bend and then another four miles to the small community of Gardena—home to approximately thirty-six humans and roughly ten times that many rattlesnakes. Gardena was as memorable to me as the fresh scent of pine at Christmas. I zeroed in on the old farmhouse where Grandma and Grandpa had lived for twenty-some years. "How come I used to think Grandma's house was a mansion? It shrinks every time I see it," I said with a short laugh. The fifteen acres of scenic property where Grandpa Fred had once grown alfalfa had sprouted a row of homes that lined the west bank of the Payette River.

Back in the 1950s and '60s, our childhood visits to my grandparents' home in Gardena required us to cross the Payette River on a narrow wooden bridge. With eyes tightly shut I'd hum a song, Jingle Bells usually, until we reached the safe side. As soon as Dad pulled up to Grandma and Grandpa's house and shifted the beige Country Squire station wagon into park, the car doors would fly open and ten occupants would spill out. Grandma Winnie's and Grandpa Fred's arms would fold around three to four kids at a time. Within minutes, we'd stampede into their house, where the smell of chicken and dumplings made our stomachs growl. Grandma always started the feast by removing from her well-stocked refrigerator a pitcher filled with cherry Kool-Aid topped off with lemon slices that floated like see-through yellow rafts.

On these family excursions, having the longest legs of the brood, I was privileged to sit in the front seat between Dad and Mom. The four kids who sat in the back seat and the three squished into the rear storage area envied my position. It didn't occur to them that with the legroom came a carcinogenic fog that billowed around me. Mom and Dad were both chain-smokers. My brothers and sisters could not see past their own discomfort, which, granted, was significant. My younger sister, Tootie, experienced mysterious and serious asthma attacks that would interrupt our trips with visits to the hospital emergency room. And my brother Eddie once required an ER visit for acute hyperventilation from a panic attack. Secondhand smoke was never considered to be the culprit. The doctor did advise Mom to keep the jockey box supplied with brown paper lunch bags to put over Ed's nose and mouth if it happened again. Being fully aware of all the possible risks involved with sitting in the back seat, I'd occasionally surrender the front seat so that others could experience the throne. Of course, I never admitted it, but the back seat was far worse than the front because of the inevitable skin touching, almost as disgusting as the squeaker farts that no one claimed. The one good thing about riding in the back seat was that I could hold my baby brother, Johnny—nicknamed Teeto—on my lap. With his chubby cheeks, piercing black eyes, cuddly body, and an attachment to me, I often pretended he was my own baby.

As children, the only time we traveled farther north than Gardena, and the scary bridge, was when we were headed into the mountains on what was my parents' idea of a vacation. The station wagon's cartop carrier would be stacked high with a fifteen-man canvas tent, fishing gear, lanterns, cookstove, sleeping bags, pillows, clothing, coolers, food (heavier than the tent), toilet paper, and enough cloth diapers for a newborn and two toddlers. Other travelers on the road would gawk, point, and laugh. And they couldn't even see inside the car, which was no laughing matter. There wasn't a molecule of unused space, which worried me because I'd been saving my babysitting money for an iron lung for Tootie, and there was no room for it. With the concave car roof only inches from our heads, claustrophobia took over and oxygen seemed scarce. Even stinky fart and ciggie air was better than no air. Eddie was lucky. He got a paper sack to put over his face to filter his oxygen.

On this Sunday morning, however, the atmosphere was different. Together, Dad and I enjoyed quality air, space, and time. Nine miles beyond Gardena, Dad pulled off the road onto a wedge of land overlooking the Payette River. There were several buildings, one of which was a restaurant that appeared abandoned. Two large signs dominated the scene. One read FOR SALE and the other PONDEROSA. Dad and I nearly leaped from the moving vehicle and Tuffy's excited bark mirrored our enthusiasm. Could this be the *foreclosure*?

I pulled the wrinkled classified ad from my purse and matched the info from the FOR SALE sign with the Realtor's name and phone number. Bingo! Dad's hunch was correct—the Ponderosa was for sale.

We found ourselves standing on four acres of incredible riverfront property, where old-growth pines filtered the sun into beautiful beams. "You know, Annie…this has been a well-known business for many years. Your grandparents patronized it," Dad revealed. Although Dad's pale blue eyes showed the same joy he felt every time one of his sons won a Cub Scout pinewood derby, I detected profound loneliness for Marie—my mom's absence on this day cut through my jubilation, but I temporarily brushed the sadness away.

Of course, I remembered. The Ponderosa was as memorable as the large black bear icon painted on the largest sign. A childhood song flashed through my mind. Every time my family drove past this spot, Dad would generate an atypical baritone and burst into improvised lyrics: "Oooohhhh, the Pond-ah…the Pond-ah…the

Pond-ah-ros-sah…home of the big black bear…it's only nine miles from Gardena…and it's a mighty nice place to be…oooohhhh, the Pond-ah…the Pond-ah…the Pond-ah-ros-sah!" It was our favorite song growing up because it meant Dad felt lighthearted, something we rarely witnessed.

For the next hour, we pressed our noses against the windows, jiggled locked doorknobs, and poked around the abandoned property. With each peek, anticipation built up, and I became increasingly eager to contact the Realtor. It didn't matter that neither Bill nor I knew anything about operating a restaurant, bar, or motel—we were entrepreneurs at heart and that gave me confidence. Even the thought of Idaho's intense summers and winters didn't dissuade me. Besides, the heat and chill of Idaho wasn't an immediate problem. At the moment, my most pressing need was to get my hands on a phone—the precursor for a conglomeration of events.

Chapter Two

JUST BUY IT

On the drive back to Dad's house, we jabbered simultaneously to one another—too preoccupied to sightsee this time. Thoughts ricocheted through my head as I rough-drafted a menu, designed a new deck, and made plans to remodel the motel rooms. Back in Kuna, Dad paced from kitchen sink to table while I tapped the redial button, held my breath, and prayed that someone would answer.

"Hello, this is Doris."

Somewhat surprised that a real person had answered the phone, I regrouped my thoughts and then spoke. "Hello. My name is Anna. I called earlier this morning about a property foreclosure." I took in a gasp of air, watched my hand shake, listened to my heart pound, and started to speak again, when I was interrupted.

"Yes, Anna. I did receive your phone message." Then Doris added, "Let me give you some information about this foreclosure. The property is owned by a bank, and I've had it listed on the market for over six months. Because the bank is desperate to sell, yesterday they significantly dropped the asking price, hoping for a quick sale." She paused for a second and continued. "I didn't receive any calls on Saturday but have had several today. However, because you were the first to call this morning, you'll have the first opportunity. Can you meet me at the property tomorrow morning, let's say nine o'clock?"

"Doris, I'm visiting from out of state, and my husband and children aren't with me. I would really like to speak with them. May

I call you back in a few minutes?" I wanted to move fast, but logic kept me focused. Dad, on the other hand, moved fast—right to the refrigerator for a beer, then sat down in his recliner, which signaled Tuffy to jump on board. There was a slight hesitation on the other end of the phone line, but I couldn't wait a second longer for Doris to speak. In my most professional tone of voice, I tried to assure her, "I'm more than casually interested in this particular property. I promise to call you back."

After phoning home with no one answering, I left a long-winded message hoping Bill knew me well enough to decipher it. As promised, I called Doris. "I'll meet you at nine o'clock tomorrow morning. I'm trying to get my family here from Oregon so we can make a mutual decision."

"Tomorrow morning will be fine," the Realtor answered.

As we waited for Bill's callback, I nervously paced from the living room to the kitchen, where Dad was heating up a kettle of his homemade stew. Dad knew how to cook—my mother taught him—and thankfully, I'd picked up the knack from them both. The level of a culinary school graduate I was not. However, I was a decent cook and enjoyed the sometimes-daunting task. Although I had waitressed at Al's Coffee Shop during my high school years, the closest I came to cooking in a restaurant was picking the meat from chicken necks for Al's popular chicken-salad sandwich spread. Uncertainty about my qualifications ripped my gut for a minute, but my high spirits returned when I recalled how Big Al, an extra-large man with a short fuse, had worked the flat-iron grill like a piano.

"Dad, are the batteries in your clock working, right?" Dad chuckled. He *knew* those hands weren't moving fast enough. "It's been two hours—why hasn't Bill called back?"

Adrenaline had me pumped-up and wringing my hands together like a twisted pretzel, but Dad and Tuffy were apparently unaffected because when the five o'clock news started, the well-worn recliner had swallowed them both. The local news distracted us for a few minutes—and then the phone rang. Dad got to it by the third ring. When I heard him say "Hi, Bill," I quickly grabbed the receiver from him.

"Where have you been?" I asked my voice unusually high.

Bill's response seemed far too casual, considering all I had going on. "I took the kids fishing. What's up?"

"You remember asking me to find a business for sale? Well, I may have found one."

Bill listened tolerantly as I described every detail of what had transpired over the past twenty hours.

"Just buy it," he said. Bill was serious.

"There's no way I can do that. This should be a family decision."

"Well, I guess the kids can miss a couple of days of school. And I'm not working until next Friday, so we're on our way."

My smile was so big it showed all my gums. Sherm, confident his second oldest daughter would soon be moving back to Idaho, relaxed and clicked the television remote.

Chapter Three

LET'S MAKE A DEAL

Shortly after 6:00 a.m., the sound of a vehicle in the driveway triggered Tuffy's annoying hullabaloo and disrupted my sleep. Wrapping myself in a terry cloth robe, I raced to the front door, mindful of the magazine rack in my path. The old blue Ford pickup (dubbed Ol' Blue) with Oregon license plates was right on schedule. I gave Bill a hug and then playfully teased him about his red puffy eyes, stubble, and breath so bad, it made me question why I had the urge to kiss him. Suddenly a stiff green tarp in the bed of the truck moved and two heads popped out. "Hi, Mom," they groaned in unison. Their gloomy, heavy-eyed faces told me their trip had been rough. Mike and Lisa had adventurously chosen to lie their sleeping bags in the bed of the pickup, and to avoid the cold air, they had covered themselves with the mold-speckled, smelly tarp. Although increased independence might be a perk of hanging out with Dad instead of Mom, freedom brought consequences.

"I'm cold."

"I'm hungry."

"I'm tired."

"This sucks!"

I listened to a few more of my children's complaints before interrupting, "Good, this trip has already toughened you up." I smiled, grabbed the squawkers, and covered them with kisses. Mike and Lisa were crabby, but they both favored a trip to Idaho over a day in a boring classroom.

Back in the house, Grandpa Sherm served up coffee, cocoa, and Tupperware bowls of Rice Krispies, and made an effort to get rid of the overripe bananas from his fruit bowl. "No thanks, Grandpa," the kids said, inconspicuously swatting away tiny fruit flies and trying to be polite.

"I'll take one of those, Sherm. Bananas are only good when they're extra ripe," said Bill. Sherm lit up. He hated seeing food go to waste.

Bill, who had planned to get a short snooze in before starting the day's activities, gave me the stink eye when I informed him that wouldn't be happening. No time for a nap! There were too many important matters to discuss before our nine o'clock gathering at the Ponderosa. Time passed quickly, especially for the two exhausted teenagers, who had crashed, partially sitting up, on the once over-stuffed sofa. I gently awoke the twosome. "We need to get a move on," I said.

Reluctantly, Lisa struggled to her feet and hardly gotten her teeth and hair brushed before revealing her worries. "Mom, if we move here, I won't be able to graduate from middle school with my friends."

"I realize that, but we'll figure it out. Just wait until you see this place before you decide thumbs down on it," I replied.

Upon our arrival at the Ponderosa, I noticed plenty I'd missed from the day before—snow piled up under the tall pine trees and against the north side of each building, where the sun rarely hit. How could I have missed the service station and towing business next door or the half dozen small cabins and doublewide mobile home across the highway? Lower Banks, Idaho, appeared to be a small community. In spite of the sun glare, the temperature held steady at barely above freezing, and I shivered while waiting for the Realtor to unlock the restaurant's door.

We entered the main building naively expecting the lingering aroma of onion rings and bacon cheeseburgers. Instead, the uninviting concoction of wet wood, mold, and stale grease punched us in our nostrils. There we stood, our morale deflated, inside a gutted-out structure that had suffered through years of neglect. The odor and stains on the ceiling and floor indicated a leaky roof. Dirty windows, worn and stained carpet, and several piles of debris were all that remained of the former occupant, but I ignored the muck and sprinted across the room toward the large picture windows lining the entire back wall. "Hurry, get over here! Look at this spectacular view," I blurted out. Only steps away and down an embankment, the Payette River flowed by, its power and majesty holding my gaze. "Don't you agree this would make an amazing place to sit and eat a meal? Can you believe this place is for sale?"

Sherm moved his head up and down in agreement, but Bill's response was verbal. "Seriously, we should buy this place," he said.

Lisa, brow furrowed and eyes moving like windshield wipers, glared at us as if we each had grown an extra head. "Of course it's for sale! This place stinks! Why would anyone want to buy a dirty old restaurant with no stuff in it except garbage? It's a *dump*!" she spat.

"But, Lisa, look at all the possibilities. We can fix it up." I tried to be empathetic and reassuring but could tell my words weren't shifting her reluctance. She was thirteen years old and I was knocking on forty. Our respective aspirations weren't even close.

Fifteen-year-old Mike, on the other hand, who considered fishing one of his ultimate purposes in life, eyeballed the river. "Think there're any fish in there?" he asked.

"Of course there are," Bill and Grandpa Sherm answered in unison.

Instantly, Mike became keen on getting moved in as soon as possible.

Flashing his quirky smile, Sherm finally spoke up, "I know you two can turn the Ponderosa around."

"I agree, Sherm. We can make this work," said Bill.

"We'll fill this place up with tables, chairs, waitresses, and busboys," I added.

With Doris in the lead, we left the cavernous three-thousand-square-foot building and walked to a small adjacent cabin. Lisa and Mike picked up the pace, racing the short distance—a hint Lisa might become more involved. On the outside, the cabin appeared neat and tidy, which gave us optimism. That changed instantly when we opened the door to our prospective new home. "Yii...Yii...Yii," was all I could muster, while almost biting off my tongue. Cobwebs hung like Halloween décor, and the bathroom sink had been torn off the wall and tossed aside like a used paper plate. In each room, piles of petrified scat caused a stench even more putrid and unsettling than that in the restaurant. I looked at Mike and Lisa's expressions, and before anyone could utter a single word, I exclaimed, "Come on, kids, let's try not to be so pessimistic. We can clean this up, put the sink back on the wall, and live here comfortably." The words "yuck" and "gross" flew around the room like flies in a barn.

Lisa took one look at my face and knew my intention. She spontaneously raced upstairs to take dibs on the solitary bedroom. "This is my room. I call it," she squealed.

"Why does she get the good room?" Mike complained to no response.

Because the cabin offered only two bedrooms, a spare room suitable for use as a sleeping area would grant Mike his own space, but sharing it with a washer and dryer further displeased him. The only room missing was a kitchen—but who needs one when there's a full-service restaurant only a few steps away? The Ponderosa would be our kitchen.

Doris, familiar with the scheme of the Ponderosa tour, held up the key chain and shook it. "We better continue, there's a lot more to see," she said, as if to say, *hurry up and move it.*

The atrocious living quarters concerned me, but I covered my feelings and enthusiastically coaxed everyone toward the motel. The three-unit motel, constructed of cinder blocks and small windows, was in the same neglected condition as the restaurant and cabin. Again, I tried to reassure the two disgruntled teenagers: "Some cleaning, furnishings, and decorating will make this motel cozy and charming." I got the words out but turned away to roll my eyes and hide my scowl.

Bill tried to make me feel better by saying, "It's the *only* motel for miles." Recognizing he needed to say more, he added, "Let's check out the other cabin at the end of the property." Bill offered his friendliest smile, but I knew it was phony. I felt a bit nauseated.

The six of us proceeded south from the motel, trudging through wet weeds and passing over several RV parking spaces to reach the second cabin, which we had no reason to expect would be any more habitable than the cabin we had toured ten minutes before. But we entered the building and stood inside a spacious great room. There was a kitchen, dining room, and living room. Now *this* place had some real possibilities. The best part—Rambo hadn't ripped the sink off the wall, the toilet hadn't grown a beard, and the bathtub didn't look like it held the remains of a beef stew. All of a sudden, things didn't seem quite as dismal, giving us renewed vibrancy as we rushed to scope out the bedroom situation. Bedrooms one and two were just the thing for Mike and Lisa. When we entered the whopping master bedroom, we were greeted with a picture window with another spectacular river view. Then without warning, we all gasped in unity—but it wasn't the scenery that made us feel like we'd been punched in the pit of the stomach. We shared a similar sensation that we were standing on the brink of a possible disaster. Aghast, we eyeballed each other, silently calculated our total group weight, and then crept from a room that seemed to suspend precariously over the riverbank. Without discussion, the group decided the first cabin, adjacent to the restaurant, was the best of the worst.

Doris suggested we walk the lengthy strip of land sandwiched between the highway on the east side and the Payette River on the west side. Mike scouted the approximately nine hundred feet of impeccable riverfront property for possible fishing holes and Lisa followed close behind him. At a standstill among the tall pine trees, I felt at ease listening to the fast-moving river's constant roar. It was close, loud, and one of the most soothing sounds I'd ever heard.

Bill interrupted my thoughts. "This will take a lot of hard work—like mending a broken spider web. But I think it'll be a good challenge for us," he added.

"Just wait!" I said. "I have to show you my idea for a new deck, which has to be the first thing we add after getting the doors open for business." When I described the deck I visualized, my arms flew around so excitedly that Sherm laughed. My animation didn't stop. "This deck will be amazing—a perfect way to attract customers. It's crazy this restaurant has been here for so many years without one."

Sherm and Bill nodded and smiled while the Realtor remained silent and uncommitted.

By the time Lisa and Mike joined us, a few storm clouds had formed, eliminating the sun's warmth. "We have to leave now," Bill said, abruptly ending the tour.

As the five of us headed toward our car, where Doris patiently waited, I heard Sherm yell. I swung around in time to watch Mike instinctively reach out and snag his grandpa's left arm. Sherm had slipped on a patch of ice—both of his legs pointing east. Regaining his footing and composure, Sherm put a shaky hand on Mike's shoulder and squeezed it affectionately, saying, "Hell, that was a close call." For me, it wasn't difficult to construe what Sherm meant, but I'm certain Mike would have valued a thank-you over a bruise on his shoulder.

The sound of the real estate agent's voice brought us to attention. "Bill, why don't you and Ann take some time to discuss this purchase? I'll be in my office all afternoon if you have any questions, but I have to remind you both that the bank wants this sold quickly."

Bill promised Doris he would call her by the end of the day. As the car left the parking lot, I swiveled around where two signs caught my eye: PONDEROSA, CAFÉ-MOTEL-BAR and a drab reader board that read CLOSED. *How sad,* I thought. *Somebody lost their motivation.*

The sound of Bill's voice drew me out of my thoughts. "How much time do we need to discuss this?" Bill asked me. "We have the money from the sale of the Lindberg Grocery. Why not reinvest it? The price is definitely right. As far as I'm concerned, we don't need to waste time, do we?"

"I love the place, and you're right—they're almost giving it away. Even though we don't know the first thing about operating a restaurant, I'm positive we can fix it up and get it functioning again. My vote is to put down earnest money, find a renter for our home, and notify Mike and Lisa's teachers," I said.

Bill didn't pause before speaking. "I'll call Doris and have her get the paperwork started, and then tomorrow morning the kids and I will drop off a check before heading back to Oregon. Annie, whatever needs to be done here, you can finish up without me."

Back in Kuna, I watched Dad enter his trailer house. Before removing his jacket, he lovingly scooped up his poodle with close-set black eyes, white curls, stained whiskers, and bad breath. Several years after Mom died, Tuffy became Dad's companion, and as difficult as it was, I had grown to accept Tuffy's sometimes aggravating presence.

While Bill made his phone call to our real estate broker, Dad and I put together a quick meal. Soon, sleeping bags, pillows, and motionless teenagers stretched across the hide-a-bed. I bent down to kiss them good night, smiled, and switched off the table lamp. Back in the bedroom, Bill, undeterred by the hard mattress, was curled up like a piece of cooked bacon. I snuggled up close to him and prayed my mind wouldn't start organizing a to-do list. Gratefully, I drifted off to sleep.

Early the next morning, I watched as Ol' Blue left the driveway with three arms waving from the rolled-down windows. I listened to the sound of a single honk, grabbed Dad's arm, and we hurried back to the house. "Brrrr, Dad, it's just like I remember as a kid—it feels like it's twenty degrees below zero out here." I squeezed his arm tightly to draw warmth.

Later that morning, Doris called. The bank had accepted our offer and expected to close the deal by the first of the month. "Dad, is it even possible to get a million things done in only two weeks?"

Chapter Four

PULLING IT TOGETHER

To get started, I sat at Dad's kitchen table, scoping out the Restaurant Equipment section of the *Idaho Statesman*'s most recent edition. With a tight budget and a lot of purchases to make, my best option was to bargain hunt for secondhand restaurant furnishings. There were plenty of options listed in the newspaper, but only one stood out. I dialed the Boise number and talked to a soft-spoken gentleman named Scotty, a local contractor who needed to liquidate existing fixtures from a restaurant before he could start its remodel.

I called out to Dad in the backyard, "We might have scored here!" I repeated everything Scotty told me and added, "We're meeting the guy in Boise at ten o'clock."

Dad came through the back door holding a purring Chester Boy in his arms. "We better head on out then," he said, releasing the plump feline back into the chilly air. In vain, he tried to brush off the multicolored cat hair covering his dark gray sweater. Dad retrieved a thick roll of masking tape, wrapped the tape around four fingers, and unwearyingly dabbed at the cat hair.

On the way to meet Scotty, I asked Dad, "What do you think we're going to find?"

"I think that restaurant is a pretty nice place, but it's been closed-up for the last several months. You'll recognize it, it's over by the university," he answered. Even if it wasn't true that the restaurant was a nice place, it's exactly what I needed to hear and loved Dad for saying it.

"I hope so. Thanks for all your help, Dad."

Right on schedule, at ten we were shaking Scotty's hand. And Dad was right again—the restaurant looked extraordinarily nice. It had been remodeled less than five years earlier, but now the new proprietors required furnishings to fit their Asian cuisine. Scotty pointed out the items for sale, and it wasn't easy for Dad or me to keep our poker faces when he announced his more than a bargain price. Tables, chairs, and booths all needed to be removed from the property, including an enormous one-piece section with six booths and a service counter. Not only was this one-piece section a monster made of wood, it contained small squares of beautiful blue tile that would need extra caution in dismantling. The entire lot would add a zippy personality to the Ponderosa. The only catch—it must be removed without delay.

Is everybody in Idaho in a hurry? I laughed to myself.

"I'll start the remodel in the kitchen area, that way you'll have some time to clear this out," Scotty said.

"That's great! We've got a deal," I said, reaching out to shake Scotty's hand for the second time.

Back at my desk, Dad's kitchen table, Sherm handed me a tuna sandwich and a freshly brewed cup of coffee for some needed rejuvenation. Once again, my eyes and index finger searched the seemingly lucky classifieds. *Let's see, I need a flat top grill, fryer, ovens, freezer, dishwasher, and what else?* I asked myself. Rapidly, I moved down the list. *Thank goodness there are walk-in coolers in the kitchen and bar. That will save time and money.*

Soon it became apparent the classifieds weren't so lucky anymore. Thinking about my next move, I noticed Sherm stretched out in his La-Z-Boy with the dog perched on his lap like a guardian. Dad sipped on his favorite beverage, a warm beer. Most of the time, he drank Milwaukie's Best, but today it was the grocery store's special, Olympia. "That looks good. May I have a *cold* one?" I asked.

"You sure do love that dog," I said and hoped my tone didn't reveal the slight jealousy I felt about the tenderness between Dad and his poodle.

Sherm smiled and gently patted Tuffy's head. I smiled, too, and wondered—*did he love his eight little kids that much?* I couldn't recall him being so attentive and patient with us.

After a light dinner, dishes washed and put away, I headed down the dark hallway toward the guest bedroom. "Night, Dad." When I said, "I love you," I realized I couldn't recall the last time I'd said those words to him. Had I ever?

Sherm replied, "Love you too, Annie." And I was fairly certain that I'd never heard those words from my father before.

The next morning, savoring my first cup of coffee, I brain-stormed. "Dad, I have an idea about the kitchen equipment. What about contacting the Ponderosa's prior owners? Maybe they're storing the appliances and would sell. If the grill and fryer came out of there, it'll fit back in perfectly."

"Good idea," Dad replied.

I called Doris and explained my plan. She released the name and phone number of the previous owner, which I scribbled onto an old utility bill envelope.

An hour later, I dialed a Garden Valley, Idaho, phone number, and a woman answered, "Hello?"

After giving my name and briefly explaining the situation, I learned the missing Ponderosa equipment was being stored at her res-idence, only fifteen miles north of the Ponderosa. Within two hours, Dad and I arrived to meet a young woman with oversize earrings that hung like chandeliers. She led us to a dilapidated shed that looked unlikely to survive another winter. We watched her wrestle with the warped door—the hinges squeaked in protest. When it finally sprung open, the entire slab fell from its hinges.

"Now we know what happened to the bathroom sink in the cabin," I whispered to Dad.

Dad tried not to laugh as he whispered back, "Yeah, we've seen these cobwebs and smelled this smell before too."

With dollar bills in her large blue eyes, she stated, "Everything works fine, just needs to be hooked up to the gas lines."

My nostrils flared, and my eyes popped when she announced her inflated price. No doubt she knew I needed what she had. I saw her tilt her flawless complexion and full lips toward the sky, and I swear she smiled. She was visibly pleased—maybe she considered it restitution for the bank's confiscation of her family's livelihood. I stood back, folded my arms across my chest, and scrutinized the stack of greasy, grimy appliances. They'd fit into the kitchen's empty space, and I needed to make a swift decision—haggling wasn't an option.

"I'll take everything that came from the Ponderosa," I stated, worried she might try to get rid of additional rubbish from the heap. "I'll be back in a couple of weeks to move it out."

Back in the car, I blurted, "Those appliances are atrocious—it's going to take a ton of cleaner and a whole lot of elbow grease!"

"You got that right," said Sherm.

Before leaving Garden Valley, we stopped to talk to a well-known contractor named Marty, who owned every sort of construction tool you could think of. After describing in detail the restaurant's neglected condition and the fixtures to be installed, Marty concluded the work was feasible, gave me his hourly rate, and said he could start the job when he got the go-ahead. His words and attitude took three tons off my back and eased the sting of the lady's hard bargain. I shook Marty's oversize calloused hand. "Sounds like we've got a deal," I said.

I awakened to a soft knock on my door. "Coffee's ready," Dad announced.

I set my suitcase down near the front door and joined my father at the kitchen table. "Well, Dad, it looks like you got your way—I'll be living back in Idaho!"

"You can do this, Annie." Dad must have thought a little reassurance was as good for me as being coddled was for Tuffy.

I loaded my car, said goodbye to Tuffy, and hugged my dad for the second time in a week. At that moment, I promised myself to hug my dad every time I saw him.

With the heavy rain blasting my windshield, I glanced back to wave goodbye and saw the tall, slim figure standing in the open doorway again. His six-foot-one physique hadn't changed much over the years—his shoulders still broad, especially in contrast to his thin body. Sherm took pride in his posture, always standing straight, unless he had fallen victim to the ghastly alcohol slump. This morning in the early dawn, I saw him wave back. His wave made me cry! And not seeing mom standing next to him ripped at my heart.

The best thing about the long drive home was that it gave me time to sit and mentally organize my tasks for the next two weeks. Hours later, I pulled into my own driveway and tapped a couple of quick beeps on the horn, and the garage door lifted up. "Mom's here!" Lisa screamed and flew into my arms.

"Hi, Leecee! It's so good to see you, honey." I squeezed my daughter tightly.

Bill and Mike waited patiently indoors, seeing no need to face the cold—I'd come inside eventually. The hugs weren't even finished before Mike and Lisa began bombarding me with questions.

"When do we move? Where will we go to school? Can I take Minnie?"

"Okay, here's the plan," I said, exhausted but excited. "We should be ready to move in two weeks, which means every one of us will need to step up our paces. Mike, you'll go to Garden Valley High School and Lisa, you'll be at Horseshoe Bend Middle School, and of course, Minnie will go." Six years prior, I had spotted Minnie, a terrier-poodle mix, at a shopping mall. The brown-and-black furball, no bigger than a can of corn, was sleeping undisturbed in the pet-store window. The moment I saw her, I had to hold her and that was the end of her stay at the pet hotel. Minnie, adorned with a red bow, became Lisa's unforgettable Christmas Eve gift—and now was an integral part of the family that soon would be moving 450 miles away.

Bill was the first to respond. "Well, today, I notified Mike and Lisa's schools to have their records transferred. Also, my part-time job at the tavern will end after this Saturday, and Harvey has a guy lined up to help with his hardwood-floor jobs."

My bed felt soft, my pillow smelled of fruity shampoo, and I drifted off to sleep, unaware of the devastating structural change that occurred that very day at the Ponderosa.

Chapter Five

MEMORIES LEFT BEHIND

The next morning began with something totally unexpected—a phone call from Idaho.

"Hello," I said.

"Is this Ann?" a female voice asked.

"Yes, it is."

"Good morning. This is Doris."

To my ears, Doris's voice contained more of a worried tone than a friendly tone, and my heart started to pound in my chest. "Hi, Doris, how may I help you?" I asked nervously.

There wasn't much of a pause before she answered. "I'm calling to inform you and Bill of a problem at the restaurant. It seems with all the rain we had yesterday, the restaurant's roof collapsed. I've been in touch with the bank, and they have decided to file a claim with their insurance company. Actually, Ann, it's a good thing, because the insurance company will pay for a new roof and repair all the water damage."

"Really?" was all I could say. My hands shook, and my heart beat even faster.

"Yes, it's true. I'll keep you posted on the developments," Doris said. She hung up and didn't hear me yelling down the hallway, "Bill, guess what?" After telling Bill the bad news about the collapsed roof, I continued on a happier note. "Until we sign the closing papers, the buildings belong to the bank, and they know it can't be sold until it's repaired. So we'll be getting a new roof!"

For the next two weeks, we were busy as mosquitoes at a nudist camp. Lisa and Mike's schools were given the addresses to mail their records, and a property manager was hired to maintain our home in Rainier, a duplex we had built eight years earlier. After a one-day garage sale and a trip to the secondhand store and the county dump, most of our accumulated junk was cleared out. Whatever didn't fit into the back of Ol' Blue and the small U-Haul trailer it towed was stored in the basement of the duplex.

On a wet Thursday morning, Ol' Blue sat waiting with our belongings stacked higher than the cab, leaving zero space between any two items. Numerous bungees fastened down the old green tarp that covered the giant mound. Bill locked up the place we had called home for the last eight years, and then, without saying a word, he slid into the driver's seat. The new renters would arrive this same day, moving into a space that only looked empty. To us, the home was still full—all our memories of family life remained. I tried not to think about our friends and the lush Oregon greenery we were leaving behind. It felt bittersweet.

I drove the Hatchback, stuffed with clothes, pillows, and blankets, leaving barely enough room for my children and teeny Minnie. If not for the sound of them breathing, I would not have known they were in the car. "Is anyone back there?" I asked in an effort to break the silence. "Just think, in only eight hours, we'll be back at Grandpa Sherm's, listening to Tuffy bark."

Another fifteen minutes passed before Mike spoke, "Mom, can I at least come back to visit my friends sometime?" His tone of voice echoed his disdain for being uprooted from his life in Rainier.

"For sure! I promise," I replied.

"Me too?" asked Lisa.

"Of course," I said, glancing into my rearview mirror, forcing a smile, and seeing only long faces—even Minnie appeared distraught. Guilt became my front seat companion, and I sought to change it fast. "Why can't one of you sit up here with me?" I asked.

"We're okay," they answered back with a touch of defiance.

"Well then, tell me about your last day at school yesterday," I asked, trying to spark a chat.

Lisa went first. "My homeroom teacher gave me a cupcake, and my best friend, Amy, cried which made me cry too."

"How about you, Mike?" I asked.

"Nothin'."

"Oh, come on. You must've had some kind of a farewell happening."

"Well, people said 'goodbye' and 'I'll see ya later, Mike.'"

"Well, that's good," I replied. "You know you'll both make lots of new friends in Idaho."

"It's not the same, Mom."

"Who knows what you'll find and who you'll meet at your new schools—maybe a really good friend, the best you ever had. You know there's more to life than living in Rainier. Expanding your horizons is always good," I said, doubtful either of the kids believed it.

"Leecee, do you realize that you'll be making lots of money being a waitress?"

"I can't wait," she said sarcastically.

"You'll be the best waitress in Idaho, honey. Customers will love you and the better the waitress, the better the tip. I know you'll be happy with your new school too." I knew I was rambling, so I shut up.

Finally, we arrived in Kuna, where Grandpa Sherm had no doubt kept himself busy peering out his window. The first hug came from me, but Mike, Lisa, and Bill were close behind.

Many things had changed from the time I'd pulled into Sherm's driveway three weeks earlier—some things, however, remained the same—Tuffy would always protect her master with a million yaps. "Tuff, it's just me," I said while stretching my arms up above my head as far as they would reach. I rubbed at my low back and felt the start of a headache.

We gathered up as much as we could carry and shuffled to the mobile home.

"Is anybody hungry?" Sherm asked.

"I am, Grandpa," Mike said without hesitation.

"He's always hungry," Bill interjected.

When we opened Dad's front door, a delicious aroma hit us. On the back burner of the stove sat a kettle with a copper bottom and dented lid. I recognized the pot Mom used every morning to prepare oatmeal with raisins for eight ravenous kids. Today, ham hock and bean soup slowly simmered, puffs of steam escaping through the misshapen lid. "Sit down, Mike. I'll get you a bowl," said Grandpa Sherm, who rarely had dinner guests and cherished such moments. He lined up four bowls and proudly ladled up the thick soup.

"This is good, Grandpa," Lisa said shyly, looking down to avoid eye contact with an almost-unfamiliar relative.

Grandpa Sherm, a man of few words unless he was telling one of his overly detailed stories, patted her on the shoulder. I understood exactly what he was trying to say, even though I could tell by the look on Lisa's face she expected more of a conversation. I hoped she'd learn to interpret his manner of affection.

"You two better get to bed. It's going to be a crazy day tomorrow," Bill said as he washed the soup bowls. "Brush your teeth and roll out those sleeping bags," he added. Mike and Lisa followed his order because complaining would have taken too much energy.

By the time the coffee finished percolating the next morning, Grandpa's home grew lively. "Hurry up, Annie," Bill said for the second time in five minutes.

I stood at the bathroom mirror and applied mascara to help make my tired eyes look awake. "Simmer down, Billy boy—we have a full hour before our appointment with Doris," I fired back, smiling.

"Sherm, we'll be back as soon as the paperwork is completed," Bill said and climbed into the car. Sherm followed us outside, and Mike and Lisa, wearing their sleeping bags like Superman capes, waved through the living room window.

The enormous stack of papers that sat on Doris's desk was in perfect order, just waiting for our signatures. Within an hour, we were officially the newest owners of a neglected wreck of a business called the Ponderosa. During the drive back to Sherm's, skepticism poked at our confidence like shards of glass. We ignored it.

Back at Sherm's, two bored kids and an anxious grandpa awaited our arrival. "Let's get moved into our new place on the river," Bill said. He looked over at Dad, "Sherm, if we can't get the cabin cleaned and our beds set up by nightfall, we'll be back."

Ol' Blue led us out of Kuna and up the canyon—my Chevy followed close behind. I couldn't take my eyes off the flapping green tarp, worried it might end up on my windshield.

In less than an hour, we were driving into the parking lot. "We're here," Mike bellowed, leaping from the truck. The mountain air smelled fresh and piney—this was the life I wanted, or at least I thought I wanted.

Fortunately, the bank was obligated to reattach the bathroom sink, giving us running water. With dozens of cleaning supplies and a vacuum, we all went to work, soon realizing the cabin's small dimensions were actually a blessing. Sprucing up eight hundred square feet didn't seem too intimidating.

Bill sensed Mike's yearning to check out the river but wasn't quite ready to set him free. "Son, let's get those waterbeds set up."

"I'll find the sheets," Lisa offered as she rummaged through a large box. Not having to deal with mattresses and box springs was a huge space saver in the move, but, on the other hand, the hot water tank emptied out three times.

After setting up a card table in the living room, I found the electric skillet, plugged it in, and announced, "I'll cook up some bacon and eggs."

"We had that for breakfast," complained Mike.

"Well, now it's going to be our dinner too."

As the sun disappeared behind the mountain, the shadows took shape on the walls. We took turns in the shower, put on clean socks and sweatshirts, and decided our beds were warm enough. I tucked Lisa into bed with Minnie at her side. "Good night, honey."

I peeked into the laundry room and saw Mike in bed but still awake. "'Night, Mike, see you in the morning," I whispered from the doorway.

"'Night," came a mumbled voice.

I was the last one in bed. Not wanting to disturb Bill, I gently pulled up the heavy quilt and listened to the newest sounds in my life. At night, the roar of the river seemed much louder than in daylight. I looked forward to warm nights when we could leave the bedroom window open and allow the sounds to soothe me to sleep.

The alarm clock, sitting atop a cardboard box, buzzed loud enough to get me up. Swathed in a fleece robe, I stepped into a pair of slippers and moved to the temporary cooking setup I had arranged—an electric skillet and coffeepot on a wobbly card table. Even before turning up the room heater, I had Mr. Coffee brewing. By seven thirty everybody was out of bed, dressed, and motivated. Bill must have thought Mike and Lisa deserved a break because he gave them his blessing as they ran out the door to explore their new surroundings, rationalizing that on Monday morning, they'd be facing strangers and new rules at school.

But for Bill and me, it was a time to get cleaning. Toting Windex, ammonia, buckets, a broom, and a mop, we headed to the motel.

"Marty said he'd be here at eight o'clock Monday morning to start the remodel and promised he'd have the job finished within two months," I said to Bill. "We'll get Marty on track and then head to Boise to meet Mr. Scotty, who I'm sure is anxious for us to get those furnishings out of his way.

"Hopefully, we'll be ready to open for business by Mother's Day."

Bill groaned aloud, wiped his hands on his untucked T-shirt, and decided it was an appropriate time to complain. "This place should be bulldozed."

"I can't hear you—my head's in the toilet," I yelled back. "Hurry up," I teased. "The faster we get this motel cleaned, furnished, and decorated, the sooner we'll have some sort of income. Twenty-five bucks a night is better than nothing." After sixteen years of marriage, Bill and I could still work together and find time for a splash of humor.

At the end of another vigorous day, the four of us congregated back in the cabin.

"Mom, what's for dinner? Bacon and eggs?" Mike asked, showing me his impish grin.

"No, we're having grilled cheese sandwiches, but if you want me to add bacon, I will." *This skillet is deep enough to cook a pot roast, carrots, and spuds—I'll surprise them next week,* I thought. We sat on boxes, eating sandwiches and listening to stories of Mike and Lisa's adventurous day. When their anecdotes started to wind down, I nudged my way into the conversation. "If you two would help us tomorrow, we can get those motel rooms finished."

"Sure, Mom."

When the sun tucked away, the nighttime sky took its place. The decreased highway traffic, weary bones, and my alertness to the sound of the river all signaled it was time for bed. Everything seemed quiet, at least inside the cabin.

Chapter Six

BUTCH

Sunday morning began with a soft knock on the door.

"Who the hell would be at our door this time of morning?" Bill asked without moving a single body part to get up.

"Well, why don't you get out of bed and find out?" I asked. My hubby's outstretched body suggested he had no intention of putting his warm feet onto the cold floor. "Don't worry, I'll get it," I said and moved toward the knocking sound. Slightly shifting the sheet aside that covered the front window, I saw a man standing on the stoop. I thought I recognized him but wasn't positive. His head tilted down with one hand on the frayed brim of his misshapen cowboy hat, obviously holding it in place from the wind, and his other hand held the lapel of his stained suede jacket together. "Bill, I think it might be Butch from Oregon," I exclaimed. Butch, an outgoing guy in his early forties, was a permanent fixture at the tavern in Rainier where Bill had poured draft beer on weekends. I'd only met Butch on one occasion, so not being certain who was knocking, I kept the door shut and waited for Bill.

Bill jumped out of bed, threw on his robe, and had the door open by the fifth knock. "Butch, what are you doing here?" Bill asked, droopy-eyed and baffled.

"Aren't ya gonna invite me in?" Butch asked in a semi-joking tone. Bill and I stepped aside, and Butch entered the living room, where Mike and Lisa, curious about the commotion, had added to the crowd. They watched with puzzled stares. Minutes ticked by as we waited for a squirming Butch to answer Bill's question.

"Heard you guys moved to Idaho, so thought I'd stop in to see ya." Butch's voice dropped, his shoulders slouched, and his eyes scanned the small room before adding, "And I sure could use a place to stay."

This guy doesn't even have the couth to schmooze us before making requests, I thought.

Bill spoke up right away, "Well, Butch, you can see we don't have any extra room in here, but we're in the process of cleaning and furnishing the motel rooms."

Hell, is my husband still asleep?

Butch's shifty eyes lit up. "Great. I have a sleeping bag and my own pillow. Would ya happen to have an air mattress?"

Dumbfounded, I practically yanked Bill into the bathroom, and wanting to wag my finger at him, I asked, "What are you saying, and why does he think we owe him a place to stay?" I knew two things about Butch—he was unemployed and he was a drunk. The buzz around Rainier had been that Butch, a gifted jewelry designer, couldn't make a go of it because of booze. With my voice lowered, I continued, "Does he look like he has money to pay for a motel room? We have a million projects to finish before we can open our business, and the last thing we need is to babysit a drunk."

Without saying a word, Bill turned and left the room. I didn't follow, but I listened and watched through a crack in the door. Bill asked Butch, "How long do you plan to stay?"

Butch's answer sounded genuine. "Not sure—might be awhile, but maybe I could help out around here."

Bill hesitated a moment, then replied, "I suppose you can stay in one of the motel rooms."

Although pissed off at both Bill and Butch, I felt more worried than angry. Bill had likely extended his hospitality to Butch because he was a Vietnam vet like himself.

"Phew! Something stinks," Lisa said, pinching her nose.

I looked down at the small rug in front of the door where Butch had stood. "Good God, Butch walked in dog crap and tracked it into the house." I quickly rolled up the carpet piece and slung it outside, almost hitting the row of mailboxes. "Now that's what you call a throw rug," I said.

"Luckily, he didn't walk around the house, Mom," Lisa said, giggling.

"See, I told you! Things are already going sour," I said. Now, my first task of the day would be to set up living quarters for Butch. Was I supposed to feed him too? Do his laundry? Clean his room? The only way to come to terms with my anger was to give him the benefit of doubt. Although I had no need to wear custom-designed jewelry while flipping burgers, it was possible he could be helpful in other ways.

Early Monday morning, the alarm clock buzzed, announcing that the first day of school had arrived. Mike and Lisa rushed through breakfast but took their time getting dressed, carefully selecting the right attire. "Mike, your bus will be here in five minutes," I fretted. "Are you about ready, Leecee? Do you need any help?"

"I'll be down in a minute!" she yelled down the stairs.

Mike ran out of the door, caught the bus just in the nick of time. "Have a good day," I hollered after him.

Lisa's anxiety showed in her guarded posture. "Honey, don't worry, everyone will like you. Give them and yourself a chance." I gave her an extra strong hug. "See you this afternoon," I said and watched her walk to the school bus with her head down.

Marty, along with a couple of workers wearing carpenter belts, arrived on schedule. While Bill and I prepared to leave for Boise, we noticed Butch leaving his motel room. "Wonder where he's going?" I asked.

"Who knows," replied Bill. If Bill shared my feelings about being used, he didn't show it.

We met Scotty, and with help from Sherm, my brother Eddie, and my sister-in-law Connie, we dismantled tables and booths, and soon three pickup trucks were loaded to their limits. As usual, easygoing Eddie, who happened to have inherited the best of both Sherm's and Marie's characteristics, had agreed to help.

Bill looked at what remained. "I'd say it'll take another trip with all three trucks to get the rest. Wouldn't you, Sherm?"

"Yep, at least," Sherm replied.

Once the caravan of three trucks piled high with chairs, tables, and decorative objects had arrived at the Ponderosa, we unloaded and restacked everything out of Marty's way. "We sure could have used Butch's help here," I commented under my breath and with my eyes nearly crinkled shut.

After a gentle hug and a quick kiss on his cheek, Dad got into his truck to leave. I could see him fighting his hip pain—the constant climbing up and down ladders from his days as a fireman and painter had damaged both his hip joints.

Bill and I lingered out in the cold when we caught a glimpse of our nonpaying motel guest pulling into his parking spot. "Looks like Butch is back," said Bill.

"It would've been nice to have his help unloading the trucks," I repeated, not even trying to hide the bitterness in my voice.

"Annie, I hope you're not expecting any help from him," Bill said, winking at me.

"Well, he'd better not get in my way. And, Bill, would you look at that guy? He's totally hammered." I shook my head in disgust as I watched Butch stagger from his car to the motel.

Inside the cabin, the events of Mike's and Lisa's first day of school provided dinner conversation. By all indications, it had been a good day for them both. Aside from Butch's unwanted presence, all seemed well, and I would have slept soundly through the night had it not been for the brutal attack of a charley horse, and some tingling in my right hand.

The following morning, Lisa stepped aboard the school bus headed thirteen miles south to Horseshoe Bend. Bill and I, also driving south on our way to Boise, got a kick out of trailing behind the huge yellow vehicle transporting our daughter—we'd done the same thing on the sly when she started first grade. This time, however, when the bus turned into the school parking lot, Bill tapped the horn twice, and we waved, hoping Lisa could see us. Without her Little

Mermaid backpack and hair ribbons, she looked more grown-up than I had realized.

Ol' Blue's radio hadn't worked in years, so we entertained ourselves by planning the Ponderosa's menu. "We need an inexpensive meal to draw in customers," I said. "On the big reader board, we'll advertise *8 oz. SIRLOIN STEAK SPECIAL $3.95!*" For several weeks, I'd been calculating the value of this meal—at least $10, I determined. So at $3.95, our profit margin would be negligible, but the goal was to build clientele, and a steak dinner at such an affordable price would draw plenty of curious patrons.

The day went smoothly, and once again, three overloaded trucks headed north up the narrow canyon. "Glad this is all of it," I said. "I can't wait to see it reassembled. Poor Marty—it's going to be a huge job putting together that enormous one-piece section with all those tile pieces that have fallen loose. I just can't imagine how long it's going to take—and the longer it takes, the more it will cost, and the longer we'll have to wait until we're open."

"Annie, stop fretting. Marty will get it done. You're making me nervous."

While driving through Horseshoe Bend, I strained to see the middle school, hoping to get a peek at Lisa, but had no luck. When my eyes shifted from the schoolyard, I caught a glimpse of Bud's Place, the neighborhood tavern. "Guess who's at the bar," I said to Bill.

"Oh yeah, that's Butch's car all right." Bill laughed. "Don't expect his help unloading."

Back at the Ponderosa, we unloaded Sherm's truck first to get him on his way. Just as Sherm's truck left the parking lot, the school bus pulled in and dropped Mike off. He plopped down his backpack and helped unload the last of the fixtures.

Suddenly, thunder rumbled over the treetops, and Bill looked over at Ed. "You guys better get going—it looks like a downpour is headed our way," he said.

"Hey, Mom, what's for dinner?" Lisa yelled from the cabin door.

Once inside, I surveyed the card table, which looked way too scrawny for the load it held. Mr. Coffee and the electric skillet now shared space with a washtub, dish drainer, plates, and an array of utensils. "How does fried chicken sound?"

For the remainder of the week, we concentrated on cleaning, unpacking, and decorating. A carpet remnant was laid out in the living room of our cabin, then a sofa was positioned next to the lazy boy, and the white sheet that stretched across the front window was replaced with colorful paisley curtains tied back by a braided rope. When a Boise appliance store delivered a washer and dryer and installed them in Mike's bedroom, I had to promise not to do laundry before noon or after midnight.

Lisa spent five days organizing her belongings. "Where did all of this stuff come from and how'd you get it all in here?" I teased. Her upstairs bedroom, cluttered with stuffed animals, ran the entire length of the cabin, one window facing the river and another facing the highway. No one would have guessed that behind the medley of pictures, posters, and school memorabilia were beautiful, knotty pine walls—and undoubtedly, someone's hidden secrets. Lisa had created a cozy, private domain and was adjusting to her new life in Idaho.

Chapter Seven

BUTCH FLIES

While the kids attended school, Bill and I picked up trash around the property, filling one black garbage bag after another. The best part of the project was meeting our closest neighbors—Doug, a stocky man with straw-colored hair, and his wife, Adelle. They operated the Chevron Service Station adjacent to the restaurant. It only took a short conversation to know we would be close friends.

As we exchanged some personal information, Doug pointed across the highway and up the hill. "We live in double-wide over there, and my dad, Doug Sr., lives in the trailer next to those cabins," Doug revealed.

"Who lives in the cabins?" I had to ask.

"Those are rentals, and you'll meet the tenants soon enough." Doug snickered. Apparently, Doug was saving the "renters" for another conversation.

Right off the bat, Doug's sense of humor captivated both me and Bill. "We've lived here for over ten years, and up until about a year ago, the Ponderosa sustained a good business," Doug said. "We're happy to see somebody fix it up and get it open again—so whatever we can do to help, just ask." His grin was as wide as he was tall.

I watched Doug's wife, the sweet and energetic Adelle, cleaning a customer's windshield with her youngest daughter straddling her hip. I had done the same thing with Lisa during my ownership of the Lindberg Grocery and Gas.

Suddenly the dialogue ended—Adelle needed help for a customer waiting for gas. Doug pulled a blue grease rag from his back pocket and said, "Well, I'd better get busy. A fellow is picking up his vehicle in an hour, and it's not ready." Besides working the gas pumps and two service bays, he and Adelle operated a towing business. Obviously, these people were not afraid of hard work or getting their hands greasy.

While lugging a heavy bag of rubbish to the dumpster, I noticed Doug coming toward me. When he was within earshot, he called out, "Hey, Annie, I meant to ask you about the fellow staying in your motel."

Just the thought of Butch increased my heart rate to a dangerous level, and tersely, I explained, "He's an acquaintance of Bill's from Oregon. We barely know him. Why do you ask?"

"Well, apparently he's been hanging around the bars in Horseshoe Bend all week and telling everybody, 'He owns the Ponderosa!'"

"*What!*" I yelled. "Are you serious?"

"I'm serious as a car without brakes," Doug replied, showing off his trademark smile.

I raced off to find Bill, which didn't take me long. Behind the motel, lying flat on the ground, Bill was struggling to clean out a clogged drain. My tight jaw and bulging eyes warned him he could expect a vocal outburst. When I told him what Doug had said, Bill's initial reaction made me as happy as a surfer riding the perfect wave.

"When Butch gets here, I'll talk to him," Bill promised me. "What a loser," he added under his breath.

Right now, I compared Butch to a nasty problematic goathead thorn, also known as a puncture vine. *A propane weed burner does a good job for eradication, I'd heard.* I tried to overcome my temptation to say, "I told you so." But the pull was too strong.

By bedtime, Butch hadn't returned to his motel room. Had he got wind we were onto him? "Bill, we are *not* going to stew over this tonight. Tomorrow—you can thump his noodle."

It was Saturday, and the kids were glad to be out of school. Lisa slept in, but Mike got up early, hooked up his fishing line, and made some big plans. "I'll catch dinner," he told me as he darted out the front door—the only door.

From his recliner, Bill could see the motel. "Butch isn't there," he said. Again, the annoyance in Bill's voice pleased me.

Once showered and dressed, I called my sister Tootie, who had survived the parental secondhand smoke and become the athlete of the family. "Tootie, don't you have a friend who operates a used furniture store?"

"Yes, what are you looking for?"

"The motel needs furnishing, so I'm searching for three double beds, three chairs, a small table, and a love seat. Oh yeah, and a few pictures—nothing too flowery or prissy."

"Sure, I'd love to do that for you," Tootie said in her typically energetic voice.

Whereas Lisa and Minnie spent the last of the morning lounging in the comfort and clutter of Lisa's bedroom, Mike wandered home, grim faced and carrying only his fishing pole. "Fishing wasn't too good," he commented.

"There's always next time," I said. He ducked as I reached out to ruffle hair that he kept short to manage the kinks and coarseness.

By afternoon, a bored Mike hollered up the stairwell, "Lisa, c'mon, let's find a place to put a horseshoe pit."

As the two of them ran from the house toward the riverbank, I called out, "I'll start dinner in an hour, so don't go far."

Sunset was about an hour away when I stood at the card table, heating up the overused electric skillet, and noticed the coating on the bottom had started to peel. Fried rice with Teflon bits would be our entree. After a typical strenuous day, our world seemed quiet and, at that moment, peaceful. Bill relaxed in his vinyl recliner, reading yesterday's newspaper.

The card table, positioned in front of the window, gave me a clear view of the highway. As I stood there, staring absently out the window, the sound of squealing tires interrupted my daydream. A tornado of dirt and debris with a large object at its nucleus was speeding toward the motel. A roadside boulder as big as a refrigerator stopped the object abruptly and propelled it high into the air.

The scene unfolded so rapidly it was difficult to comprehend—yet somehow, I realized it was a *car* spinning in circles like a whirling pinwheel without a handle. After the vehicle disappeared from my view, everything became eerily quiet. Horrified, I shrieked, "Bill, a car just crashed into the motel!" Bill hadn't seen it, but he'd heard the pandemonium and was instantly out of his chair. Mike's and Lisa's screams propelled us forward, and I instinctively ran to the area where I'd lost sight of the airborne auto, Bill on my heels. Within seconds, we reached the motel and saw a car lying on its side, and heard its engine running and radio blaring. With no human being in sight, a driverless vehicle did not register, but something else did. The mangled blue two-door sedan belonged to Butch.

The color faded from Bill's face, and he bolted toward the river-bank, yelling out, "Butch! Butch! Butch!"

Meanwhile, I scanned the property in an effort to zero in on my children's frantic cries. When I discovered the two terrified teen-agers standing behind our cabin, about fifty feet from the wrecked automobile, I ran toward them and noticed Butch lying at their feet. "Bill, he's over here!" I shouted toward the river. The sight of the large white propane tank only inches from where Butch lay made my heart sink. Had he hit the tank? Was he dead? What should I do? I leaned over to examine him and discovered he was alive but barely. "Hurry, Bill, call for an ambulance!" I screamed. "Mike, Lisa, it's going to be okay," I told them but felt like it was a lie.

"Mom, he flew over the motel roof and almost landed on top of me," Lisa cried out.

"And he flew over the power line too," Mike's added, his voice quivered at a high pitch.

Mike and Lisa, both hysterical, would have to wait for my com-fort because my immediate attention focused on the broken body at my feet, which showed no sign of movement. I bent over Butch, lis-tened to his soft gurgling sounds, and silently begged him not to die. He was drunk and smelly—yet I pushed my breath into his mouth and clumsily pumped his chest. The kids slowly calmed down and huddled together to watch. When I heard sirens, I realized Butch was breathing.

Once the paramedics took over, I put my arms around my children, whose faces matched the color of the propane tank. We all stared as they loaded Butch into the back of the ambulance.

"He should've worn his seat belt," Lisa declared in an adult tone of voice.

No one responded to Lisa's words, but for the next hour, we discussed the details of the accident and Butch's troubled life.

"Mom, do you think Butch will be okay?" Mike asked.

"Let's hope so. There wasn't any blood, which may be a good sign, but saying a prayer for him wouldn't hurt—he needs lots of prayers."

Chapter Eight

RENOVATION COMPLETE

The following weeks passed as quickly as a vacation on the Oregon coast. Marty and his crew worked fast and proficiently, and in only a few days, the interior space displayed beautiful blue-tiled counters, booths, and service areas—all topped off with a new roof. The Ponderosa was taking shape.

The outside reader board lit up MOTEL OPEN—VACANCY. "This should attract a few sleepy travelers," Bill said exhilarated to have at least *part* of the business in operation. While we were at it, we added the words RESTAURANT OPENING SOON.

Several days were spent fine-tuning our menu and determining the initial food order. While Bill envisioned his bar section supplied with beer kegs, wine racks, and glistening glasses, my mental picture covered more space—kitchen shelves filled with utensils, spices, industrial-sized pans, and a fully stocked walk-in cooler. After consulting with several food and beverage distributors, our provisions list was compiled, and clean-cut Frank, of Frank's Meats, received the first order for four dozen eight-ounce sirloin steaks. And when he told me his bacon was the best flavored in the state, I ordered fifty pounds of the thick-cut.

Meanwhile, in the backdrop, Lisa talked nonstop about her upcoming middle school graduation, even though the first of June was two months away. Mike found friends when he joined the freshman baseball team and grew especially close with Tim, his most compatible sidekick. Both of my children seemed to be adjusting reasonably well.

While Butch lay in a hospital bed, recuperating and hopefully making new living arrangements, plenty of changes were happening at the Ponderosa. God only knows why, but Bill still felt a need to keep in touch with Butch, so when Butch was finally released from the hospital, we drove to Boise to return his belongings. He had moved into a studio apartment as rundown as the woman he shared it with. Still, Bill's compassion toward Butch remained intact. Vietnam vets forever, I suppose, but it turned out to be the last we saw or heard from him. I have to admit that there was a side of me that appreciated Butch and all his melodrama—he taught me a lesson. Indeed, Butch helped the Ponderosa—he convinced me not to hire a drunk.

Back in the kitchen, Marty connected the gas lines and checked the kitchen grill and fryer for leaks. "If Marty gets it up and running by tonight, I'll cook dinner here," I told Bill.

"Hey, Marty, need any help?" Bill asked eagerly. Marty smiled, picked up his wrench, and moved to the back door. "There's good news, Annie," Bill reported.

Eliminating the card table and its cluster would be an occasion for a party. "Let's surprise the kids tonight and serve our first meal from the Ponderosa kitchen," I said, mimicking Bill's expression.

Bill hummed loudly and prepared a table for four in front of the window that overlooked the magnificent Payette River.

It took Marty another day to complete his final task, but by midafternoon on a Friday, while I washed windows and daydreamed of the grand opening, his loud voice rang out. "Well, I think my work is done here," he said. "Everything turned out okay, don't you think?"

"Everything looks wonderful, Marty."

"I'll get the final bill written up and drop it by on Monday," Marty said, then gathered up his tools and walked away, leaving behind one of the most handsome restaurants I'd ever seen.

Both Bill and I were excited for the kids to get home from school, so the instant they came through the door, I shouted, "Welcome to the *new* Ponderosa! Remember what this place looked like two months ago?" They both rolled their eyes, but I could tell they were happy.

Lisa asked, "When are we opening?"

"Very soon," I answered.

"Looks good. What's for dinner?" Mike asked.

"Well, what about that big trout you caught yesterday?"

"Oh, Mom, there're only *little* fish in that river."

"Mike, how about we cook dinner for Mom and Dad?" Lisa suggested. Mike must have liked the idea because he tossed his backpack aside and moved toward the kitchen.

Bill poured a couple of beers from the keg—foam rolled off the mug as he handed one to me. He tapped his mug against mine. "Lordy, this has been a long three months. C'mon, let's dance," Bill said. A pool table and jukebox had been installed the day before—the only things missing were a couple of quarters and the press of a button. We turned up the volume and danced around the restaurant. Lisa ran from the kitchen to join in.

"Put in more quarters," Lisa shouted as she twirled around tables and chairs.

It wasn't long before we heard Mike proudly announce, "Dinner is now being served." He carried a tray filled with baskets of finger steaks and curly fries to the same table Bill had set up earlier. Lisa, who'd stopped dancing, served four salad bowls filled with leafy greens.

"Great dinner, you two," I said.

"Let's dance some more!" Lisa interrupted.

"Sure, but first, I want to propose a toast—to us and the Ponderosa!" Soda glasses and beer mugs clinked together, making us laugh. Not being a school night, the party continued, and for another three hours, the jukebox gobbled up quarters. Bill and I unwisely accepted Mike and Lisa's challenge to a game of pool—and they kicked our butts.

"Where did you learn to play pool like this?" I asked them both.

"Remember, my friend in Rainier had a pool table in his basement," Mike answered. Mike didn't have to tell us how much he missed his friends from Oregon—it was obvious from the look on his face.

After losing three straight games, Bill and I cried "Uncle." Everyone pitched in to put things away and restore the Ponderosa to brilliance, untouched by the public. We left the restaurant through the side door, the most direct path to our cabin, which was to become the most well-worn walkway of our lives.

Chapter Nine

UNDER NEW MANAGEMENT

Early Saturday morning, even before Doug opened his business, I handed Bill a cup of coffee brewed at our new coffee station. At the counter, we sat on chairs facing a six-levered soda machine and a milk dispenser Bill said looked like a stainless-steel beast with a white hose for a mouth. I stared into the kitchen through the large opening designed for waitresses to call in orders and where plates of food would wait in queue prior to being served. I wondered how many breakfasts, lunches, and dinners would pass through that window.

"I'll touch base with our wholesalers on Monday morning, and with any luck, the deliveries will begin by Wednesday," I said.

"And I'll pick up the menus from the printer on Monday," Bill offered.

"Thanks! That reminds me, Beth called from the bank yesterday—our business checks are ready. Can you stop there too?" I asked.

Beth, my youngest sibling and now a thirteen-year bank employee, was only ten years old when Bill and I married and left Idaho to begin our life together in Oregon, where I discovered lush greenery (referred to as moss by many) and a pleasantly mild climate. Now, I looked forward to having a renewed connection with Beth.

Mike strolled into the restaurant wearing baggy stretch pants and trailing Lisa, who wore mismatched PJs and a blue bath towel wrapped around her wet head. When they proceeded to the kitchen like they owned the place, I turned to Bill and whispered, "It's a good thing we don't have customers."

"Speaking of customers," Bill said, "we need to plan our grand opening."

"Yeah, I guess we'd better discuss that," I replied, starting to feel some jitters. This topic made us both anxious, so we'd been sidestepping it for a while.

"Bill, since I've never done this type of cooking, and Lisa hasn't waitressed, maybe we should have a small rehearsal opening—we can invite Doug, Adelle, and their girls and pretend they're customers. Lisa can waitress, I'll cook, and you and Mike can help out where needed. After that, let's start business on a weekday rather than a busy weekend."

An hour later, our plans were firm. The practice run with our good-natured neighbors would be on a Sunday evening, and then the following day, a quiet Monday, would be our soft opening. We surmised that five low-key weekdays would warm us up before getting clobbered with weekend patrons.

Although the schedule looked good on paper, I felt scared, like a patient waiting for a root canal. After three months, the real deal was upon us, and there was no backing out.

A week of deliveries had the shelves, freezers, and walk-in coolers stocked with food and supplies. When I slowed down long enough to arrange salt and pepper shakers and decorative placemats on each table, a heart-stopping insight hit me. "Bill, do you realize we can serve almost a hundred people in here? How can I cook for that many people?"

"Well, I have to wait on them," Bill replied, biting at his fingernails. Normally, he could hide his nerves, but not this time.

Bill, in charge of sign making, had a knack for writing precise straight letters. "How does this look?" he asked, holding up an extra-large placard that read OPEN—NEW MANAGEMENT.

"That's perfect! Nobody can miss that!"

Back in the far corner of the room, Mike and Lisa had their own project. "We have all the letters and numbers ready for the outside reader board," Lisa announced.

I walked over to see what they had displayed on the table: *8 oz. SIRLOIN STEAK SPECIAL $3.95.*

"Great job—that's exactly right," I said, smiling.

Doug and Adelle had kindly agreed to our proposed mock opening. Plus we owed Doug a free meal for rectifying Bill's unsuccessful attempt to repair the leaky water pipe in the motel.

All afternoon, we prepared for the tryout dinner, and when the time arrived, I handed Lisa a pen, order book, and a dark maroon waitress apron. "Mom, I'm scared," she admitted. Her molasses-brown eyes seemed larger than usual.

"It's just Doug, Adelle, and the girls—they'll be really sweet to you. You'll do a wonderful job. And you look really cute in your new apron," I added, hoping to give her confidence.

I tied the strings of my new crisp white four-way cook's apron into a loose bow, cringing at the thought of drawing attention to my long, flat derrière. Then approaching the flat top grill, I worried about everything—about the grill being too hot, or not hot enough, and how to make certain that everything in an order of more than one item would be ready to serve at the same time. I wished I had *my* mom for reassurance.

At six thirty sharp, Bill unlocked the front door of the Ponderosa. With every indoor restaurant light on, the grill at the correct temperature (I prayed), and all four of the restaurant's employees in position to give their best performance, Bill ushered Doug's family to a booth overlooking the river. Lisa, responsible for the first part of the relay, bashfully approached her first customers. She spoke softly, "May I take your order?" From the kitchen, she looked like a little girl playing waitress, but she wrote down their order with the poise of a professional server, then she walked up to the open window in front of me and announced the order: "Two steak specials, medium rare, a plain burger with fries, and an extra plate." She tore off the first page of her order book and snapped the green slip into a clip on the order wheel. I winked at my grown-up daughter, then turned around to face my own fear—how to gauge when a steak is medium rare? For a couple of moments, I nervously fiddled with the spatula and told myself, *This is the same as cooking for my family,* which I had done for half of my life. Slowly the layers of anxiety peeled off like the leaves of an artichoke.

Doug ordered a beer, which gave Bill a job. While Mike delivered three sodas, Lisa served them two salads. Just as I concluded, the steaks were now medium rare, I heard several strange voices and looked up to see a group of four unfamiliar faces shuffling into a booth. This wasn't the plan and I knew instantly what had happened and what hadn't—people had noticed lights on in the restaurant, and Bill had forgotten to lock the front door.

"Mom, what do I do?" Lisa quietly cried out.

I quickly responded, "Well, go take their order."

Bill scurried in the direction of the door as another couple passed through, but instead of asking them to leave, he escorted them to a table as if that had been the idea all along. We had inadvertently opened the restaurant.

At the end of the night, we cleaned the grill and helped Mike, who'd been the dishwasher at the end of the relay. And we all laughed at how our idea of serving four friends a simple meal turned into an honest-to-God business adventure.

"Oh yes, income!" Bill said, counting the till and beaming.

Lisa reached into her apron pocket and pulled out a wad of dollar bills and some loose change. "Mom, I made $12.50," she squealed in amazement. "Do I have to go to school tomorrow?"

"Yes, but you'll be here after school for more waitressing, and don't you think you should share some of that with the dishwasher?" I said, laughing. I watched as Lisa handed Mike some coins, then happily skipped off to bed. Lisa had discovered wealth.

Pulling up my bedcovers, I couldn't resist bragging a bit. "All the customers seemed to really enjoy my food."

"You cooked those steaks perfectly!" Bill said.

"I did, didn't I?"

"Do you have the alarm set?" he asked.

"Yep—5:00 a.m.!"

When the alarm buzzed, we both jumped out of bed, anxious for the day to begin—it was Monday morning, our first *official* day of business. Bill unlocked the front door of the restaurant, turned on every light, and then placed his OPEN—NEW MANAGEMENT signs so both northbound and southbound traffic could spot it easily. Unexpectedly, I froze and stared at the hot, empty grill, dreading the thought of my first order of eggs over easy. Flipping eggs without breaking yolks is not a skill to be taken for granted. Almost in tears, realizing nobody was coming to my rescue, not even Big Al from the coffee shop where I worked during my high school years. I inhaled heavily and exhaled lightly. *Ann, you don't need Big Al's help, you need to* become *Big Al and do this,* I told myself without speaking the words.

For almost two hours, nothing happened, and Bill and I paced around empty tables, looked at each other, and asked, "Where are the customers?" But our worry was needless—by eight thirty the grill was covered in bacon, pancakes, and hash browns. Bill rushed around taking orders, serving food, pouring coffee, bussing tables, washing dishes, and putting money in the cash register. I swear I could hear circus music.

Every time I got snowed under that day—which occurred at least once every thirty minutes—I'd tell myself, "One order at a time, Ann."

Bill was elated when he spotted Lisa and Mike get off the school bus. Help had arrived.

The next four days flew by—working sixteen hours a day at such a frenzied pace, we slid right into our first weekend.

As wonderful as it was to build clientele and put cash in the till, reality hit—our inventory was critically low. "Bill, don't get too attached to that money—I'll need every cent when I boost my supply order for next week."

On Friday, Frank's Meats delivered fifty-five pounds of boneless prime rib in preparation for our Mother's Day event. "This Sunday, everybody's help will be needed for the entire day, so don't make any other plans," I announced to the family. "Remember, this is a *family* business." Adelle offered to juggle the needs of her service station with those of the Ponderosa if the parking lot filled up. After advertising over the last couple of weeks, we expected two things—a flood of customers and to see Adelle wearing a Ponderosa apron.

On the big day, the door never stopped swinging open, and unoccupied tables were scarce. By the end of the day, we were dog-tired—relieved that Mother's Day was behind us. Lisa and Mike added to their cash stash.

"Seeing Sherm today was nice," Bill said.

"It *was* nice he showed up unexpectedly. The best part—he washed dishes for four hours," I said, yawning.

Chapter Ten

FREE BED AND BREAKFAST

On Tuesday morning, the restaurant had been open for exactly fifteen minutes when the side door swung open. I didn't have to look up to know who had entered and that it was a quarter past six. My first customer knew the location of the coffeepot. "Morning," I called from the kitchen.

"Good morning," he shouted back. I couldn't see his face, but trusted he was wearing a huge grin, clean blue uniform pants, and a matching shirt with *Doug* embroidered on its pocket. Our neighbor always started my day with a big shot of sparkle. Before the start of his twelve-hour shift at the Chevron station, a shift that excluded his 24/7 towing business, we'd share a quick cup of java. The black grease smudged on his clothing and face by the end of the day would only enhance his bright smile.

One of Doug's friends, Deputy Buck, had also become a regular patron. Whenever Buck arrived, I knew Doug would return for his break. A routine had begun. The days and weeks moved along rapidly.

"I'll be late getting home from school today," Mike revealed.

I looked up from the grill to see Mike sitting at the counter eating his usual bowl of cold cereal. "Why, what's up?" I asked.

Casually, he answered, "I have driver's ed class after school. Tim's mom will bring me home."

"What? Wait a minute! I don't want you driving on these dangerous roads!" I said eyeballing him through the food-pick-up window.

"But, Mom, I'm already signed up. And where do you think I *should* drive?"

"Don't I have to sign the form? Besides, the roads around here are too narrow and windy and get slick in the winter. Likewise, people drive too fast on this highway, there's way too much traffic, and there are no guardrails along the river. Mike, we need to talk about this." Mike ignored me, grabbed his backpack, and ran to catch the school bus.

"Why can't he learn to drive like other students, on freeways and downtown streets during rush hour?" I mumbled. "Better yet, a cemetery. He can't get hurt there. Next, he'll want his own vehicle." I took a couple of deep breaths before telling myself to simmer down and let Mike continue to grow up.

Mike's new driver's ed class shook me up, and Lisa filled me with additional concerns. "You can't come to my graduation?" Lisa cried. Her disappointment broke my heart.

I tried to explain. "Honey, the restaurant can't close, and there's nobody else to cook for me. I'm sorry, Lisa, but I have a really full plate. Aunt Kat, Aunt Beth, and Aunt Tootie will be there—they love you and are looking forward to seeing you graduate. And you remember how your Aunt Kat always takes lots of pictures to share." My family had generously volunteered to fill the gap that my new career created, but I tried not to think about how many more milestones I might miss.

"Good morning!" Like a song, the sound of Doug's words rang out. The creak of the side door preceded him at precisely six fifteen.

Two customers, already enjoying the $1.99 breakfast special— two pancakes, two strips of bacon, and one egg—chatted together in a booth.

"Morning, Doug." I scurried past him, carrying syrup and silverware, then took the time to refill coffee cups before I stopped to visit. It had started to get light outside, and the traffic was getting heavier. "The highway seems busy—is there some event up at McCall this week?" I asked Doug.

"Not that I'm aware of, but the jet boat races are this coming weekend," Doug reminded me.

"That's right! Can't believe boats race *up* the Payette," I said.

"It gets a lot of spectators, so you'll be swamped," Doug added.

For the past month, we'd been observing rafters, tubers, and kayakers nonstop. All of which provided a welcome entertaining sideshow for our customers. Of course, the jet boat races would bring an audience—undoubtedly a hungry one.

"My plan for next year at this time is to watch the races from our new deck," I said.

"That'll be nice, but do you really want more business?" Doug asked, laughing aloud and refilling his cup. Suddenly, something out the window caught Doug's attention, and he walked over for a better view. "What goofball would be walking down this busy highway?" he asked.

I peeked out the window to see this uncommon sight. "What the hell? That's my motel guest who hasn't paid. He arrived late last night after we'd all gone to bed, so I gave him a key, told him we'd square things up in the morning. That jackass!"

Doug had never heard me cuss, but if he was shocked, he hid it. Calmly, he walked across the room to the phone on the wall. "Hey, Buck, it's Doug. I need you to pick up a fellow walking north of Lower Banks. He owes the Ponderosa for a motel room."

"Thanks, Doug," I said. He waved and left the same way he had come in.

It took less than twenty minutes for the sheriff's car to pull into the parking lot. Deputy Buck had company. He ushered a guy in his late thirties through the side entrance and introduced him as Russell. I scrutinized the man who had just tried to dupe me. His shaggy beard, speckled with premature gray, suggested that a razor wasn't an item in his knapsack.

"Well, Russell, it's obvious you were trying to stiff me for last night's lodging," I said.

"I don't have any money," he answered honestly.

"Did you really think you could stay in my motel for free?"

"Well, I'd planned to leave before you got up," Russell admitted.

"You owe me $25 for the room, plus tax—a total of $26.50."

Russell struggled to avoid any eye contact with me. "I can't pay you," he said.

Buck must have sensed that I could handle Russell, or maybe he was showing me the way disputes are settled in Idaho. For whatever reason, he decided his presence wasn't needed for the time being and slipped out the side door. "Annie, I'll be back in a few minutes," he said, heading toward Doug's station.

"Sit down right there, Russell, until I decide what to do—I have an order to cook." I directed him to the counter where I could keep an eye on him through the opening. As I flipped pancakes, an old saying popped into my head: *'You can't get blood out of a turnip.'* It also occurred to me that I was partially to blame for not collecting the money before giving out the room key. I was irked, but Russell, like Butch, had taught me another lesson. I studied him through the service window, and from his sniffling, could tell he was fighting off a cold. He wore a faded flannel shirt and dirty worn-out jeans, but after using the motel's shower and soap, he looked remarkably clean. I watched as Russell stared at a menu in deep contemplation.

When I returned to resume my interrogation, he spoke first. "I can design a better-looking menu."

"We already have a nice menu," I retorted.

"I'm a graphic designer, and I can make it look even better. Do you have a piece of paper?" Before I could answer, Russell picked up a napkin and began sketching out different designs, which suggested he had talent. "If you had someone do this work for you, it'd cost a minimum of $300, but if you give me a couple of weeks and your mailing address, I'll mail you my illustration." He must've seen the skepticism on my face. "Trust me, I'll do this for you," he added.

Oh hell, don't give me that cockamamie load of crap, I thought to myself. *And don't suggest that my menu is lackluster.*

Buck returned to find Russell, who apparently was not only a talented artist but also a pro when it came to conning restaurant ladies, devouring a large breakfast. "Looks like you have things worked out," Buck said. He stared at me with an expression of amusement mixed with curiosity as to how I'd gotten tricked out of more.

In only a few words, I explained how Russell planned to pay off his tab.

With a full stomach and a lot of attitude, Russell sauntered toward the front door. "Can I get a large coffee with cream and sugar to go?" he asked.

Before exiting the restaurant and leaving the warmth and breakfast smells behind, Russell reassured me one last time but without eye contact, "It might take a month to get this mailed, but don't worry."

As I watched the lonely man resume his stroll along the busy canyon highway, sipping coffee from the Ponderosa's deluxe-sized to-go cup, I felt certain this would be the last time I'd see or hear from Russell. My menu design would stay the same.

Occasionally I would speculate about Russell and presumed he had lost my address. This time it felt okay to be hoodwinked.

Chapter Eleven

STRETCHING AND GROWING

"Bill, we'll need help for this coming weekend. Doug says it gets pretty crazy around here on race day."

"Yeah, I know. There've been at least two dozen people who've mentioned they'd be back on Saturday."

The upcoming event had Mike counting down the minutes. Next to food, girls, and cars, the thing a fifteen-year-old boy likes best is watching high-speed motorboats rip up a narrow, rocky river. Throw in 1,200 decibels of open exhaust, and you have total bliss.

Directly behind the restaurant was a particular rapid that routinely caught rafters and kayakers off guard, always creating some riveting amusement for the Ponderosa patrons. Bill, the kids, and I decided this rapid deserved a name. After chucking out a few unmentionable words that promoted some loud laughter, we selected KYBR. Initially, only we knew what the acronym meant, but the name was too good to keep a family secret, and eventually *kick-your-butt rapid* became well-known. Mike knew even a motorboat was no match for KYBR and eagerly awaited the wipeouts.

Four days before the boat races, Adelle came in to treat herself and her youngest daughter, Sophie, to a chicken breast sandwich. Mike also loved this lunch favorite and used every opportunity to order it. After overhearing Adelle's order, Mike called out, a smidgen too loudly, "Hey, Mom, can I get one of those chicken-*booby*-sandwiches too?"

"Mike, don't say that in public," I reminded him for the hundredth time, unable to hide my smirk.

While Adelle waited patiently for Sophie to finish her portion of the sandwich, I had a few minutes of respite in the kitchen, so I decided to say hello. Neither Adelle nor I had much of a social life—grabbing free time with each other was rare. "How are you girls today?" I asked, approaching their table.

"Pretty good, now that Sophie's over her ear infection," she replied. We chatted for a few minutes before she asked me, "Have you met our newest neighbor? Her name is Moriah. She just moved into one of the cabins across the road—she's the blonde gal, sitting over there with her friend, Paula." Adelle gestured toward the table behind her.

When Adelle and I looked at the girls, they both waved, acknowledging us.

"Hi!" I said and waved back.

Adelle leaned in and whispered, "I think Moriah is looking for a job. She seems really nice."

Instantly, I jumped into motion, heading straight to Moriah's table. I reached out my hand—promptly getting right to the point of the matter. "I'm Ann—it's a pleasure to meet you. Are you looking for a job? Because I sure could use a waitress for the weekend," I said.

"I've never waitressed before," Moriah responded hesitantly. Somehow the look of panic made her big blue eyes and curly hair even more darling.

I had a good feeling about this petite blonde in her late twenties and wasn't going to let up. "We're all new to this!" I laughed.

"*Order in!*" Lisa yelled.

"Just a second. I'll be right back—don't leave!"

Within minutes, I sat down next to the young woman whom I hoped would be my new employee. "Maybe you can drop by tomorrow and work with my daughter, Lisa, just to see if you like it. Can you come in tomorrow morning around eleven?"

"I can definitely give it a try," Moriah said, timidly.

"Lisa," I called. "Come here—meet our new neighbor, Moriah. She'll be here tomorrow to help you."

En route to the kitchen and carrying a tub of dirty dishes, Lisa yelled, "Hi, Moriah!"

"Do you need a cook?" Moriah's friend Paula asked.

When I heard this question, I couldn't believe my luck—had I just caught two fish with one cast?

"I cook part-time at the café in Horseshoe Bend," Paula revealed.

What good fortune! My head spun, and my toes tapped the floor under the table. "Are you kidding me? Yes, I need a cook. When can you start?"

"I can start on Friday," Paula answered, excitement radiating from her pretty hazel eyes.

"Awesome!" I stood up from the table, took a step backward, and added, "I'd better get back to the kitchen. Moriah, I'll see you tomorrow morning." I twirled around, and with an upbeat stride, I walked away. Finding employees wasn't complicated—all I had to do was check out the customer pool.

When Moriah arrived ten minutes early to work, I took it to be a good sign. During their shifts together, Lisa and Moriah laughed nonstop—they hit it off perfectly. Moriah's cheerful personality and desire to serve made all aspects of the job flow naturally. She would be an asset to the Ponderosa, and if after the coming weekend she still enjoyed waitressing, she'd be on the schedule along with my new assistant cook, Paula.

On Sunday, jet boats roared by the Ponderosa at high speed, and every last one of them avoided KYBR, to Mike's disappointment. But the action impressed its audience nonetheless. With having the restaurant busy from dawn to sunset, I realized more waitresses were needed. I remembered what Paula had mentioned earlier that day—her sister needed a job. Realistically, I needed three more waitresses, in addition to Lisa and Moriah. My mission for the following week would be to recruit.

Even though her shift was over for the day, Moriah returned just as Bill locked the restaurant's front door. "Let's sit and talk awhile," I said to her. "So how do you like waitressing?" Having heard Paula call her *Myra*, I quickly added another question, "Can I call you Myra?"

"I love it, and yes, you can call me Myra," she answered.

"I'm thrilled to hear that—would you be interested in working the early morning shift, six to two o'clock, with Mondays and Tuesdays off?"

"I like the work, and really need the money—the tips are incredible," she added. "No doubt, I want the job!"

Myra, whose cute personality matched her appearance and easy smile, was raising her young son, Benjamin, alone—having a steady paycheck would help lighten her responsibility. While discussing her wages and bi-weekly paydays, Bill poured a couple of draft beers and set them down in front of us.

"Thanks, hon, that's exactly what we wanted." We toasted and laughed. Laughing was contagious around Myra.

The following week, Paula's sister was added to the payroll along with two of Mike's classmates. "Can't wait for Sherm's next visit. He'll be surprised to see we've hired a cook and four waitresses," I told Bill.

However, by the middle of June, the highway traffic had become constant, and more vehicles meant more business, which meant we needed additional help. "Tomorrow, I'll start looking for another cook and a few more waitresses," I told the family. Relief showed in everyone's faces. The Ponderosa's business grew rapidly, and I questioned if we could keep up.

Chapter Twelve

FIRE ON THE MOUNTAIN

After the lunch rush on a Wednesday, I said to Myra, "It's a perfect time to throw in a load of laundry. I'll be back in a bit."

Entering Mike's room, I winced. "He needs to clean this up," I grumbled to myself. Filling up the washer with sheets and soap, I remembered a motel room that also needed cleaning. *Will I ever get caught up?* I wondered. There wasn't time to mull over the answer—I flew out the door, ignoring the mess in the living room.

Sprinting down the driveway en route to the motel, I heard an odd sound. Across the highway, directly behind Myra's cabin and up the steep mountain, a helicopter hovered at the summit above the treetops. When three people descended down a rope that dangled from the helicopter, I thought the incident seemed peculiar—but didn't take time to ponder the situation.

Within ten minutes, I locked the door to the clean motel room and turned toward the restaurant. When I noticed a few new vehicles in the parking lot, I picked up my pace. Curious, I glanced back up the mountain where the helicopter had been, but instead of a helicopter, I saw *smoke* billowing from the summit. Alarmed, I ran like I was the one on fire, swung open the restaurant door, and ran smack into Myra. She started to speak. "I need three Ponderosa burgers and a—"

"Myra, there's *a fire on the mountain behind your cabin!*" I screamed. As I raced past her, I accidentally hit the corner of the jukebox, and my right hand crunched loudly. Intense pain racked my body, rendering me tearful and breathless. "*Yoaaawwooowwwww…you no good…quarter-sucking…,*" I muttered, holding the injured hand close to my chest.

But even extreme pain wasn't enough to stop me. A waitress's order slip, tacked on the wall next to the phone in my office, was foremost in my mind. On this small green paper, there was a pencil-scribbled number to call in case of an emergency, and in my book, this qualified as a crisis.

When a woman answered on the second ring, I gave her the specifics and answered her questions. She sounded far too cavalier for my comfort, compelling me to add, "They'd better hurry!" It seemed necessary to rev her up to an understanding of the significance of the emergency.

"Ma'am, help is on the way," she replied.

By the time I hung up the phone, our customers had become spectators. People filled the parking lot, watching flames and smoke spread across the mountaintop.

An elderly gentleman, with a cigarette dangling from his mouth, interjected, "With all those trees for fuel, it's going to burn pretty damn fast."

He was dead-on. The rugged mountainside, dry from summer heat and drought, was covered with thick underbrush, which acted as an endless supply of kindling, igniting the ponderosa pines like a string of firecrackers.

By the time we heard sirens, all the spectators had been scared off, and only the Lower Banks residents remained. We watched in disbelief as emergency vehicles filled the Ponderosa's and the Chevron's adjoining parking lots. Not long after, the highway closed, allowing only fire and emergency vehicles to pass.

A tall man in full fire gear faced me and asked, "Is this your restaurant?" His green eyes narrowed, and he looked at me intently from beneath his hard hat.

"Yes," I said, my eyes big as Ponderosa burgers.

"No need to worry about the fire coming down this far, these emergency rigs and the water tanker over there are here to protect the buildings." The firefighter's gravelly voice was confident and calm, but the increasing smoke and flames across the highway were more persuasive.

Knowing Myra would be concerned about Ben, her cabin, and her possessions, I scoped out the congested area to find her and noticed Doug moving quickly toward me.

"They can't fight the fire from the highway, so they sent a fire crew up the mountain," Doug reported using his most reassuring tone. The look on my face told him I wasn't comforted. "Annie, they won't let Banks burn. Look over there next to my house," Doug said, pointing across the highway. "What do you see?"

"Doug, how can you be so calm? That's a *gas tank*!"

"Exactly! Do you think they'll let that baby blow up?"

"I sure hope not! One-hundred-foot flames and a behemoth gas tank don't make a good combination."

Bill walked over to Doug, wearing the same expression as all the other Lower Banks residents. "Oh, there's Myra and Ben," I said, leaving the men to discuss the gas tank.

After getting through the logjam of people, I reached out for Myra's hand and wrapped my free arm around Ben's small shoulders. The sweet, easy-to-love six-year-old melted into my side. "Are you both okay? They both nodded in the affirmative. I passed on the information Doug had given me, purposely avoiding a certain topic—the oversize gas tank.

After sunset, the firefighters continued to work in smoky, abstract shadows. The firestorm that had devoured the mountaintop had dwindled, and the flames traveling downward flared less ferociously. Although less terrifying, no one could overlook reality—fire still descended toward the cabins. The small community of residents huddled together beside the water tanker, staring up at the red glow of the entire ridge ablaze. Our untrained eyes were unable to calculate the fire's proximity.

The sound of an unfamiliar voice distracted us. "Folks, let me ease your minds," the man said. "You can all go to bed. We'll be stationed here all night—don't worry about a thing. When it's dark outside, the fire looks worse and appears closer than it really is. Plus there's a fire crew up there—you just can't see them." Walking away, he added, "Sleep well. We have it under control."

When Lisa began to cough, I took it as a sign. "Well, I guess there's nothing we can do, so let's get to bed." I put my arm around Lisa's waist, and together we walked to our cabin. Even with firefighters protecting us, it would be a restless night for the eleven residents of Lower Banks.

The following morning greeted us harshly. With the thick smoke obstructing my 20/20 eyesight, it seemed as if I was peering through my nearly blind great-grandma's glasses. However, the fireman had kept his word—every building stood, unscathed by the blaze. But the danger wasn't over—emergency vehicles and firefighters still littered the parking lots, which had become the command post.

With the highway closed, there was no reason to open the business. I hustled to the restaurant and entered something rare—our eatery, empty of customers. At first, I felt a little sad but quickly told myself, "Don't be an *idiot* Ann, enjoy every second of it!"

After brewing coffee, I carried a full tray of steaming Styrofoam cups into the crowd. Most of the firefighters had been up all night, so the tray emptied quickly. I was enjoying myself, doing what I did best, fully focused on serving people, when I was caught off guard by a loud *boom* that penetrated the morning quiet.

"It's just the pitch pockets exploding in those pine trees," Bill explained when he noticed my reaction.

When did Bill become an expert on forest fires, using the lingo and everything? I wondered. It didn't matter, though, the explanation sounded good to me.

In the crowd, a firefighter also witnessed my fear. "Don't be concerned," he said. "There'll be a fire crew around here for a couple more days. And thanks for the coffee," he added with a polite nod.

"You are welcome. I'll keep the restaurant's side door unlocked, so everyone has access to the restrooms," I said. It was the least I could do for the people protecting my family, friends, and property.

"Annie, your dad's on the phone," Bill yelled from the doorway.

I ran to the restaurant, anxious to speak with him. "Hi, Dad. I tried to call you last night, but you didn't answer."

"Yeah, I went into town for some groceries." (I'm pretty sure he meant beer.) "What's going on up there? I've been watching the news and heard the highway is closed." Dad sounded concerned.

I gave Sherm a complete update and ended our conversation with the reassurance that we were out of danger. I generalized—because Dad had been a fireman, he was all too familiar with the unpredictability and mass devastation fire can cause. Suddenly, an unforgettable event flashed into my mind:

Back in 1956, when I was five years old, I recalled how Dad would take me to the fire station and show me the fire trucks, equipment, gigantic kitchen, sleeping room, and lastly, the fireman pole, which he would slide down in record speed. What intrigued my young brain the most was the line of pants and boots that were already connected, ready for my dad to step into and just pull up. I remember the fire alarm was loud, about the scariest sound ever.

Another memory, from that same time period, flooded my thoughts:

While eating breakfast, I learned why my dad hadn't come home from work—he'd gone to the hospital instead. It was in the final hours of his four-day shift at the station when the alarm awakened him. When the fire truck arrived, he discovered a house engulfed in flames and heavy smoke. My dad ran into the burning house because there was a three-year-old boy trapped in an upstairs bedroom. After spending three days in the hospital for treatment of smoke inhalation, Dad came home and went straight to bed. That same afternoon, I peeked into his room and noticed he was awake, so I took him a glass of water. Dad looked different—kind of frightening, his little eyes beet red in contrast with his pale skin. Dad's voice was also scary. He said, "Thank you, Annie," in a low, hoarse voice, and then began to cough.

"Daddy, what's wrong?" I asked in a nervous voice, confused by his strange appearance.

"Don't you worry, Annie, I'll be fine in a few days."

I pounced onto the bed next to Dad and told him I would take good care of him until he got better. After a few minutes passed, Dad stopped coughing, and I asked the question I'd been pondering for days. "Daddy, how's that little boy you saved from the fire?"

Dad stared at me with his red eyes and explained how the little boy hadn't survived the fire, but his two sisters had.

"Daddy, you needed wings," I said.

"Wings, huh?"

"Yeah, if you had wings, you could have jumped out the window," I explained.

"I suppose you are right about that," he answered. "You can go play now because I'm going to sleep for a while." When I jumped off the bed, his words were loud and clear. "You're going to make a great nurse, Annie." For the remainder of that day, those words stuck in my head. Finally, somebody had appreciated me, I thought. For me, the immense character-building lesson I learned that day was: empathy was worthwhile and would make me feel essential. No matter how often Dad's alcoholism let me down or made me cry, he would always be my hero.

Returning my thoughts to the present, I found my attitude had shifted. Instead of holding resentment for my father's endless binges, I felt admiration for a man who had saved other people's lives. I reached for the phone and called him back. After a few minutes of lighthearted conversation, I invited him to lunch. "Dad, with a bit of luck, the road should open soon. And I have a deposit for you to take to Beth." Sherm, soon to become the driver of the Ponderosa's Brinks unarmored car, loved being an important link to the Ponderosa's success.

"Yeah, I can do that for you," Sherm responded.

"Thanks, Dad. Hope to see you soon."

For another hour, Bill and Myra continued our nonstop beverage service through the side door, and by nine thirty that morning, because of the heavy smoke, most of Lower Banks inhabitants had gathered inside the Ponderosa. That day, Moriah and Ben became an important part of our family.

Forty-eight hours after the highway closed, it reopened. The water tanker left, followed by the majority of the other emergency vehicles, only leaving a few firefighters to mop up the hot spots along the blackened, barren terrain.

"In another twenty-four hours, they should have the fire knocked down and be completely out of your way," Deputy Buck reported.

"That'll be nice," I said, knowing my coffee supply was running dangerously low.

Highway traffic crawled along, every traveler rubbernecking to take in the scorched landscape. After the restaurant reopened, Myra and Lisa soon grew weary of repeating the same old stories.

After a couple of days, however, restaurant life once again returned to normal, which spelled *hectic*.

"Annie, somebody wants to talk to you," Myra said, catching my attention through the food window.

"Tell them I'll be right out." I looked at Paula and said, "I'll be back." Wiping my hands on my apron, I practically stomped from the kitchen, a tad annoyed by the interruption. There, standing beside the cash register, was a middle-aged man with chiseled features and a well-manicured handlebar mustache. He held out his right hand and introduced himself.

"Hello, I'm Ann. What can I do for you?" I couldn't stop staring at his precisely twisted facial hair.

"I understand you're the individual who called to report the fire on the mountain," he said.

"Yes, that was me."

"Can you tell me exactly what you witnessed?"

"Well, I saw a helicopter drop off three people on the summit, and fifteen minutes later, I saw smoke."

"Did you happen to see anybody or anything else?"

"No, that was all I saw."

"Okay. Thanks, Ann, for your help. I appreciate it," he said and turned and left.

I resumed my position at the grill and reached for my spatula. "Paula, I'm certain that that helicopter and those three men had everything to do with starting that fire, but I sure can't make sense of it." If the mystery was ever solved, I was not privy.

Chapter Thirteen

THE JULY MELTDOWN

Bill, his face splotchy red and covered in shiny sweat, complained loudly, "I don't think those swamp coolers are working worth a damn." The armpits of his polo shirt were soaked nearly to his waist, and he was trying to control his temper, but I could tell his agitation was only a whisker away from a full blowup.

I stared directly at him, and I wasn't smiling—not even a little bit. "I know it's warm in here, but it is a hundred and ten degrees outside. What do you expect? It's July in Idaho. And if you want to feel *real* heat, why don't you stand in front of this grill and fryer for sixteen hours."

"I don't need your smart-ass remarks," Bill sniped back.

"But it's true, and I don't need your bellyaching," I mumbled under my breath. Bill's anger trigged resentment in me I didn't even know I'd been harboring. Within seconds, I was as pissed at him as he was at the coolers. But the miserable expression on his face softened my anger, and I did my best to shift my disposition and become more helpful.

"Next time George and Trudy from the Garden Valley Store stop in, we can ask them who does their maintenance. I'm guessing they know of a good handyman. Better yet, why don't you just give them a call right now?"

Acting as if he didn't hear me, Bill yelled, "Where's Mike? He just leaves his fishing pole anywhere he wants. I just stepped on it and snapped it in half."

Lisa piped up, "He's next door, helping Doug."

"He'd rather pump gas than wait tables," I added.

Wanting to make a little more trouble for her older brother, Lisa broadcasted, "Mike wants Doug to find him a car to buy."

Her comment caught me off guard, as she had hoped, but I didn't want to give her the satisfaction. "Well, he's working to earn it," I said. Secretly, I liked the thought of Mike pumping gas and learning auto mechanics—these days Ol' Blue seemed to always need a tune-up.

Our mailman loudly announced, "Special delivery for Lisa!" He got a kick out of Lisa and knew how to make her day. Lisa pulled down a hot roast beef sandwich from the open window and let out a loud "Yahoo!"

"What are all those packages?" I asked.

Lisa sprinted off to deliver the steaming plate of sliced beef with mashed potatoes and gravy, nearly spilling it onto the gentleman's lap. I gasped aloud.

Lisa was handed six large parcels, which she could hardly carry. "These are the new clothes I ordered from the catalogs," she squealed, her face radiating excitement. "I got all this for only $189.99!"

Watching her open each package, I pretended to be thrilled with her newly discovered way of spending money. The discussion of saving for college would come later. For now, it was her cash—she'd earned every cent of it—plus I didn't have time to take her shopping. *Hell, I didn't have time for anything.*

"Order in!"

"I'm coming." Trudging to the kitchen, I grabbed a bag of M&Ms from the candy-and-gum rack next to the cash register. M&Ms always made me feel better. I considered taking a peek at Lisa's catalogs but ruled out the idea quickly—nothing looks fashionable under a food-splattered apron.

Mike moseyed into the restaurant through the side entrance, covered in grime and grease.

"It must be your lunch break," I said, staring at his attire and knowing at the end of my day I'd see those clothes in the forever-growing pile of dirty laundry. "Don't come any closer with those oily hands and clothes. I'll fix your lunch."

"How about a chicken booby sandwich with extra swiss?" He snickered.

"One chicken *breast* sandwich coming up," I answered back, grinning and feeling my mood shift a bit.

Mike wolfed down his lunch, jumped up, and announced, "Mom, I think Doug found me a cool car."

"That's great!" Thanks to Lisa's warning, I was able to muster a response more cheerful than I actually felt.

"I'll tell you and Dad about it tonight," he hollered as he ran out the door.

"Mom, George, and Trudy are here from the Garden Valley Store!" Lisa yelled.

Though I wondered why she had to shout it out from across the restaurant, I was grateful for the information. George and Trudy were well-known in Boise County and had become regular customers on their weekly trips to Boise. They would stop by for a sandwich and a cup of tea, Earl Gray for George and herbal for Trudy. "Good to see you both," I said, approaching their booth. "How's everything in Garden Valley?"

"Well, good, except that our cashier fell off of his roof last Friday," Trudy answered, dipping her tea bag into steaming water. "Yeah, he's lucky. He broke his leg in a couple of places, but he'll be fine."

"Thank goodness! Hey, I wanted to ask you both—who works on your swamp cooler?" Without waiting for an answer, I continued, "Better yet, do you have a general maintenance man? We have a few little projects around here that need attention."

George spoke up immediately, "Yeah, we use a guy named John Vander. He's new to the area and does odd jobs for the locals."

Trudy smiled and added her two bits, "He does a terrific job, and he's a real character too. I know you'll like him."

George barely let Trudy finish her comments—he wanted to be the one to tell me about John. "He lives in an old bus at the trailer park, so he doesn't have a phone, but I'll let him know to stop by if he's interested in more work."

"Looks like the waitresses are getting busy, so I'd better get back to cooking. It's nice to see you again, and thanks for the info on John."

Later that evening, Mike desperately tried to convince Bill and me of the advantages of owning a vehicle that didn't run. His enthusiasm and relentless persuasion reminded me of how I had tried to convince him of the benefits of owning an abandoned, broken-down restaurant.

Mike explained, "Doug says he'll help me restore it."

The word *restore* caught Bill's interest. "Okay, tell us about it."

"Yeah, Dad, it's a yellow 1971 Ranchero. When we're finished with it, it'll be the *best*."

"How do you plan to pay for it?" I butted in and instantly regretted it, knowing how determined Mike was once he got his mind-set on something.

"I'll work at the station. Doug says it's okay."

Bill caved in first. "Well, if Doug is willing to help you get it running, it's all right with me."

I decided to stay silent.

The following afternoon, while slicing, dicing, and otherwise getting ready for the dinner rush, I noticed a rather scruffy man sitting at the counter. Even with his uncombed red hair and loose-fitting, slightly shabby clothes, his kind demeanor showed through. When I made eye contact with him, he nodded sociably and motioned for me to come to him. "I'll be right there," I said through the opening.

"George from the store told me you needed some work done," the man mumbled cordially.

"Oh yeah. Hello, I'm Ann...You must be John Vander. Thanks for stopping by." I shook his hand and gave him the details of the problematic swamp coolers.

John asked, "Where's your ladder? I'll check them out." His soft voice contrasted with his burliness. Within the hour, John reported that the coolers had pretty much served their purpose in life. I had to stand close to hear his words. "They're just worn-out," he told me. "I can hook up a new air conditioner, if you want."

John, obviously sensing my hesitation about an unanticipated expense of an air conditioner, interjected, "I have a bunch of scraps I can use for the installation—you only need to purchase the air conditioner."

I recalled that I'd been told John was a mastermind when it came to fixing, building, and inventing. It didn't take me long to decide I should jump at his offer.

"I can start tomorrow, around noon. I don't get up too early," he said, grinning for the first time, revealing large, perfectly spaced teeth.

"Thanks, John, see you tomorrow."

John worked on the cooling system with diligence and precision, and in less than a week of drilling, cutting holes, and adding ducting for cold air to circulate, the restaurant was cool and summertime bearable. "Excellent job. So what do I owe you, John?" I asked.

When he said an amount quietly, almost under his breath, I was sure I hadn't heard correctly—it was less than half of what the job should cost. John must have noticed the shocked look on my face because he repeated himself. I had the impression he thought his fee might be too high.

"I appreciate your low charge for such great work," I said, handing him a check. "Are you hungry?"

John devoured a well-deserved meal and told me he liked to stay busy by keeping his fees low. "How about I hook up TVs in those motel rooms?"

"But you can't do that without cable hookup, which we don't have," I replied.

He cocked his head and looked intently at me. I had no idea what he was thinking.

"I'll be back in a few days," he said in that soft voice of his, which I no longer had to strain to hear. He waved his hand and ambled away. Clearly a genuine friendship had commenced.

Sunday's heavy highway traffic brought nonstop customers streaming through the restaurant. Grateful for Paula's help in the kitchen, I thanked her for the thousandth time. When Bill flew by, carrying a tray of dirty beer mugs headed for the dishwasher, he heard me repeating yet again, "I think we need extra help."

Bill, busy with a crowded bar of drinkers, spoke without missing a step, "We can talk about it later."

Sherm stopped by for a visit. He wasn't big on eating a sit-down meal, so he rarely had more than a cup of coffee. He called himself a snacker, loving salty peanuts, kimchi, and spicy pork rinds (like condiments for his favorite beverage), none of which were on the Ponderosa menu. Unless Dad stood beside me at the grill, visiting was difficult, but Sherm understood—he got his enjoyment from seeing the Ponderosa bustling with customers. But when it became time for Dad to leave, I called nonsense. *I should at least take time to say goodbye,* I thought.

Sherm, though a man of few words, hugged me back and expressed his approval aloud. "You and Bill have turned this place around. I'm proud of you, Annie."

"Thanks, Dad, I appreciate that. And thanks for scoping out the Ponderosa last February and forcing me to acclimate to weeks of triple-digit temperatures now," I said, giggling. My dad's up-front expression of praise, something rare, made me giddy, and I basked in his admiration before giving him an extra hug. I handed off the bank's deposit bag, waved, and ran back to the kitchen, which now seemed like a jail cell with a grill—there I discovered the order wheel clogged with green slips, dangling in a muddled array. The physical consequences of taking a five-minute break blew me away; well, I could only hope it would blow me away, possibly into a different county. I yanked down four slips—each covered with more food items than the previous. I placed them in a row, threw on six burger patties, picked up the spatula, and sighed.

Chapter Fourteen

LIFE FLIGHT

"*Help! Help!*" These cries, I'd heard a few days earlier, when a raft got trapped in KYBR and flipped six people into the river. Over the summer months, I'd grown accustomed to KYBR screams, a mixture of fear and joyful laughter. However, this time, the loud disruption came from a different source. This scream didn't come from the river—it came from a single voice. Again, I heard it. "Hurry call for help—there's been a bad car accident around the corner. Call an ambulance!"

Without bothering to put down the spatula, which seemed to be a permanent extension of my right hand, I rushed to the phone and dialed the emergency number, a number I had almost memorized. When the dispatch lady asked her usual questions, all I could tell her was, "The accident is close to the Ponderosa and people need medical attention." Her voice sounded annoyed. "Emergency vehicles are en route," she said.

There hadn't been time for me to enforce prudent parental censorship before calling for the ambulance, so Mike and Lisa had run off to see the accident before I could catch them.

"Traffic has completely stopped moving. That's not a good sign," Myra said, looking out the window.

With traffic at a standstill, business ceased, and the waitresses were sent home for the day. Any details of the accident were sketchy and inconsistent until Mike and Lisa returned, the color missing from both their faces, especially Lisa's.

Mike hollered, "Mom, we have to get the parking lot cleared out—they're bringing in Life Flight and I heard them say they're going to land here."

"Seriously? They're going to land a helicopter in our parking lot? How can they do that? Are you sure, Mike?"

"Mom, he's hurt really bad—there's blood everywhere," Lisa cried.

"Come here, Lisa. I wish you hadn't gone down there," I whispered, clutching her tightly, angry at myself for letting it happen.

Dusk, fast approaching, might have diminished the summer heat, but it had no effect on the tragic bedlam. Mike, busy describing what he saw, was interrupted when a state police officer approached our group, confirming that our parking lot would need to be cleared of all vehicles and bystanders. Immediately, Bill and Mike took charge of getting people to move their vehicles from the soon-to-be landing pad. The officer, concerned about flying debris, ushered everyone into the restaurant.

We all selected windows to watch the dramatic event unfold. Within minutes, we heard a whirling sound and felt the building shake, as Life Flight landed right before our eyes. We were frozen, silent, and hardly breathing as we anticipated what would happen next. Perfectly choreographed, the ambulance from the accident site was quickly positioned adjacent to the helicopter, and the doors swung open wide. Because of the dusk and the cluster of EMT personnel, the patient could not be seen in transit from one emergency vehicle to another, but the horrifying sound of pain was loud and clear. The severely injured man became argumentative and combative, indicating a possible head injury, or a totally intoxicated person, or both. It took only twenty minutes before the helicopter lifted off, but it seemed like hours.

Bill locked up the restaurant and then found Ben asleep on the padded bench of a booth, giving Myra permission to stay.

"What a night," Bill said, pouring only *one* mug of beer from the tap.

"What about Myra and me?" I sat down at a table close to the bar and waited for Myra to sit down with me. "Lisa, I think you should go to bed, honey," I said.

"No, Mom, I want to stay up."

I knew Lisa had witnessed a shocking sight and probably needed to talk about it.

"People said the guy who got hurt was passing five cars at a time, right on the corner there," Mike said, pointing south. "A big motor home, going the opposite direction hit him head-on. Jeez, the guy was driving a little sports car, and it got demolished."

We listened to Mike's gory details of the bloody scene until he wound down, and then, without being asked, he and Lisa slipped out the bar-side door, off to bed.

Bill poured another three mugs of beer, and we sat a little longer listening to Bill's version of the story. "I talked to Doug, and he gave me more details. The fire department had to use the jaws of life to extricate the man from his car. Both of his legs were crushed. Being disoriented, he verbally and physically attacked the EMTs. They eventually had to pop him with a syringe full of drugs. The poor guy probably won't survive."

"Well, for what it's worth, the version I got was that the guy drove over eighty miles an hour and passed cars on a blind curve before smashing head-on into a thirty-eight-foot Winnebago. Did he think he'd end up with a black eye or broken pinkie? What about endangering other people's lives? Or at least affecting their travels?" The horrific images made me nauseous.

"Let's call it a day. I have to face the morning rush."

"I'm glad the weekend's over," Myra responded, who didn't seem to mind that she hadn't gotten to share her observations or opinions.

Bill went to the booth, gently scooped Ben up into his arms without awakening him, and followed Myra out. I trudged to the kitchen for my end-of-the-day cleanup.

Chapter Fifteen

THE BIG PICTURE

John Vander, whom I had recently nicknamed Vandie, proved clever in hooking up three small televisions in the motel rooms. Now we fully understood what Trudy had meant when she said, "John can build a washing machine out of a penny and a battery."

"What's John doing with that big satellite dish?" Mike asked as he entered the kitchen.

Ben, who happened to be standing beside me to observe the soup-making process firsthand, answered Mike. "He's putting TVs in the motel rooms," Ben said, sounding wise for a first-grader.

Mike flipped his one-pound burger patty high into the air and watched it hit the grill, splattering grease everywhere. "That's cool!" (Did he mean the splattered grease or the satellite dish?)

"Ben, would you do me a big favor—go remind John it's time to eat," I asked politely. Without answering, Ben ran out the door to find his new buddy, John. Since John's labor charges were always below standard costs, I made sure he got fed.

A short time later, John wandered into the kitchen, looking delighted as a child who just performed his first summersault across the living room floor. He quietly announced, "I'm finished, come look and tell me what you think." John's lips turned up slightly at the corners—his perpetual smile had caused several deep creases to form around his eyes.

I watched as Paula spread mayo onto a BLT sandwich. "I'll be back shortly," I said and followed John to the motel.

When John turned on the *Ricki Lake* show in room 2, the perfectly clear picture amazed me. "You knock my socks off!" I said, patting him on the back. John stood next to the satellite dish with his eyes smiling and an *aw-shucks-it-was-no-big-deal* expression. For the first time, I realized that under the bristly facial hair and sloppy attire, there was a fairly handsome man.

The familiar background sound of screams from KYBR had John and me laughing. "Come on," I said. "Let's get you something to eat, and I'll write you a check."

During our walk back to the restaurant, we discussed the ignorance of someone passing heavy traffic on a blind corner. John had more common sense than a dozen people all put together and had strong opinions about those who were short on it. He shook his head and said, "Common sense ain't so common." He rarely tainted his quiet demeanor with ranting, but when he did—his expressions were bright, unique, and truthful. He could always put me in a good mood. The level of appreciation and acceptance I had for this man, who rarely used soap, humbled me.

"Happy sixteenth birthday, Mike. Your gift is…you get to help me cook until I find help." I tried to break the news in a humorous way, but for Mike, this was anything but funny—he'd come in the kitchen for a birthday omelet, not a job.

Mike wanted to argue with me but stopped when he saw my expression—he recognized the look. My intensity matched that of his football coach, and Mike knew he wouldn't win this battle.

"Paula decided she doesn't want to drive the distance to work anymore," I said and walked over to the freezer, fuming. Her crappy way of quitting last night just made matters worse. She had left a note on my desk right before she left the restaurant. *Why couldn't she tell me in person? Was she too embarrassed?* I ruminated. It didn't make any sense. I didn't have the answers or kitchen help.

Bill, who had been listening, tried to shift the subject to something lighter. "Mike, how's your car restoration coming along?"

Mike, grateful for a new topic, replied, "Good, Doug's helping me a lot."

"So nice of Doug to spend time working on your car. It's probably about finished, right?" I asked, attempting to be positive and to include myself in a conversation that didn't involve Paula.

"No *way*. It won't be done until *next* spring," Mike replied. His tone showed impatience with his mom's ignorance about rebuilding cars.

He didn't realize this information was a huge relief to me—for one more winter, he wouldn't be driving on treacherous roads. *With some luck,* I thought, *the restoration could take several years.*

Of course, Mike came to my rescue in the kitchen, in spite of his reluctance. He was an excellent cook, who fearful of getting stuck in the kitchen, tried to hide his enjoyment. We mostly worked well together, although the way he stood at the grill drove me crazy—as we stood side-by-side facing the grill, he'd spread his feet three feet apart, and each time I turned around or took a step, I'd trip. "Mike, put your feet together," I'd grumble, but his only response was to grin and continue to stand as though a policeman were frisking him.

A week passed by with Mike and my team cooking. Then one day, unexpectedly, Myra clipped an order onto the wheel and whispered, "Ann, there's somebody who'd like to speak with you."

I looked out and saw a young lady holding an infant. "I'll be right back, Mike." I spun around to leave, tripped on his right foot, and caught myself just before going down on my knees. I let out a small yelp, then quickly composed myself.

"Hi, what can I do for you?" I asked in a pleasant tone.

"Hello, I'm Jodi, and this is my daughter, Katie."

I guessed Jodi to be about eighteen years old and Katie no more than eight months.

Jodi's hand nervously but gently rubbed the baby's arm as she told me she was looking for work.

"Have you cooked in a restaurant before?" I asked.

"No, but I can learn. Right now, I live with my parents, who told me to get a job." Jodi seemed eager to give me all the details of her story, which, in an odd way, impressed me.

After a short interview, I smiled at the baby and said to Jodi, "I do need a cook. I will teach you. Can you start tomorrow morning at eight o'clock?" It didn't strike me as impulsive that I would hire an employee on the spot, *again,* because right now, only two things mattered—I needed a cook and Jodi needed a job.

"I'll be here. My mom will be thrilled," Jodi said excitedly, giving each of Katie's cheeks an exaggerated kiss.

I instantly liked this girl and introduced her to the rest of the work crew, feeling confident she would be a game changer. Jodi's mom would be happy, but not nearly as happy as Mike.

Dependable and a quick learner, Jodi spawned excitement about everything. The night Paula walked out on me was actually a *big* blessing—now my sixteen-hour days were more manageable.

Today, my goal was to organize the staff so they could operate the Ponderosa for a few hours without Bill or me. After seven months of endless work, we were starved for time alone. I planned a special surprise outing to celebrate our seventeenth wedding anniversary.

By August 21, I had a foolproof plan and was proud that I had come up with a gift that benefited the giver and the receiver equally. When I dropped myself into the front passenger seat of our car, I couldn't hide my smile, and Bill couldn't either. We looked like two newlyweds leaving the church to begin their honeymoon.

"We'll be gone a couple of hours, but I know you girls will do a great job." My words of encouragement to Myra and Jodi were unnecessary, but they made me feel better about leaving.

"Go have fun, don't worry," they both interjected.

"Wow, so this is what it feels like to move without using my legs," I said to Bill with a cackle. I often stood at the restaurant's side entrance, daydreaming about going north. Now the day had come, and I reveled in the joy of sitting stationary in a car moving from one location to another. As Bill and I drove up the narrow canyon, we were entertained by everything from traffic, to road signs and rafts floating down the river. We traveled north, then turned east along the South Fork of the Payette, headed toward Garden Valley. After several miles, Bill turned off the main highway onto a dirt road. We felt as adventurous as teenagers on their first road trip.

"This is beautiful country," Bill commented.

"Yeah, Idaho really is gorgeous—but if you ever quote me on that, I'll deny it," I joked.

As Bill drove unhurriedly down the lightly traveled road, we giggled about silly things. Then without saying a word, he pulled over and turned off the ignition. "This is a perfect spot," he said. With a multicolored quilt hung over my arm and Bill's wicker picnic basket swinging about, I felt acutely aware of everything from the yarns that tied the quilt to the sweet scent of balsam pine, warmed by the sun. Picking our way through the trees, we walked into the woods together, carving out our own path.

Our time away from work passed quickly, but our emotional reconnection made it seem like a ten-day vacation. We approached the Ponderosa and noticed a full parking lot. "Well, Bill, we're back to reality."

We both wore grins—even felt glad to be home. After thanking each employee for work well done, I faced the grill, wearing a clean white apron and a refreshed attitude.

Chapter Sixteen

WHO IS THE BOSS?

As anticipated, Labor Day weekend kept the waitresses flying around like tiddlywinks. The following Monday, Sherm and Tuffy stopped by for a visit, staying only long enough to enjoy a cup of vegetable beef soup. After a quick farewell hug, Sherm's Brinks mobile, the size of a toaster on wheels, left the Ponderosa parking lot with the moneybag tucked in next to Tuffy.

School started the next week, though not without incident. Mike, now a sophomore, was to show his freshman younger sister the ropes at Garden Valley High, but Lisa, independent and feisty as always, was determined to attend the school of her choice, and Garden Valley High was not on her list. On the first day of school, when the bus stopped at Lower Banks, Mike boarded it—alone.

"Where is Lisa?" I asked, shaking my head. "She just missed the bus!"

When the bus drove away, there was no sign of Lisa anywhere.

"Wait till I find her. She's going to be sorry," I said loudly. It was not only Myra's day off, but the other waitresses had gone back to school, leaving the restaurant in Bill's and my care.

"Bill, how's she going to get to school now? It's more than twenty miles away."

Lisa darted out from behind the motel and stood next to the distant vacant cabin, thinking she was hidden from view. My annoyance grew by the hour, so after the breakfast rush subsided, it was time to track her down. Bill pointed at Doug's station and called out to me, "Look, she's over there."

I watched as she left the safety of the neighbors and scurried by the restaurant's side entrance. She was caught off guard when I swung open the door. In a stern voice, I said, "Lisa, get in here! I'm not going to chase you all over all God's green earth!" She must've had enough of being on the wanted list, for she willingly came inside. "Lisa, why didn't you get on the bus?"

Tears flooded her big eyes as she tried to think of a believable excuse. "Because I want to go to school in Emmett," she answered.

"Lisa, Emmett is thirty miles away—opposite the direction of the bus route. There's no way to get you there or back."

Eventually, the truth surfaced—all of Lisa's friends from Horseshoe Bend Middle School had gone on to Emmett High.

"I'm sorry, Lisa, but now that you are in high school, Lower Banks residents are required to attend Garden Valley schools." When I reached out to give her a squeeze, she burst into hysterics. "Honey, is there something else going on that you want to talk about?"

"Mom, I'm afraid to go to school in Garden Valley because there's a girl who wants to beat me up, and she's big."

Lisa only weighed about eighty-five pounds, so her fear was understandable. "Why does some girl want to hurt you?" I asked out of curiosity.

"Molly went to middle school with me, and she thinks I'm trying to steal her boyfriend. On the last day of school, she told me she'd kick my butt if she ever saw me again."

"Oh, Leecee, you're full of spunk, and she's probably all talk. Just tell her you're not interested in her boyfriend. Besides, you're way too young for a boyfriend." I continued, "I'm sure the teachers won't let kids beat each other up. And when have you *ever* been afraid of anybody? It's only nine thirty—you haven't missed much. Dad can take you to school."

Lisa wiped her cheeks and nodded.

"I know you'll make new friends quickly. You'll be surprised how this will work out."

Bill chimed in, "You can kick *her* butt."

"Oh, Bill, Lisa needs a ride to school, not a boxing coach. When you get there, would you take her to the office and explain?" Feeling my own panic, I added, "You've got to hurry though. I don't know how long I can hold down the restaurant by myself. "Good luck, Leecee. We can talk about this more tonight." When Lisa arrived home after school, she was full of stories—the only mention of Molly was that she had given Lisa a dirty look.

That night, before turning off the cabin lights, I called up the stairs to Lisa's bedroom. "Good night, Lisa. Do you plan to catch the school bus in the morning with your brother?" I waited for the right answer.

"Yes, Mom." She giggled.

A muffled voice came from the laundry room, "What a dork."

With school back in session, the highway traffic slowed down, and so did business, which was fortunate since most of our employees were students. Jodi and Lisa only wanted to work weekends, which worked well, because Monday through Friday, Bill, Myra, and I were able to run things efficiently on our own.

Mike joined the drama team at school, but while his outgoing and entertaining personality was an asset on stage, it proved to be a liability in the classroom. The *attitude and interpersonal* skills column on his report card, marked with asterisks, indicated that his humorous comments were disruptive. Under his theory, this made him popular with other classmates.

Lisa also discovered that school could be fun. She joined every established social club, made good grades, and good friends—Molly included. At home, she enjoyed showing off her progress at becoming a well-rounded, willful thirteen-year-old who knew everything.

Late one afternoon, I spotted Lisa doing homework at the far corner table and joined her. I'd been looking for an opportunity to discuss the *correct* price—seventy-five cents—for a "served" can of soda from the cooler. It was to be our fifth conversation in as many weeks.

I sat down across from her. "Lisa, what part don't you understand about the cost difference between the price of fifty cents for a can of soda to go, and the seventy-five cents for a can of soda served at a table?"

"Mom, I'm *not* going to charge more than fifty cents for a can of pop! People can get a can of pop from the cooler and take it to go for fifty cents, and there is no reason to charge them extra if they decide to drink it in the restaurant." Lisa's voice grew louder with each word she spoke.

"Lisa, like I've explained before, it costs money to serve someone in the restaurant. Let me break down the cost, so you can understand it. I am paying *you* wages to serve that customer, and you always provide a glass with ice that must be bused from the table and washed. All of that costs money and is the reason the price for a served can of pop is seventy-five cents."

Lisa rolled her eyes, her nostrils flared slightly, and I realized that no matter how many times, or in how many ways, or how thoroughly I explained the situation, Lisa would continue to lose me money. I quickly left the table so she wouldn't notice my eyes watering from silent laughter. However, from there on out, Lisa's customer slips indicated a fifty-*five*-cent charge for a can of served pop. When I first noticed this, I thought she had made a mistake. Then I realized—she had heard me. We both had won. That day, I realized my daughter would always be her own boss, in charge of her own life, and at the same time would find ways to collaborate.

Chapter Seventeen

WHERE'S BILL?

The fall day seemed quiet, even for a Wednesday, allowing Myra and me ample time for conversation, mostly about the previous summer months. Myra chuckled. "How did we ever survive the summer frenzy?" she asked. Weren't you overwhelmed, Annie, especially considering this is the first restaurant you've operated?" "Of course, but didn't we all become frazzled at least once?" I laughed and quickly added, "I'm looking forward to a slower pace, with wintertime activities like jigsaw puzzles."

By Thursday, business was at a standstill, giving Bill, Myra, and me time to deep-clean the restaurant. While Bill scrubbed the walls in the bar area, Myra and I washed windows. When a loud, confident voice interrupted our calm, Myra and I snapped to attention. "Hello, my name is Joe. People call me Gentleman Joe."

Across the restaurant, in the bar area, I watched an elderly man shake Bill's hand. His character and voice were a hundred times larger than his small stature. A thin face illuminated by a flashy smile, full of overly large, artificially white dentures, caught my stare. His silver hair, trimmed to precision, and his attire, a suit and highly polished black shoes with smooth soles, gave him the appearance of having come straight from a Vegas casino. I wondered what he was doing at the Ponderosa. His charisma filled the room and made its way into my heart. I wanted to meet this exuberant man and quickly extended my right hand. "Hello there, I'm Ann."

Joe took my hand, but instead of a hearty shake, he held it tenderly as if I were a lovely maiden. "Very pleased to meet you, Miss Ann."

Before Bill or I could ask about the nature of his visit, Joe started in on his story. "I just retired from waiting tables in Vegas. Now I'm traveling north to visit my dear ninety-two-year-old mother, who recently fell and broke her hip," Joe explained. "I'm highly impressed with the appearance of your restaurant and would feel honored to work for you."

I'd nailed it! I knew he'd come from Nevada. "Sorry to hear about your mother. Is she really ninety-two?" I asked but didn't wait for his answer. "Joe, I have to tell you, we've started our slow season and currently don't have a position open," I added.

"Well, Miss Ann, if you ever need my help, I'll be staying in Lewiston with my mother. Her name is Flora. She's a very lovely lady," Joe proudly added.

Joe spent another fifteen minutes, talking about the restaurant's menu and the cleanliness. The longer we visited, the more enchanted I became with Gentleman Joe's charm and wit. I scribbled down Joe's name and phone number and tacked the paper onto the wall above my office desk—right next to the emergency number. Did I have some premonition, or was it just an open spot on the wall? Following Joe's departure, the restaurant seemed gloomy. I envisioned Joe in action, wearing his shiny shoes, serving food with a linen towel draped over his arm like an English butler. The image, both absurd and amusing, made me smile.

"Myra, can you, Jodi, Lisa, and two other waitresses handle the restaurant next Saturday?" I asked.

"Sure we can," Myra answered without hesitation. "Are you and Bill planning something?"

"My brother Eddie and his wife, Connie, invited us to their place in Garden Valley."

"Go have fun. Don't worry, we can handle the customers."

Myra's confidence, over the past several months, had blossomed, and I couldn't resist giving her a well-deserved hug. "Thanks, Myra."

Early Saturday morning, a cooler packed with marinated chicken ready for the barbeque, beer, and a large container of my famous potato salad, all covered with crushed ice, sat by the door. By late morning, Bill and I were en route to Garden Valley, leaving behind five dependable employees.

The air was hot and calm for late September, a perfect lawn chair day. "Judging by the steady flow of traffic, the Ponderosa could be a busy place today," I commented—it was hard to unplug. Bill, however, sick of work, wanted me to relax.

"Stop worrying, Annie—they'll be okay."

The plan was to meet Eddie and Connie at their vacation property and spend the day together. When we arrived in the early afternoon, we spotted their vintage, unpolished, silver Spartan trailer, strategically positioned in the shade. *What a welcome sight,* I thought.

Connie, the first one out the screen door, greeted us, her arms swinging wildly above her head with excitement. Her cheerful, loud voice rang out through the old-growth pine trees. "Anna Banana!" Twelve years earlier, at our introduction, she'd decided that a simple "Ann" wasn't enough.

When Ed sauntered out from the Spartan mansion (the trailer also deserved a nickname), the screen door slammed hard against its frame. He welcomed us with his characteristically small, deep smile and handed me and Bill a cold brew, which we drank in the shade while making plans for the day. The four of us unanimously decided the fun should start by visiting the nearby hot springs—after that, we'd return for the barbeque.

During our conversation, under the shade tree, Ed announced he'd quit smoking.

"Actually, Eddie is *trying* to quit—for the twentieth time," Connie chimed in.

"Cut me some slack. It'd be easier to count the wrinkles on Grandpa Fred's neck than to stop smoking," Ed said, looking embarrassed.

Having never smoked myself, it was difficult to understand the effort it took to stop the habit, but I was proud of Ed and gave him support. "Good luck, brother, I bet you can succeed this time." Being only sixteen months apart in age and exceptionally close friends, we had protected each other throughout our lives—at age eight while playing in our backyard, he gave me a bloody nose, then kindly handed me a wad of toilet paper. At age seventeen, I paid off his past-due parking tickets—he eventually paid me back plus bought me lunch at Taco Bell.

Forty-five minutes later, the four of us were simultaneously relaxed and energized as we leisurely soaked in the natural warm water that bubbled from an opening in the rocky mountainside.

Ed loved the experience of warm water cascading over his shoulders—perhaps because it helped to alleviate the nicotine withdrawal. "Hey, I heard there's an even better pool that not many people know about, called Dreamer's Delight. It's just up the road—should we go find it?" he asked us all.

"I've heard of it, and think I know where it is, but it's not close," Connie replied.

Bill and Ed were hell-bent on going, and after months of being cooped up, I was ready for the adventure.

"Hey, Bill, we'll follow the girls in my truck! Connie knows the place, so she and Annie can lead the way in the car," said Ed.

The expedition began immediately. Without trepidation, we drove through new territory—along the narrow, winding dirt road, so excited that even the dust and washboards didn't slow us down. I led the caravan, leaving a plume of dust as large as the smoke clouds from the Lower Banks fire. In an effort to avoid the veil of filth, Ed followed a far distance behind. Connie and I, oblivious to the miles rapidly clicking by, stayed absorbed in conversation. As dusk began to set in, my car speed decelerated, waiting for Ed's truck to catch up. After almost a mile of barely moving forward, I glanced over at Connie. "I don't think they're behind us. We'd better turn around. Plus it's getting dark." The uneasiness I felt took the fun out of the trip.

"Annie, you're right. Let's get back to the Spartan. I'll bet they turned around and they're grilling chicken."

But back at the Spartan, we found no sign of our husbands and no clues as to their whereabouts. "Do you think they returned to the Ponderosa?" I asked.

"That would be weird, but they must've. Where else would they go?" Connie said.

Clueless and not considering the worst possible scenario, we drove back through the narrow canyon, wrapped in eerie darkness. Unexpectedly, fifteen miles short of the Ponderosa, we encountered several emergency vehicles, whose piercing flashing lights made the darkness seem even darker. As we inched closer to the lights, I could see the road was partially closed, leaving only one lane open to traffic. On our right was the hillside—on our left, the South Fork of the Payette River. Slowly, I drove past three police vehicles before encountering an ambulance parked in the closed lane. As my car passed by, I peeked inside the stationary ambulance.

"*Oh my God*, is that Eddie?" I screamed at Connie. "*It's Ed! It's Ed!*"

Bending down to see, Connie screamed in horror. Leaving the car in the middle of the highway, we raced to the ambulance's open back doors, and after a quick glance, it registered that Ed was sitting upright and coherent. "Where's Bill?" I screamed, my panic escalating.

Within seconds, I stood face to face with the Boise County sheriff. "Annie, you've got to listen to me," he spoke articulately, trying to calm me. "Bill's been in a serious accident. He's being brought up from the river." I darted to where six men were climbing up from the cliff's edge, lugging a person on a stretcher. When they stopped for a moment to catch their breath, my eyes focused on the body strapped to the narrow board. It was Bill, motionless and covered in dirt. The air went out of my lungs, and I struggled to make sense of what had occurred over the past hour. "*Are you okay? Please wake up!*" I called to the man I'd loved for over half my life. There was no answer. "Please answer me, Bill...*please*," I begged.

With the smothering darkness, I couldn't see anything beyond the cliff, but did catch sight of Deputy Buck, brandishing a flashlight. Somehow, I moved my paralyzed legs and ran to him. "What's wrong with Bill? What happened? How far did he go over the cliff? Did he go into the river?" The details didn't really matter, yet I had to know.

The Boise County sheriff joined Buck and me, and again he tried to answer my questions in a slow, calm voice. "Annie, their truck went off of the road, plummeted about 150 feet and landed just short of the river." As he finished his sentence, a paramedic pulled him aside to confer.

"Yes, we'd better do it," were the sheriff's only spoken words to him. When he turned back to face me, he stared directly into my terrified eyes. His eyes looked frightened, too, but his demeanor stayed composed. "I'm very sorry, Annie, but Bill's injuries are critical enough that he'll require Life Flight to fly him to Boise. Life Flight is being notified, and the other fellow will be taken to the hospital by ambulance." Before turning away, he added, "Annie, go back to the Ponderosa, pick up Mike and Lisa, and get to the hospital. And *please* drive safely!"

"Annie, get in the car, I'll drive." Connie blurted out.

"*Wait!* I have to tell Bill I'll meet him at the hospital."

As I moved through a crowd of police and paramedics, instinct pulled me toward Bill. Staring down at him, it hit me, and I went completely numb—Bill might not survive. I bent down, put my face next to his, and whispered, "You have to hold on, baby. I'll see you at the hospital." My lips quivered when I kissed his gray cheek. He was cold and still. "I love you, Bill." My tears dropped onto his neck and formed miniature mud puddles. I could see gravel in his ears, nose, and the corners of his turned-down mouth. All I wanted was to take him home, wash him up, and put him to bed in our little cabin on the river.

When I gently placed my hand on his forehead, miraculously, Bill's left eye opened to a small slit. He responded in a barely audible voice, "Okay, honey." If Connie had not grabbed my arm, I would've continued to stand there.

"C'mon, Annie, let's go get the kids."

On the way back to my car, with Connie in the lead, we stopped at the ambulance to reassure Ed. He sat immobile as a statue, with a confused and vacant stare. "Connie, I think he's in shock," I told her. "Ed, we'll see you at the hospital. You're going to be all right. We love you." It felt awful to leave him, but we had to.

Connie drove but had only gone a couple of miles before I asked her to pull over. I threw open the door and vomited like a carsick child.

Back at the cabin, Lisa and Mike were awakened. It took effort to maintain some composure in explaining the need for a middle-of-the-night drive to a Boise hospital. "Hurry, get dressed, we have to leave *now*," I said.

Once in the car, Connie and I skirted around the specific details of the accident, but my stomach wouldn't cooperate—during the forty-mile drive to Boise, Connie made two emergency puke stops. Each time, I apologized.

"Mom, are you sick?" Mike asked.

"I'm just upset." Silently I prayed, *God, please keep Bill alive.*

We stood at the trauma unit's reception desk, where an older woman with thin silver hair tucked into a tight bun told us, "I'm sorry, but we don't have a patient here by that name."

"Please, you have to find him. He's been airlifted to the hospital," I cried.

"Hang on, ma'am," she said. She opened her left hand and moved it toward me like she was going to give me a high five. She placed it close to my face as if to hush me, and then, with her right hand, she answered the phone. She stared at me while listening intently to a voice passing through the receiver. After she hung up, with a hint of empathy, she said, "Life Flight just arrived with your husband." She pointed to a row of straight-backed, armless chairs lined up against the wall. "Please have a seat with your children. Somebody will be out to talk to you." With crippled emotion, my worries continued to soar.

When Connie's name was called out, she was escorted through the white steel double doors to visit Eddie. *That's a good sign,* I thought.

Lisa laid her head on my shoulder, and I squeezed her hand. "Mom, will Dad be okay?" she asked.

Under the harsh fluorescent lighting, her eyes glistened, and her lips quivered with worry. I touched her face and answered, "I'm praying so." It took a great effort to keep my emotions in check.

The image of Bill's motionless body stuck in my mind. I couldn't imagine life without him. We met when I was seventeen, starting my senior year of high school, and Bill, newly discharged from the military, was twenty and beginning his freshman year at Boise State College. It seemed our twenty years together had passed as quickly as a Christmas morning.

Mike sprawled himself across three mauve chairs, his body appearing huge against the tiny teal stripes on the hospital furniture. *When did he get so big?* I wondered.

"I'd better call Grandpa Sherm," I told the kids.

Dad answered on the fifth ring. "Hi, Dad. I'm at the hospital."

After receiving a few pertinent details, he replied, "Annie, I'll be right there.

Chapter Eighteen

ICU

By the time I returned to the waiting room, Lisa had also laid herself across several chairs, and both kids were asleep. In less than half an hour, Sherm arrived. The instant I saw him, I broke down and wept on his shoulder, and he held me securely. It wasn't something I'd done before, nor could I remember his arms ever comforting me. Many times throughout my childhood, I had yearned for this connection, and now his support was what I needed to get through the news I was about to hear.

Minutes later, the double doors swung open automatically, and Connie appeared. "Hi, Sherm," she said with surprising calmness. "Ed's probably fine, but they're concerned about his lungs and spleen, so he'll stay overnight for observation."

"That's good news, Connie. Did you happen to see Bill back there?" I had to ask.

"No, Annie, I never saw Bill. You mean you haven't heard anything yet?" Connie looked worried.

"No, I haven't talked to a single person!" Just then, I heard the familiar sound of the automatic doors and watched as a young man in need of a shave and dressed in blue-green scrubs walk out. His eyes scanned the large room, intuitively landing on me. I bounced to my feet, moved toward him, and asked abruptly, "Are you looking for me?"

"Are you William's wife?" he asked, never losing eye contact.

"Yes, I'm Ann." Something about saying these three words made my voice tremble and tears form.

He motioned toward the closest empty chair. "Please sit down."

I felt like yelling, "I've been sitting for hours, just tell me if Bill's alive," but my Catholic school manners took hold. I sat down and listened respectfully.

The young doctor spoke in a matter-of-fact voice. "Bill has a broken back in two places and some internal bleeding—he's being prepped for an angiogram. We should know more in a couple of hours."

I watched the doctor's immaculate-white sneakers disappear from sight. For a few seconds, I sat in silence, and when his words sunk in, I cried out, *"Dad, Bill's back is broken!"*

Instantly, a woman squared off in front of me and spoke. "Please be *quiet*." Her presence startled me, and I wondered if I had missed the sound of the automatic doors. Gawking blankly at the woman, I tried to figure out who she might be. Then more of her stern words followed. "Sit down and *listen*," she demanded and waited, making sure she had my full attention before continuing, "I'm Dr. Blankenship. I'm treating your husband's injuries. I'll tell you everything we know about Bill, but you *must* stay calm." Like a child whose been scolded and decides to behave, I nodded obediently—my eyes met hers as I tried to comprehend her words. "Bill's in critical condition. He has two broken vertebrae in his lower back, three broken ribs, and a damaged liver and lungs. Also, there's some internal bleeding around his heart with a possibility that he may have a problem with his aorta. I ordered an angiogram, which will determine the cause of the bleeding. I need to get back to him. Oh, by the way, Bill is not paralyzed." As fast as she appeared, she disappeared through the big doors.

"Oh, Dad, what's happening?" I said, using a wadded clump of damp Kleenex to wipe my drippy nose.

Within minutes, the receptionist gave Dad and me permission to visit Ed, who appeared physically unscathed but was visibly upset.

When Ed saw me, he apologized, "Annie, I'm so sorry about Bill. I don't know what happened."

I hugged his shoulders. "It is okay, Eddie. You need to get better. Please don't worry."

"They're going to keep me in the hospital overnight," Ed told us.

Relieved the topic shifted away from remorse for Bill, I reassured Ed, "That's good—we have to make sure you're all right."

A young male orderly pulled back the floor-length curtain and announced he was moving Ed to ICU. When we questioned the need for ICU, which seemed extreme from our perspective, he answered, "That's where his doctor wants him for observation." The ICU sounded scary, but the orderly's calm affect reminded us that Ed's condition appeared stable. We watched Ed's bed move down the long corridor decked out with medical equipment of different shapes and sizes.

Back in the waiting room, we found Connie antsy to leave. Sherm offered to drive her home, and I promised to call them both with updates. The receptionist escorted Lisa, Mike, and me to another waiting room, about the size of a large walk-in closet, then a hospital volunteer brought us three flat pillows. We struggled to get comfortable.

I couldn't sleep, and when claustrophobia set in, I cracked open the door and found a direct view of the nurse's station. The constant buzz of phone calls, paper shuffling, and conversation provided a welcome distraction. The fear of missing an update on Bill kept me alert. Besides, who, but a kid, can sleep in a chair? Mike and Lisa had pushed two chairs together and were sleeping, curled up like newborn kittens. I watched them sleep, feeling protective and envious.

I remained upright with a pillow scrunched between my head and the wall, skimming the surface of sleep. When a shadow moved into the room, I tried to discern who had entered. The silhouette gradually took the shape of a man, though his voice remained more distinct than his image. "Bill's in ICU. His aorta is intact. The bleeding is from a badly bruised heart muscle, which we expect to heal, and as for his liver, lungs, and ribs, they, too, will heal over time. Sometime during the next couple of days, he'll be fitted for a body cast, and in about twenty minutes, you should be able to see him." The shadow figure reported the facts, then left the room.

I gently awoke Mike and Lisa. "Dad is going to be okay."

After phoning Sherm, I made the dreaded call to Bill's family in Oregon. Though his mom took the news hard, I calmed her fears by promising to keep her informed of any changes in Bill's condition. After the phone calls, my body collapsed onto the chair, my chin rested on my chest, and tears rolled down my cheeks. *Thank you, Jesus!*

The room was dark, except for a dim glow coming from above Bill's bed. Asleep (the nurses called it comatose) and lying on his back, Bill looked peaceful. Even with the noisy hum of a breathing machine and the buzz of a motor attached to his bed, the room was strangely quiet. It was so quiet that when Bill's blood pressure cuff suddenly inflated, all three of us jumped. We were startled yet elated—it seemed to us a sure sign that Bill was really alive.

"Can Dad hear me?" Mike asked.

"Sure he can, he just can't answer back," I answered for Bill.

"Mom, why is Dad's bed turning?" Lisa asked.

"I'm not sure. We'll ask someone. It looks funny, huh?"

When a nurse came into the crowded room, the only thing Lisa asked about was the moving bed. The nurse, a large, imposing woman with an easy smile and gentle manner, patiently explained, "Patients with broken backs benefit from a bed that rotates from side to side. Your dad's doctor wants him to sleep on it so he'll heal quicker."

Lisa and Mike pushed chairs to each side of their father's bed like bookends, staking out permanent stations. Though I understood how they felt, we'd been on the edge of our world collapsing for over ten hours—now it was time to take care of us. "It's after six o'clock— we need to go home, get a bite to eat, and shower. It'll make us feel much better. I promise we'll come right back to Dad."

Back at Lower Banks, Myra had tacked a note onto the door of our cabin, asking us to contact her. The thought of notifying Myra hadn't crossed my mind, and for the first time in nearly a year, the Ponderosa wasn't my primary concern. I contacted her immediately.

At first, the details of the past sixteen hours rendered Myra speechless, and then she broke into tears. "Myra, we'll be closing the restaurant for a couple of days."

"Whatever you need to do, Annie. You know I'm here for you guys."

After a quick shower, a change into clean clothes, and an attempt to eat breakfast, I posted a sign on the Ponderosa's front entrance that read: *Temporarily closed. Bill is in the hospital.* I considered a less detailed sign, but knowing how many of our customers were like family, I decided to include the detail about Bill, so they wouldn't speculate or bother our neighbors for information. When I gave Doug the news, I discovered I'd been beaten to the task—Deputy Buck had notified him hours ago that his towing service was needed to retrieve Ed's truck.

"Annie, I've already checked out the site. The highway will need to be shut down while I recover your brother's truck. I'll tow it back and park it out of sight."

"I appreciate that, Doug."

While talking with Doug, Lisa, and Mike sat in the car, their restlessness to leave undiminished by their exhaustion.

"We should be back at the hospital by ten thirty," I promised, dropping into the driver's seat.

"Do we have to go to school tomorrow?" Mike asked.

"Do you want to?"

"No."

"Well, then how about you spend today and tomorrow with Dad? I think he needs you as much as you need him." En route to the hospital, I answered dozens of questions about the accident, but for the first time since the tragedy began, our conversation included a smidgen of hope—all of us had survived the trauma, at least for the moment.

The elevator vibrated just before the doors separated in the middle, to let us off on the sixth floor of Saint Alphonsus Hospital. We moved down the extrawide hallway and slipped into room 608, which seemed cheerier by day, with a spot of sunlight spilling in through the large window facing the parking lot. We noticed a blanket that covered Bill to his waist and the tubes and wires that connected him to several machines. As the bed turned his body from side to side, he received three intermittent kisses.

"Dad's still sleeping," Lisa noted.

"Yes, honey, but sleep is good for him, so don't worry."

Both Lisa and Mike seemed satisfied with my comment and promptly pushed chairs close to the bed and plopped down.

"Hey, kids, I'll be back in a bit," I said. "I'll be across the hall, visiting Ed."

In room 605, Sherm stood gazing out the window, his broad shoulders slightly slumped. Noticing Ed's bed was empty except for the heap of bunched-up white sheets, I felt a jolt of panic. "Where's Ed?" I asked.

"They took him for another x-ray," Dad answered.

"Oh no! What's going on?"

"This morning, Ed complained of neck and back pain, so the doctor ordered more pictures. Apparently, last night's x-rays weren't clear. How's Bill doing? I peeked into his room when I got here an hour ago," Dad said.

"Exactly the same. The kids are with him."

Our discussion ended when a doctor and an orderly pushing a wheelchair entered. The wheelchair's unfamiliar occupant, a pale man wearing a white neck brace and a disoriented expression, spoke as he entered. "Hi, Dad, Hi Annie." We recognized Ed's voice.

The doctor holding a clipboard immediately explained, "Ed has a broken neck." He said it like Ed had just been diagnosed with a wart. "However, at this time, surgery isn't necessary, but he's required to wear the neck brace for three, maybe four months. Because of his injuries, he'll remain in the hospital a few more days."

Too stunned by the diagnosis to ask questions, we didn't notice when the doctor left. Our attention was focused solely on Ed and his comfort as we awkwardly assisted in lifting Ed from the wheelchair onto the lowered hospital bed. A hush enveloped the room until the orderly exited, pushing the empty wheelchair.

Ed spoke first. "Annie, I have to tell you about the accident."

Chapter Nineteen

PAINFUL REGRET

E d's pained expression twisted my spirit. "Annie, Bill's like my brother, and I almost killed him. I don't know what happened. I'm so sorry."

I gripped Ed's hand. "I don't blame you for anything, and I'm positive Bill doesn't either. Ed, it was an *accident*. I'm just thankful you both survived."

But an unconvinced Ed needed to get things off his chest, so he continued. "After the wreck happened, I didn't know where I was, but do remember getting out of my truck and hearing Bill crying out, *'It hurts, it hurts.'* Bill moaned loudly and then he got quiet. The only thing I wanted to do was help him, but I couldn't find him. Annie, it was so dark, and the ground was so steep I felt like a blind person tripping over rocks and bushes. No matter how fast I moved, I couldn't find Bill. Finally, I realized he was still *inside* my truck." Ed stopped talking for a moment, took in a deep breath, and asked me a question. "Did they tell you the passenger-side door of the truck, where Bill sat, was wedged against a tree and dented in more than two feet?"

"Oh, no, Eddie, I haven't heard any details or seen your truck. Are you sure you want to talk about this now? It's okay if you want to wait."

"Yeah, I have to tell you about it." Ed's eyes blinked fast several times. "The tree held Bill's door closed, so I sat beside the truck and talked to him. I reminded him about his strength in surviving the Vietnam War as a machine gunner, and that he would survive this too. But his only words were, 'Ed, it hurts…I can't breathe.' I couldn't help him, Annie. When I reached into the truck to touch Bill, I felt him hunched over with his head below his knees. Once I heard voices and saw flashlights shining down on us, I yelled out for the people to hurry. I didn't know how far down they needed to come, but it seemed like it took them forever to reach us. When I tried to help them get Bill out, they ordered me to climb the hill and wait in the ambulance. I didn't want to leave Bill behind. It's one of the hardest things I ever had to do."

Ed's eyes were red and on the verge of tears. "I'd change places with Bill," Ed said, breaking into stifled sobs.

Again, I tried to reassure him. "I know you would, but you have your own problems—like a broken neck. Speaking of which, I can't believe you climbed 150 feet with a *broken neck*, in a place so steep that it took six men with three ropes to get Bill out."

"I bet they're glad Bill only weighed a hundred and seventy-five pounds," Sherm added.

When Ed's food tray arrived, I spoke up, "Go ahead, eat your lunch while I check on Bill and the kids. Do you want to come with me, Dad?" Sherm nodded and followed me out the door.

"Poor Eddie. The neck is nothing compared with what he's doing to himself inside," I said to Dad.

The ICU was Ed's home for another day. After that, they moved him to a different floor and gave him a much larger room with a lousy view and an extra bed but no roommate.

Mike and Lisa reluctantly returned to school. For the next week, the CLOSED sign stayed put, and we all waited for Bill to wake up.

"Mom, are we doing anything for my birthday tomorrow?" Lisa asked calmly.

I stared into her brown eyes. "Ahhh, September 27—I'll always remember that very important day fourteen years ago. May I surprise you with something special?"

"Sure!" she said and ran out to catch the school bus.

Back in Bill's hospital room, with nothing to do but watch him sleep, I reminisced about the jubilance I felt when Lisa was born. *"The true moment of splendor,"* I called it.

After spending so many days in room 608, we had developed friendships with many of the nurses. When I mentioned my birthday dilemma to Norma, my favorite nurse, she graciously offered the nurses' break room for a gathering place. "It would be good for Bill to celebrate Lisa's birthday. Bring in a cake, decorations, and a few guests. The room is yours."

"Thank you so much! Lisa will love it."

The following evening, Mike, Grandpa Sherm, my siblings, several good-natured nurses, and I sang "Happy Birthday." Leecee blew out the candles and then slices of chocolate cake were passed around. A smiling Norma stood in the doorway waiting to catch Lisa's attention. "Make sure you go look in on your dad," she told Lisa.

Lisa, eager to include her dad in the celebration, headed toward Bill's room, Norma and I following close behind. At first glance, all appeared the same—a motionless man in a rotating bed. But as Lisa moved closer to her dad's bedside, she froze in place. The timing was perfect—the bed rotated, giving her a view of her father's face. His eyes were open and looking at her. "Dad's awake!" she screamed with excitement, perhaps a little louder than she should have. Norma slipped out and closed the door behind her.

Chapter Twenty

THE ROTISSERIE

Although Bill remained in the hospital for another week, his absence from the restaurant wasn't going to stop me from reopening. With Myra's help I'd give it a try. I wanted our lives back to normal—reopening seemed like a step in that direction.

"My plan is to serve breakfast and lunch, then close the restaurant when Mike and Lisa get home from school, so we can make it to the hospital in time to have dinner with Bill," I explained to Myra.

Myra, my steadfast cheerleader, always supported whatever plans I would conjure up. "Great, I'll work every day from six to four, then."

"Thanks, Myra, but how about we shorten our day and make it eight to four."

It didn't take long for Mike to discover how he could make his dad laugh *and* cry by running from one side of the rotating bed to the other. "Dad, how"—he went over to the opposite side of the bed—"are you"—he went back to other side—"feeling today?" Bill laughed until his eyes watered and his ribs screamed for mercy. His hearty and contagious laughter loudly announced that he was back in the game and we couldn't hear it enough. Mike found creative ways to expand the game and taught Lisa the sport. She quickly became proficient, and poor, helpless Bill had to contend with both kids. Strapped down securely, he couldn't escape, or even launch a few choice words while holding eye contact before his rotisserie bed turned away.

I tried to protect Bill by saying, "Come on, you guys, this is cruel. Don't forget he'll be able to get you back someday, and you know what they say about payback." Bill appreciated me defending him, but nothing could've been more healing and fun for him than being able to laugh with his children. His joy was worth the discomfort. Bill's room was full of life, and we looked forward to spending time at the hospital. The accident, a brutal sucker punch in the gut that knocked the wind out of us, turned out to be a breath of fresh air. With his stint on a rotating bed, Bill corralled the family playfulness which had been lost while building our business.

"It's four o'clock, will you put up the CLOSED sign?" I asked Myra. The words were hardly out of my mouth, when the side door swung open and Doug, Adelle, Deputy Buck, and his wife entered, displaying mischievous smiles.

"You're not going to close the restaurant tonight, because we're here to keep it open," Adelle said.

"You and the kids go visit Bill. Don't worry about a thing," Buck added. "I'm a pretty good cook, you know!"

"How often do you cook?" Doug asked, crinkling his brow and showing off his perfect teeth in a wide smile.

"Well...never," Buck replied, avoiding eye contact with Doug or me.

Everyone laughed and took their stations. Myra generously offered to stay and help guide them through. As I watched my friends take charge, I did my best to stay collected, but it only lasted a few seconds. Touched by the blessing of caring friends, I found my tears of gratitude couldn't be contained. Keeping the restaurant open for an extra couple of hours didn't seem profitable, but how do you turn down a gesture of such kindness? I couldn't.

Bill's condition improved rapidly, and the time came to say goodbye to ICU and the rotisserie. As the orderly pushed Bill's rolling bed from the elevator, he said, "Bill, we have a nice room waiting for you, and a good roommate."

"Hey, brother Bill," Ed said, the second he saw us enter the room.

Bill, surprised by the identity of his new roommate, laughed. "Hey, Ed, how're ya doing?"

Another orderly joined the crowded room to assist with Bill's transfer to his new bed. "Wow, this bed feels strange—it's not moving!" Bill exclaimed.

Ed laughed. "Yeah, now maybe you can get a good night's sleep."

The rapport between the two, battered by the same misfortune and blessed with similar luck, was palpable. The guys loved each other. Each would help the other heal.

Chapter Twenty-One

HELP ARRIVES

Myra flipped the sign over to the CLOSED side and switched off the outside lights. It had been a long day for us both.

"It's time to relax, Myra," I announced, walking to the bar for a couple of cold mugs. "Haven't the last two weeks felt like a hundred years? We've got to find some help," I said.

"What about that guy with the fancy suit and shiny black shoes?" Myra asked.

"Oh, do you remember him?" I asked with a grin.

"Are you kidding? How could anyone forget him?"

We collapsed into chairs, clicked our mugs together, and laughed. "Cheers!"

"Hey, I haven't had a chance to tell you the good news. Supposedly, Bill can break out of the hospital at the end of the week."

"Annie, that's *great*." Myra's eyes twinkled, and our mugs smacked together again.

"Of course, Bill won't be of any help around here, and I'll have extra work taking care of him at home. I'd better give that Vegas character a call in the morning." Something about the way I said this made us both break into hysterics, making me almost wet my pants.

The following morning, I dialed the Lewiston phone number, and a sweet, shaky voice answered, "Hello, this is Flora."

I introduced myself, told her where and how I'd met her son, and then asked about her fractured hip.

"I'm doing fine, dear. Thank you for asking. Would you like to speak to Joe?" She'd didn't move the phone from her face before calling, "Joe, a nice lady named Ann from the Ponderosa Restaurant wants to talk to you."

"Hello, Miss Ann. How may I help you?" Joe asked courteously.

I updated him on Bill's accident, noting only relevant details in an attempt not to keep him on the phone for days. Although I barely knew this man, his response wasn't a surprise.

"I'll be there tomorrow, Miss Ann."

"Thank you, Joe." The relief I felt in knowing I had reinforcements arriving far outweighed my trepidation about hiring such a unique character—and over the phone, no less.

The following day, both Myra and I eagerly awaited Joe's arrival. When Joe finally walked through the front door, the lunch rush was in full swing, and the best I could do was to give him a quick wave through the food service window. He waved back, diverted his path, approached Myra, introduced himself (as if he needed to), and asked for an "order book with a pen." Out of the corner of my eye, I watched Joe move with proficiency and ease. His customers' expressions showed delight. Indeed, Gentleman Joe was a pro.

Fresh mushrooms were being sautéed on the grill next to a sizzling half-pound burger patty, and a plate embellished with lettuce, tomato, onion, and pickles waited. After melting a slice of Swiss cheese into the cooked mushrooms atop the cooked burger, I used an extra-wide spatula to place the entire mound onto a toasted extra-large sesame-seed bun. The sight and aroma of the famous Ponderosa burger, a guaranteed five-napkin delight, along with Gentleman Joe's presence made me feel much better about life. For the first time in weeks, I cooked with a smile on my face. The tailwind just got stronger.

When the opportunity came to leave the kitchen, I approached Joe, grabbed his hand, and nearly shook his arm from its shoulder socket. "I'm so glad to have you with us Joe. Come on, it's quiet in here now. Let's get you settled in your motel room. While I get the key, you can park your car next to room 3."

My urge to do cartwheels down the driveway to the motel almost won.

"So, Myra, what do you think about Joe?" I asked.

"I think the three of us can take care of business!"

Mike and Lisa got off the school bus just in time to see Joe walking from the motel. We'd discussed Joe previously, so they knew immediately who he was. When the bar-side door to the Ponderosa swung open, I saw three happy faces passing through. "Looks like the three of you know each other," I said with a grin.

"How's Dad?" were Mike's first words.

"He's doing so well that after you get home from school Friday, we can bring him home." Their faces lit up.

Early Thursday afternoon, Sherm delivered a rented hospital bed and a wheelchair to Banks II. Before assisting with the bed setup, I had several lunch orders to prepare, but as soon as both grill and order wheel exhibited no sign of disarray, I rushed to the cabin. I was greeted by a beefed-up bed that devoured most of the living room. "Thanks, Dad. Sorry I didn't help you build this monster. I'll bet Bill will enjoy the privacy of lying in front of a huge picture window facing a parking lot and a highway," I added with a laugh. "But obviously the bed won't fit anywhere else, unless we set it up in the restaurant. Hey, that would be a convenient way for me to take care of him," I added and laughed again. "Come get a cup of coffee and meet Joe, and you'd better eat something. You know, Dad, I'm the bossy one! Do you remember how, when we were growing up, the other kids called me Bossy Priscilla?" We both laughed. I grabbed Dad's arm and we walked together to the restaurant.

"Annie, why don't you sit and visit with your dad? Joe and I can handle the restaurant," Myra offered.

Dad and I slid into a booth. "This view will always amaze me," he said quietly, letting out a happy sigh.

"How's Ed feeling?" I asked.

"Did you hear about his neck brace?"

"Oh no, what now?"

Sherm tilted his head and stretched his thin lips into a slight grin, and I knew that a good Sherm-style story was about to unfold.

"It's the damnedest thing. On Tuesday night, while Ed sat on the couch watching television, Connie noticed some writing on his neck brace. When she looked closer, she saw the word *TOP* upside-down and at the bottom—the hospital sent him home with his neck brace on *upside-down*."

"You're kidding."

Snickering, Dad continued his story. "Before Connie made the discovery, she said Ed kept complaining about the pain, and she kept reminding him that a broken neck was bound to hurt. In other words, she told him to stop his bitching."

Although the story was funny the way Dad told it, I couldn't help but think Ed's suffering seemed to have no end.

Joe brought over the coffeepot and refilled our cups. "Thanks, Joe," we said simultaneously.

"You know, Dad, looking back on this ordeal, I'm astonished that neither Bill nor Ed required a single stitch—absolutely no blood on either of them. Well, except for Bill's right butt cheek where his pocket comb scratched him!" The image of the minor abrasion appeared in my mind and made me laugh out loud, and Dad followed suit.

"If you look at the damage to Ed's truck, it's a miracle they both survived," I continued.

"Oh my, that reminds me—I almost forgot to tell you what Doug revealed yesterday. Doug noticed that one of Ed's rear tires had blown out. He said that having a blowout on those extrawide tires would make it difficult to maneuver on a curve. Ed needs to know that—it might help him feel less guilty about the accident. Next time you talk to him—will you tell him?"

"For sure, he'll be relieved." Sherm continued, "Well, I'd better get back to Kuna, so I'll have time to drop off your deposit at the bank."

Outside in the parking lot, Dad and I noticed the air had a cool bite. "Sure hope Idaho has a mild winter coming, like those Oregon winters I love so much," I said, showing off my best phony smile.

Sherm smiled back and countered, "But, Annie, you're in Idaho now." The expressions on both of our faces revealed how much we enjoyed our ongoing banter, meaningful only to the two of us.

Chapter Twenty-Two

RIDING OUT THE STORM

L isa dashed to the car, screaming, "Hurry, let's go! Dad's waiting!"
"Hold your ponies, I'm coming," I called back. I scurried
out the door, telling Myra, "I'm not sure what time we'll be back, but
you can lock up after the dinner rush."

Bill had been gone for three weeks, so for Lisa bringing her
father home was exciting as discovering little Minnie, her puppy,
under the Christmas tree. "Mom, will Dad be able to do anything
besides lie in bed all day?" Lisa asked, her frown told me this thought
concerned her.

"That's all he'll be able to do for a while—so my full plate just
got fuller. Your help and Mike's help will definitely be needed."

With the aid of the hospital staff, we loaded Bill into the car.
Bill, thrilled to be out of the hospital, didn't complain once during
the hour-long ride home. A few stifled groans were the only clue that
the unyielding body brace encasing his torso was uncomfortable in
a sitting position. The fact that Bill had lost weight wasn't a good
thing—but one positive thing had come from the tragedy—Bill said
goodbye to twenty-five years of nicotine intake. In his words, "It's
easy to quit smoking—just get knocked out cold and hooked up to
pure oxygen for ten days."

Exhausted, Bill made a courageous effort to get nestled into the
living room's largest piece of furniture and fell asleep immediately.

The following day turned out to be a learning experience for everyone. By late evening, I'd traveled from the cabin to the restaurant at least two-dozen times. I'd always dreamed of being a nurse—but not while juggling being a chef, bookkeeper, human resource manager, custodian, supply clerk, and mother of two teenagers. My new role as caregiver left me with little time, and I missed Bill's daily sponge bath that first day, partly because I expected the procedure to take a lot of time, but mostly because the thought of it intimidated me as much as I had been uneasy when giving a newborn Mike his first bath.

By the second day, Bill's bath couldn't be put off any longer. While Bill lay immobile on his back, I cautiously unfastened the Velcro straps on the brace and then gingerly rolled him over onto his side. As I rolled him back and forth, I listened to my heart pound in my ears and prayed I wouldn't hear a pop in his back. After accomplishing his bath, I refastened the body brace that looked like a turtle shell, drained the sink water, threw a load of towels into the washing machine, then bolted off to the restaurant.

Forty-five minutes later, I delivered a late lunch to Bill—turkey on sourdough, his favorite. When I entered the room, he could barely speak, "I don't feel good. I'm having trouble breathing."

"What? Why can't you breathe?" I asked.

Panic showed in his flushed face. "I don't know. I just can't breathe," he struggled to say.

"I'll call an ambulance." I rushed out the cabin's door and heard it slam behind me.

The school bus let the kids off just as Bill was being loaded into the ambulance. "What's wrong with Dad?" they both yelled, running toward me, the breeze swinging their coats open. They stopped at the ambulance's closed doors, straining to see inside.

"I don't know, just get in the car. We'll follow him to the hospital." My voice sounded abrupt and louder than I wanted.

We made the trip to Boise in silence, broken only by Lisa's cough and sneezes. Not feeling the need to keep up with the ambulance speed, I crept along at a mere fifty-five miles per hour, anticipating another long hospital wait.

I approached the ER triage desk, holstering a bit of reluctance, unsure if I could cope with a setback.

The receptionist, with large-framed glasses propped on her head, responded swiftly. "You can go back and see him," she said, a little overzealous for my mood. "Go through those doors and a nurse will take you."

This is way too easy, I thought. A nurse pointed to the end cubical, and we rushed off. When we pulled back the floor-length curtain, there lay Bill, looking perfectly healthy, wearing his turtle shell and a gigantic grin.

"What happened, Dad?" Mike asked.

Bill didn't have time to answer before a doctor, noticeably oversize at the waistline, entered the small space, also smiling. "Bill is doing well, considering," he announced.

"Considering what?" I asked quickly.

The physician tried to contain his impulse to laugh but couldn't keep his belly from jiggling. "As you know, Bill was struggling to breathe. Apparently, his body brace had been cinched up too tight."

"Did I do that?"

"I'm afraid so," he said, with a Santa laugh.

Chapter Twenty-Three

NO TIME FOR PUZZLES

Over the succeeding weeks, we kept to a strict schedule. Besides taking care of customers and cleaning kitchens and restrooms, Bill was being fed and bathed on a daily basis. The late fall weather brought rain, which, as the season progressed, gradually turned to snow.

Gentleman Joe was always punctual, dressed in a wrinkle-free suit, freshly showered and shaved, and doused with a hefty splash of cologne. Customers didn't seem to mind the overpowering scent—they appreciated his appearance and gregarious personality.

Bill's broken back healed slowly, and his attitude stayed mostly positive. He hoped, as we all did, that he would be in a wheelchair by Thanksgiving.

Our routine had more or less fallen back into place as if it had never been disturbed. Doug came in for his morning coffee, and Doug Sr. stopped in for his afternoon glass of wine. In optimistic anticipation of an easygoing winter, three new puzzle boxes, each holding a thousand pieces, were placed on the far corner table that overlooked KYBR.

Surprisingly, business didn't taper off much, and the weekend before Thanksgiving brought on fourteen-hour days of nonstop cooking. While I rushed back and forth between Bill's room and the kitchen, Lisa, Myra, and Joe labored at a frantic pace to keep up with customer orders. Sunday took up where Saturday ended (like a tornado riding on the back of a hurricane) with a full parking lot and a packed restaurant.

Shortly after two o'clock that Sunday afternoon, I remembered Bill hadn't eaten since breakfast. I slapped a grilled ham-and-cheese sandwich onto a plate with chips and a sliced pickle—which drooped over the plate's edge—and dashed out the side door to deliver another meal in bed.

Instead of saying thanks, Bill asked, "Aren't you going to give me a bath today?"

"What? Can't you see the parking lot is full?" I yelled.

"Oh, I'm sorry," he said with a gloomy look.

Bill's expression and tone hit a chord of sympathy in me—though my life seemed difficult, it must be horrible for him. I couldn't imagine anything more boring than lying in bed, day and night, week after week staring at paisley curtains. "I'll try to get back over here to give you a bath," I promised before running out the door. Earlier that week, a nurse's aide had offered to take over Bill's bathing duties, but Bill, abashed and defiant, declined the unfamiliar female's proposal.

Bill's most basic needs added hours to my workload, but that wasn't the main problem. Before the accident, I thought I knew how much manpower he contributed to the business, but I'd had no idea. He stocked, managed the bar—including all customer service. He took pride in making sure the restrooms were the cleanest in Idaho. He was always just where I needed him. I'd lost my right-hand man. Most of all, I'd lost the spunk—so much a part of my day—that came from his laughter, his sense of humor, and his sweet and flexible nature.

Later that afternoon, when there weren't enough customers to fill up an elevator, I whispered to Myra, "Bill wants a bath. I'll be back."

I pulled the paisley curtains together for privacy, removed the hard brace, and dropped it on the floor. Bill lay flat on his back, buck naked and displaying a cheeky grin. The ritual was simple—I'd travel back and forth the ten feet between the bed and the bathroom sink, where I'd rinse out the washcloth. The fearful handling and painstaking care I'd given Bill on his first days at home was no more. I could do the entire bath procedure blindfolded, as quickly and efficiently as flipping burgers.

Everything was going well until Bill made a comment that he soon regretted. "Can't you use *warm water?*"

"Excuse me? I'm using the hottest water coming from the faucet."

"Well, it feels cold to me."

With my face contorted, I stomped six feet to the front door, and in a tone of voice I'd never used before, I said, "*This* is what cold feels like!" I swung the cabin's door open to reveal the icy-patched, congested parking lot and busy highway. Hysterically waving the door back and forth, I fanned frigid air into the room and onto Bill's naked, shivering, and shocked body. I didn't give a rat's ass. Worse yet, his discomfort gave me a hint of sadistic satisfaction. An uncontrollable feeling of anger had derailed me. I don't remember snapping back to sanity, but when I did, I resumed giving the bath avoiding any eye contact. Neither of us spoke a single word.

The amount of relief I received from letting my anger loose didn't compensate for the enormous shame. Finally, I spoke. "I've got to get back to work." I didn't look at him or give him a chance to respond before leaving the cabin.

The last thing I needed was to face more demands at the grill or to fake cheerfulness, so when the soothing sound of the river tugged at me, I moved in that direction. I stepped carefully and deliberately, so as not to slide down the slippery bank into the icy water. I searched for a place to sit, when a perfect rock, smooth and dry, showed up in my path. With a quick glance around to make sure I was out of everyone's view, I sat down on the rock, and the tears, sobs, and moans started immediately. What had happened to the joy and gratitude, I had experienced when Bill had survived? I felt frazzled, as if I was torn into little pieces like the jumbled mess in the unopened puzzle box, and I wondered if this might be a nervous breakdown. After what seemed like hours of wallowing in dark despair, I heard an echo of words from out of my past: *"Let it be, let it be. Speaking words of wisdom. Let it be."* I'd loved Paul McCartney since I was twelve years old and knew his wisdom wouldn't steer me wrong, especially at my worst hour. I climbed up the slippery bank and checked on Bill, who had fallen asleep propped up on pillows. The expression of peace and innocence on his face should have made me feel better, but instead, I felt a violent stab of remorse. I bent down, kissed his cheek and whispered, "I'm sorry, honey. We'll get through this together." From this moment on, I decided I would allow Bill his idiosyncrasies and go with the flow. For now, this small room was his world. I quietly shut the door behind me and hurried back to the restaurant. My body felt as if it had been on earth a hundred years instead of thirty-nine.

As scheduled, Monday morning found Bill and me waiting in the doctor's exam room. The doctor entered and announced, "Good news, Bill—I don't see any reason why you cannot use a wheelchair. Also, you can take off the brace and stand in the shower, provided you have help." Bill's face glowed with renewed hope that life would be worth living again—seven weeks without a shower can cause a deep depression.

On the drive home, Bill winked at me and said, "I'll bet you're glad I won't need any more sponge baths." It was Bill's way of thanking, apologizing, and forgiving me.

"You're lucky I didn't *completely* unravel and cinch up your brace too tight again. The only thing that saved you was that it would've meant another trip to Boise, and I didn't have time for that."

"So you didn't *completely* lose it?" Bill asked as he let out a huge, long laugh.

I laughed, too, and silently thanked God that I had Bill in my life.

Chapter Twenty-Four

BETTER TIMES

We decided to close the restaurant on Thanksgiving Day, choosing instead to host twenty-eight family members. Sherm, my siblings, their spouses, nieces and nephews, and Myra and Ben all pitched in to make the event easy and fun. Bill, manually rotating his new wheels, maneuvered around tables and chairs and found ways to make everyone merry.

"It sure feels good to be out of bed," Bill said to Sherm.

Dad put his hand on Bill's shoulder and gave him his customary squeeze.

The day filled with excitement and connection wouldn't end before my niece and nephew, Michelle and Buddy Lee—both four years old—climbed onto the jukebox and made the flat top their tiny dance floor, underlit like a Vegas stage. They boogied to the song "Louie, Louie," which blared from the two large speakers mounted above the bar. Buddy and Michelle's identical rhythm amused their audience. The adults cheered and egged them on. Meanwhile, the older cousins enjoyed the pool table and soda dispenser.

After many prolonged goodbyes, Bill and I sat alone—enjoying the Ponderosa's stillness. "This will be the start of a new tradition. From now on, our family will celebrate every Thanksgiving at the Ponderosa," I said to Bill.

"Count me in," Bill said, covering his mouth in an attempt to hide a big yawn.

I pushed his wheelchair out the side door and through the thick gravel. "How about a shower tonight?"

Monday morning brought a cold windstorm, indicating that an aggressive Idaho winter was upon us. There were no orders for me to cook, but I lingered at the grill, reveling in its radiant warmth. I bent down to straighten the heavy rubber floor mat when a strong whiff of cologne hit me. Without looking up, I said, "Welcome back, Gentleman Joe! How's Flora?"

Joe had spent Thanksgiving in Lewiston with his mother. "Hello, Miss Ann. Mother's doing very well, taking her age into consideration." Joe looked around the nearly empty restaurant.

"Go ahead and take another day off if you want, Joe. Myra, Bill, and I can handle this crowd."

Bill must've smelled the cologne too and came wheeling himself into the kitchen. "Hi, Joe!"

"It's sure good to see you out of bed," Joe said.

"It feels wonderful," Bill answered.

"Thanks for the offer of a day off, Miss Ann. I think I'll go to my room and enjoy a small glass of scotch or two."

Joe disappeared in a wink. And while I soaked in the kitchen's heat and the silence of the restaurant, I poured a fair amount of pancake batter onto the grill and listened as it sizzled. I placed an almost perfectly round pancake onto a plate, drenched it in whipped butter and maple syrup, picked up my fork, and began to eat. Indeed, better times had arrived.

Chapter Twenty-Five

UNC'S SECRET

"Mom, where do you want the Christmas tree?"

I caught sight of Mike and his best friend, Tim, standing in the middle of the restaurant next to a misshapen fir tree. "Right where you have it is good. The tree is perfect," I fibbed. "How about a couple of Ponderosa burgers with extra fries for your effort?"

"Sure!" they both replied.

Tim seemed like a good guy, so it pleased me that he and Mike had become close friends. They both enjoyed outdoor activities—mostly hunting and fishing—and played high school football and basketball at the same caliber, which was pretty darn good. When I handed them two plates, each piled high with curly fries and a burger, I asked, "So you boys are sticking around to decorate the tree for me, right?"

Mike answered loudly, "*No*, Lisa can do that." It was the response I expected and chuckled aloud.

Mike reached for the ketchup bottle and announced, "I'm going to the dance after the game tonight, okay?"

"Are you asking me or telling me?"

"Please, Mom! Tim is driving, and I'll be home by ten thirty or eleven at the latest."

"Okay. Go have fun, but no later than eleven," I said, giving them both my sternest look.

As I drifted back to the grill, I mumbled to myself, "I love that kid." Then turning back to face them, I added, "Tim, make sure you drive that Jeep safely."

My relief at making it through the dinner rush was short-lived—within moments, Lisa appeared at the service window and called out, "Two steak specials, medium well."

When I reached up to grab the only green ticket from the order wheel, I noticed an older man with a young girl, about five years old, sitting at the counter. I assumed they had ordered the steaks, which seemed odd, considering the size of the child. The man, a bald, unkempt guy in his late seventies, wore a vinegary look. He caught my gaze and stared back through narrow pale-gray eyes. I disliked the man instantly. Lisa served the child a coke and the man a cup of coffee and a slice of apple pie.

Ding. I hit the button and number 1 lit up, notifying Lisa her steak order waited. My far-reaching curiosity propelled me to study the child as she sipped her soda through a straw. She had uncombed wavy brown hair. I wanted to make eye contact, but she wouldn't look up. Still inquisitive, I left the kitchen and stood at the counter in front of the odd twosome. "Is there anything else I can get you?" I asked pleasantly.

The old man answered in a sinister voice. "No, this is all we're having."

I felt compelled to speak to the bashful child, "Hi there, sweetheart. How are you today?"

She squirmed a bit on the stool before turning her round face up to me. Dark eyes peeked through long bangs and grabbed at my heart. She quickly looked away without saying a word, obviously too shy to engage in conversation.

"Chef salad and a side of garlic bread." Lisa's voice nudged me back to my cooking duties.

Through the service window, I could see and hear Lisa asking the unfriendly man if he'd like a coffee refill. He shook his head no and asked coarsely, "How much do I owe you?" Lisa began to write out a ticket, but the man didn't wait. He stood up and threw a five-dollar bill on the counter. The child's entire hand disappeared into the grumpy man's palm—she remained expressionless. From the small window in the kitchen that faced the parking lot, I watched as they climbed into a dirty white Toyota pickup with a beat-up camper shell. The man pulled out from his parking space and headed north on Highway 55. Swirls of gray smoke billowed from the truck's tailpipe, while a raggedy bluish curtain flapped from the canopy's missing window. The truck vanished into the canyon shadows.

"Lisa, your order is ready," I called out.

After all the diners had left, I locked the front door and switched off the lights. My nightly kitchen cleanup duties were so routine, the job no longer required mental focus, which was good because I had something else muddling my mind—the child's sad demeanor had troubled me all evening.

As I thought about her, my breathing grew unexpectedly quick and shallow. I needed to sit down. The only light filtered in from the bar area, where capable Bill (the parameters of his wheelchair wouldn't stop him) tended to a couple of Horseshoe Bend locals enjoying a late evening beer. Alone in the corner booth and certain my presence was concealed, I hid there as a flood of memories from 1957, the year I was six, washed over me. Although the events had occurred thirty-some years prior, the details were amazingly clear, even the colors and smells. Drifting back to my early childhood days, I recalled being my uncle's favorite kid. Out of all my siblings, he had paid me the most attention, and my parents had thought it was nice that I had such a special relationship with Unc. A particular incident clawed the air and I drifted deeper into the abyss.

"Annie, come sit on my lap," Unc hollered from across the sprawling yard. Unc sat on a swing that hung from a tall, strong tree.

"Can I swing too, Unc?" I squealed. My skinny, disproportionately long legs transported me across the lawn, which had more weeds than grass. The wind caught my curly, shoulder-length brown hair and blew it into my face. "I want to swing too," I said, grinning and pushing away my hair.

Unc was smiling and seemed to be having fun. "Annie, do you want to sit on my lap so we can swing together?"

I said, "Yes," and started to climb onto Unc's lap.

"Wait, it might hurt," he said. Words I'd never forget.

An expression flitted across Unc's face, which confused me—how could it hurt to swing? It seemed like all the fun was spoiled, but I didn't know why.

Unc stood up, told me it was my turn to swing, and walked away.

"Are you mad at me, Unc?" I called after him. Unc didn't answer.

"Wait, Unc," I called. "Instead of swinging, can we play in the hay barn?" I remembered how much fun I'd had before, jumping from the hayloft into a huge mound of hay. When Unc stopped and turned in my direction, my heart raced with gladness—he wasn't mad after all, and I wouldn't have to play alone. "Hurry up, Unc!" I raced ahead, clucking my tongue to sound like horses' clomping hooves. But it turned out Unc wasn't much fun in the barn. It was a lot better to play with my brothers and sisters. But where were they, and where were my parents and grandparents? I was left alone with my great-great-uncle.

The hot blue sky of summer loomed over the multicolored hollyhock flowers growing on stout stalks lining the pathway to the two-story farmhouse. The weathered red barn, the chicken coop, and the smelly old outhouse resided in the distance. Red-checkered kitchen towels and a faded green apron with rickrack around the pocket hung from a sagging clothesline. My family and I were visiting my grandparents at their ranch in the mountains far away from any town. On this occasion when I was alone with Unc, I followed him into the farmhouse for lunch and sat waiting at a long wooden table. It looked as if someone had tried to paint the table dark green over yellow but hadn't finished the job. A long bench, painted a purplish blue, stretched along the wall side of the table, and six mismatched chairs were pushed in around the other side. All the chairs were ugly scratched wood and I thought they should be painted red, my favorite color. Unc placed a peanut butter and honey sandwich in front of me and handed me a cup of milk with a floating ice cube (this meant the milk was warm, and I wouldn't be able to gag it down—the ice cube trick never worked). The milk smelled awful and triggered a nasty image of the yucky bucket Grandpa placed under the cow while he milked her. I had seen him carrying it to the house earlier, full of white liquid with globs of cream, gnats, cow poop, and straw. The bucket sat on the counter, waiting to be poured into drinking cups. After I finished my sandwich,

Unc removed the empty plate, collected the untouched cup of milk— which no longer showed a trace of ice—and told me to go upstairs for my afternoon nap. I had just settled into my bed against the wall when I heard the wooden stairs creak. Unc was coming upstairs. He moved slowly to my bed and sat down next to me, then without saying a word, he slipped his hand underneath the bed quilt. My eyes grew large with fear—I wanted someone to be there to save me but didn't want anyone to know Unc's secret. I didn't understand what Unc was doing or why he was doing it. After a while, Unc stood up, and once again, I heard the stairs creak—the good sound of him leaving. I wanted my mom, but she was nowhere to be found.

It was night at the farmhouse. The air felt cold and damp and smelled like old people. Darkness surrounded me and heavy quilts covered every inch of my small body. I lay motionless in a twin bed with a rusty iron headboard. Grandma and Grandpa's featherbed was on the far side of the room. Were they in it? I couldn't tell for sure. I had to pee and remembered the chipped and dented pee pot under their bed but was afraid to use it. I was only six years old and afraid of everything. The thought of finding my way down the steep, constricted stairway to the outhouse in the pitch-black place made me reconsider using the porcelain pot, but I couldn't leave my bed. And what if Unc came up? I tried to make myself disappear so I could reappear in a new place, and when it didn't work, I tightly shut my eyes and prayed that the dark of night would be safer than the light of day.

An apricot orchard near the outhouse provided a safe place to pee. One day, squatting next to the tree, I realized the orchard also made a good hiding place and found the largest tree to lie under. Facing up, I stared at the branches, mesmerized by their twisted growth, and noticed a bird's nest safely tucked into a fork in the highest branches. I considered climbing up to take a peek at the baby birds, but the nest was too high. Instead, I watched and listened from the ground, imagining how perfect it would be to have wings.

For another eight years, Unc continued his unconscionable behavior, and no adult ever thought anything but good came from his fondness for me. I kept a secret about a smelly old man with sharp whiskers and chipped yellow fingernails. Unc had told me early on, "You can't tell anybody, because they'll get mad at us. They'll be so angry they might even kill me." The tone of Unc's voice made me sure I was doing something wrong, and it felt wrong, so I knew he must be right. I loathed this thing, this terrible thing that made me feel ashamed and sick to my stomach, but if anyone found out the secret, they would think I was stinky like Unc. And though I hated him, I didn't want him to die. And besides, my mother and father loved Unc, so they probably wouldn't believe me anyway. There were too many uncertainties, so no matter how bad it got, Unc's secret remained a secret. For the last three years of his life, Mom and Dad gave Unc a room in our home so he wouldn't have to live alone. I avoided him as much as possible, yet somehow, he found ways to get me alone. I turned thirteen the year Unc died. He was eighty-four. When I heard the news, I tried to look gloomy by pinching my face into a frown, but my heart sang with happiness.

Suddenly, a loud laugh came from the Ponderosa's bar area, startling me. I glanced in that direction and noticed Bill had acquired an additional beer drinker. The entire time I sat having these flashbacks, they had been oblivious to my existence in the dark corner. In place of a therapist, I reached for a bag of M&Ms, slipped quietly out the side door, wondered about my young counter guest, and prayed my suspicions were wrong. Unc's secret and my distrust for eccentric old men would indubitably haunt me for the rest of my days.

Chapter Twenty-Six

MISSING PIECES

Christmas came and went, leaving behind more than a foot of snow and a dried-up grand fir. Doug graciously extended snow-removal services from his parking lot to ours. Weekdays were fairly slow, giving us ample time to work on a nearly completed jigsaw puzzle. Deputy Buck provided amusement by secretly placing a single solid-blue piece onto the molding ledge above the window, hiding it from everyone's view. Later on, he got to complete the puzzle's cloudless sky.

However, weekends were different—there wasn't time for games. A steady crowd of hungry guests traveling from Boise to McCall for the winter carnival, ice sculpturing, skiing, and snowmobiling bombarded the Ponderosa.

For two weeks, the outside temperature stayed below freezing, keeping the narrow canyon's curvy roads snow-packed and icy. Mike and Tim had only one basketball game remaining, so my worry about their driving on dangerous roads would soon be over.

Early Friday evening, Mike raced to the door at top speed, his Nike bag slamming hard against the wall. "Bye, Mom. Tim's here. See you after the game!" he yelled.

"Good luck! Remind Tim to drive safe, the roads are slick!" I shouted back.

"Tim's a good driver, Mom, don't worry!" Mike's reply faded as if swallowed by the cold.

Estimating that Mike would be home by nine thirty, I was shocked when he and Tim walked through the door before nine o'clock, both soaked to the bone and shivering.

"What happened?" I called out as I rushed toward them from across the room. "Hurry, stand next to the woodstove," I said, shoving them both in that direction.

Mike's lips were blue and seemed to have a hard time making them move when he tried to speak. "Mom, you won't believe what happened on the way to the game tonight."

This cannot be good, I thought, and instantly spoke up. "You're nearly hypothermic. First, go to the cabin and put on dry clothes, then you can tell me about it."

In dry attire and sitting close to the woodburning heat, Mike began his story. "Just so you know, Mom, Tim wasn't driving fast, but the car in front of us probably was."

Bill and Lisa joined the group, and Mike had our undivided attention. "About eight miles short of the high school, the car in front of us missed the curve and disappeared over the bank toward the South Fork River. Tim stopped the jeep, and we both jumped out. When we found the tire tracks in the snow, we slid down to the river on our butts," Mike explained. His eyes showed echoes of panic as he continued. "When we saw the car upside-down in the river, we just stared at it, trying to figure out what to do next. Then all of a sudden, a man popped out of the driver's side window. We were relieved until he started swimming to the wrong side of the river. We hollered at him. *'No, come this way! You're going the wrong way! There is no road on that side!'* But he must've been disoriented or maybe he couldn't hear us. When he got to the edge of the river, he could hardly stand up. We thought he was looking at us, so we waved our arms at him. It was hard to see his face, but he acted like he couldn't see us at all."

Mike then told us how Tim had raced up the hill and drove his jeep to the nearest phone. Meanwhile, Mike did his best to encourage the man. "Hold on! Help is coming!" he shouted, not knowing if his words were reaching the man or even if what he was saying was true.

When Deputy Buck and Sheriff Alex arrived ten minutes later, they brainstormed different ideas on the rescue and came up with two options—trek the mile of snowy terrain along the opposite side of the river to the man's location, or somehow get the man to swim back across in the frigid water. Both Mike and Tim referred to the second option as "completely ridiculous." But the time required to carry out the first option didn't make it a good choice either.

"I can't believe it, but some bystander thought he had the perfect solution—he tied a rock to the end of a rope and attempted to throw it across the river. Even if the guy could've grabbed it and held on, which was about as likely as him swinging across the river holding onto a tree limb, he would've been dragged back fifty feet through a river of ice chunks and rocks." Mike paused, looked at me, decided it was okay to cuss, and continued, "Shit, the guy was getting weaker and colder by the minute. Tim and I decided to go get him before it was too late. Nobody stopped us or volunteered to go—so we took off, drove back down to the bridge, parked the jeep, and began to hike."

"I wish we'd had snowshoes. The snow was up to our crotches, in some places," Tim interjected. "The full moon helped us to see, but the hillside was really steep, and a few times we slid into the river's edge." Tim's eyes blinked nervously.

But neither wet shoes or frozen pants could deter Mike and Tim from their mission. When they spotted the flickering flashlight signals coming from across the river, it guided them to where the nearly unconscious man lay on the frozen ground. Like most sixteen-year-old boys, who seem to think that building a fire is a must in all emergency situations, Mike and Tim wanted to warm the man and themselves before transporting him back to the highway. Mike pulled out a pack of matches, surprised to find them completely dry, and flashed them at Tim. Both boys rifled through their wallets, looking for paper fuel. When their hunting and fishing licenses failed to produce enough heat to ignite the small pile of damp twigs, they gave up the fire idea. With Mike's help, Tim was able to lift the stout stranger, positioning him over his shoulders like a veteran fireman. Then taking turns carrying him, the boys retraced their trail over the slippery terrain back to Tim's jeep, where, thanks to Sheriff Alex, an ambulance awaited.

Deputy Buck congratulated and thanked the exhausted two-some. "Do you know *who* you two carried out of there?" Buck asked.

"No, who?" they both asked, puzzled.

"The referee for tonight's basketball game—a game the *three* of you missed."

"Really?" Tim asked. He looked at Mike and exclaimed, "Hey, dude, we missed our game tonight!" They laughed, jumped into the jeep, and cranked up the heater.

"Hey, Tim, did you hear what the ref told me while I packed him?" Mike asked.

"No," Tim replied.

"He called us his angels in blue jeans and thanked us for rescuing him," Mike said.

"I couldn't be prouder. You both saved a man's life. I'm sorry you missed your game tonight, but without a referee and two key players, there probably wasn't a game anyway. Oh, and I'm *really* sad you no longer have fishing and hunting licenses," I added. "Are either of you hungry?" Without waiting for an answer, I headed to the kitchen, pausing only to suggest to Tim, "You should call your mom, let her know you're here, and ask if you can spend the night."

Chapter Twenty-Seven

SURVIVING OUR FIRST IDAHO WINTER

My anxiety couldn't be contained a second longer. "Be careful up there!" I yelled up to Mike, who paid no attention. The chore of shoveling the heavy snow off the roof seemed dangerous to me, but to Mike, it was just another job. When an avalanche of snow slid off the roof with a horrific crash, I decided I had had enough and returned to the warmth and safety of the restaurant.

The temperature for the past two weeks had been in the teens at night, and several inches of new snow fell each day—it was winter in Idaho.

Mike stood at the side door and yelled across the customer-less restaurant, "The roof's done! Now can I go snowmobiling with Doug and Adelle?"

"Me too?" Lisa chimed in.

"I guess so," I answered flatly. The kids had been talking about this outing for days, but I'd been unenthusiastic about their plans—more likely than not, I was a bit envious.

Gentleman Joe decided to brave the thirteen miles of hazard-ous road conditions so he could patronize the Horseshoe Bend gro-cery store, a clear indication that his supply of scotch and cigarettes must've been dangerously low. Alone in the restaurant, Myra, Bill, and I planned to spend another boring day indoors.

In an effort to liven up the doldrums, I tried to spark a conversation. "As soon as this weather breaks and the snow starts to melt, I plan to ask Marty for a cost estimate to build a deck. What could be better for the summer crowd than a new deck?" But neither Bill nor Myra had a chance to respond before my attention was caught by a person entering the restaurant, a man with a drab stocking cap pulled down so low that it nearly covered his eyes and a coat collar pulled up so high that it covered his mouth and nose. The man moved slowly toward the woodstove, and that's when I recognized my handyman, John Vander. Happy to see my friend, I moved quickly in his direction. "Good to see you, Vandie! It's been over three weeks—where've you been?"

"I've been sick with a rotten cold, probably pneumonia," John replied.

"Oh no, that's awful. But you're out and about, so you must be feeling better?"

John grabbed his cap and, along with his coat, draped it over the back of a chair, and plopped down as if his body weighed two tons. My heart sank. John was a mess. I tried not to show my shock at the sight of his face with whiskers, runny red nose, and puffy, bloodshot eyes. I knew John loved my homemade soup, and fortunately, a pot was simmering on the stove. "Hold on, John. I have the perfect antidote. What you need is a bowl of my chicken noodle soup."

After downing two large bowls of the hearty soup, John sat up straighter and regained his shy smile. He reached into his pocket and brought out a worn wallet, but before he had a chance to say or do anything, I said, "Put your wallet away. You aren't paying for a darn thing."

He muttered a quiet thanks, replaced his wallet, put on his stocking cap, zipped his coat, and left. "Hey, John, get healthy and don't stay away so long," I called out before the door shut.

Officially released by his doctor and confinement of his wheelchair, Bill strolled into the kitchen. "Wow, it's almost twenty-nine degrees outside!" he commented sarcastically.

"Wow, and it's also astonishing to see you walking around so effortlessly," I replied back while giving him a high five.

"Order in! Ham-and-cheese omelet, hold the ham!" Myra announced.

Myra and I locked eyes. "Isn't that a cheese omelet?" I asked quietly, wearing a quizzical expression.

Myra seemed to think the situation was too funny to ignore, but she couldn't comment within earshot of customers. She whizzed back into the kitchen to explain the odd request. "I know, Ann, when I nicely asked the guy the same question, he repeated, 'I want a ham-and-cheese omelet with no ham.' Maybe he thinks you'll add extra cheese since he's not getting the ham." Myra worked so hard at holding back her laughter her eyes watered.

I couldn't help but lean forward and whisper to her, "Or maybe these drab winter days are making people nuts." Myra grabbed at her stomach and bent at the waist. Though her laughter was contagious, we both knew we had to keep a lid on it—which made the situation even funnier—like getting the giggles in church. "All-righty then, one ham-and-cheese omelet with no ham, coming up," I said, rolling my eyes back so far the pupils almost vanished.

As I put an extra handful of cheddar on the ham-less omelet, Joe poked his head into the kitchen and announced, "Miss Ann, there's a fellow here by the name of Woody who'd like to speak with you."

"Okay." I took a minute to compose myself and finish up the order. Joe pointed out a nice-looking young man, who waited at the counter.

"Hi, I'm Ann. How can I help you?" I asked.

"Hello, nice to meet you. I'm Woody. I noticed the FOR RENT sign in the window of the cabin at the far end of your property."

"Are you looking for a place to live?" I asked.

"No. I own a rafting company and need a place along the river where I can operate my business." With a touch of arrogance, he added, "It's a successful, established operation."

Turning around to find Myra, I asked, "Myra, can you work the grill until I get back?"

Once I located the key from underneath a pile of invoices, Woody and I walked down the long driveway past the family cabin, the row of mailboxes, the motel units, and the vacant RV spots.

Finally, we reached the unoccupied building and entered. Woody's eyes lit up. The large, open space and generous-sized bedrooms seemed to appeal to Woody, and his enthusiasm couldn't be camouflaged. He told me, "This is exactly what I'm looking for!"

"Well, I have one more room to show you," I said, and ushered him into the back bedroom. His expression turned from excitement to unease—exactly the reaction I had expected. Watching strangers experience that sensation for the first time was always entertaining.

The oversize window drew Woody as gravity draws a falling apple. He gawked out at the white frothy water, not far downriver from *KYBR*. "What a view! But is this safe? It feels like this room is tilting toward the river," Woody said.

"You're right, it does slope that direction," I said, with a straight face, enjoying shaking Woody's smug composure. However, I couldn't keep him in discomfort for long and confessed, "Awhile back, a contractor inspected the pilings below, and he assured us of its sturdiness."

"Well, okay. I'm very interested in renting the building," Woody said. Losing most of his swagger, he nearly tiptoed back to the living room. "And I may have an excellent business proposition for you. I own a dozen rafts and guide seven days a week, and some of these raft trips need to be catered. It could be a couple of groups a day, and some might be up to a hundred people—would you be interested?"

Ignoring the reappearance of his tone of superiority, and without fully considering what it meant to add *catering* to my job description, I said, "For sure. I'm interested."

Looking in the direction of the sloping room, Woody added, "If you can give me a good deal on the rent, I'll provide you plenty of business."

I reached my hand out to shake his. "It's a deal. Let's get back to the restaurant and write out a detailed plan, including your food requests."

The decisions about rental fees and catering were hammered out in the expectation it would be a win-win situation. Cocky Woody was growing on me. After signing a simple, one-page, handwritten lease agreement, he said, "I'd like to start moving my supplies into the cabin next week."

"As soon as you pay first month's rent, you can move in," I said.

After Woody handed me a check, I passed him the cabin key and couldn't refrain from saying, "Remember, don't put too much weight in that back bedroom." His nervous laugh told me he wasn't convinced by the contractor's reassurances.

With a large dose of energy, I explained the business expansion to Bill and Myra, and a look of worry grew on Myra's face. "Ann, this sounds like a lot of extra work for you," she said very softly, her blue eyes showing unease. Myra was only trying to protect me from myself, and I loved her for it. But nothing could rain on my entrepreneurial parade or squash my ambitious plans to whip up fifty pounds of my famous Boise County macaroni shrimp salad and feed it to a hundred additional people a day, making it even more famous. "You're right," I said. "I'll need to hire more help. Bring on the summertime!"

The early spring sun raised the temperature and slowly melted the snow. Woody moved into his new business location and mounted an oversize sign on the front of the blue-gray building that read Woody's Rafting.

Marty designed a four-level, 1,200-square-foot deck that any architect would be proud of. With the eagerness of a child, he handed me the blueprints and a written bid and said, "As soon as you give me the go-ahead, I'll have the lumber and materials delivered and start building."

My enthusiasm, naïve as it might be, would have had Marty sawing and hammering before nightfall, but Bill calmly dissected Marty's bid, immune to my fervor. "Sure hope we can afford this extravagant deck," Bill said, the crease between his eyebrows becoming deeper and more defined.

"Oh, Bill, trust me! It'll pay for itself! People will come from all over to sit outside, eat and view the river," I exclaimed. Bill did trust me, and he also knew that nobody—not even he—could put the kybosh on my deck plans.

Marty showed up early Friday morning with a truckload of tools and a large work squad. "I know you want this deck finished as soon as possible, so I brought extra help. I have to tell you, Ann, this will be quite the deck."

Chapter Twenty-Eight

SLEEPING IN A CHAIR

The morning alarm wasn't set to go off for several more hours, but I couldn't tolerate the pain a moment longer. "Bill, wake up! There's something wrong with my hands." For the last couple of weeks, a painful tingling in both my hands had been waking me during the night. But expecting the pain to peter out, I hadn't mentioned a word to Bill until now. The symptoms were difficult to explain—including the strange fact that if I stood up with my hands hanging down at my sides, the numbness would subside.

Bill didn't try to muster even a speck of sympathy. "Make a doctor's appointment in the morning," he said and rolled over. At that precise moment, a distinctive sound came from under the covers. He actually had the audacity to pass gas.

"Screw you," I responded, just a little too loudly.

"Annie, what the hell would you like me to do in the middle of the night? Drive you to Boise?"

"Well, I suppose nothing," I retorted.

The conversation wasn't going the way I'd hoped, but Bill was right—I would have to wait until morning.

The next morning, after a string of phone calls to half a dozen different physicians, I located an orthopedic surgeon. "Dr. Kinsman can see you next Friday morning at ten o'clock, and if there's a cancellation, I'll be sure to call you," the receptionist promised.

Disappointed I couldn't get in within the hour, or at least that afternoon, I replied, "I'll take it."

For the remainder of the week, I slept in a chair with my arms dangling at my sides. It helped some, but I wasn't getting much rest. The simple reality—I couldn't work sixteen-hour days with so little sleep at night. My highly efficient lifestyle was going south, and my new nickname of Crabby was an understatement.

Finally, the day arrived for my appointment. After Dr. Kinsman listened to my symptoms, he asked questions and put me through a series of different hand and arm positions, and within minutes, he explained, "Normally we run tests to determine the cause of pain and numbness, but I don't think you need to waste time and money. You have a classic case of carpal tunnel syndrome. The quickest and surest way to get relief is with surgery."

I asked, "Can you operate this afternoon, and what's the recuperation time?"

Dr. Kinsman replied, "We'll get you on the surgical calendar, and of course, it won't be this afternoon. Your wrist and arm will be in a cast for several weeks. After that, it takes up to six months to complete the healing process."

My next question seemed reasonable, at least to me. "Can you operate on both wrists at the same time?"

In a tone of impatience about my impatience, he answered, "We don't recommend operating on both wrists at the same time. I realize you want to act quickly so you can feel better and return to work, but you need to know this is going to be a *process*. Let me check with my nurse for the earliest opening."

Dr. Kinsman left the room, leaving only Bill, me, and a loud, long sigh. Shortly thereafter, we were informed the following Tuesday would be the day. Bill tried to cheer me up when he noticed my disappointment. "Annie, that's good—it's only four days away." His words were pleasant; however, the tone of his voice said I should *chill out.*

"Easy for you to say—four days is like four *years* to me," I whined.

Back in the car, rolling up the canyon at a steady pace, I contemplated the surgery day. I needed to have all the details planned out. Planning and organizing were in my nature, and it also helped soothe my nerves about the upcoming operation and its prolonged healing time.

"Bill, I'll have to be at the hospital by ten o'clock Tuesday morning. The surgery starts at eleven and will take forty-five minutes to an hour, and then after a couple of hours in recovery, I should be good to go." When I finally stopped talking, there was nothing but silence. "*Hello*. Bill, did you hear anything I just said? Are you even going to take me to the hospital?"

"Of course I will," he answered.

"If you can't, I'm sure my dad will." Without waiting for Bill's answer, I continued, "Actually, that's probably a better idea because you'll be needed at the restaurant. I'll call Dad tonight."

Dad was happy to assist with Tuesday's plans, and as it turned out, I needed every second of the four days to get prepared—schedules had to be made for all employees. With winter over, business picked up daily, and to top it off, our seating capacity was about to almost double. The deck footings had been poured, and lumber was being measured, sawed, and screwed together. In a couple of weeks, the deck would be ready for paint, outdoor furniture, and customers. But I was getting ahead of myself—for the time being, I only needed to worry about getting through several more nights of sleeping in the chair.

"Thanks for the lift to the hospital, Dad," I said. During the hour trip, I recited the difficulties of sleeping while sitting up, keeping my arms dangling at my sides.

Dad's sympathy helped. "If that was happening to me, I wouldn't drive to the hospital, I'd take an ambulance!"

Finally, someone understood! "I just wish they'd do both my wrists today and get this over with."

The operation proceeded without incident, and Dad and I left the hospital just in time to combat the five o'clock traffic. Clasping a prescription bottle of pain medication, I slept soundly until Dad pulled into the Ponderosa's parking lot.

"You're home, Annie. How are you feeling?"

"Okay, I guess. Thanks, Dad, for your help."

When I entered the restaurant, everyone greeted me with warm words. I glanced at the wall clock and calculated that Jodi had put in a long enough shift. "Jodi, thanks for your help, go home to your baby girl, I can handle this now."

I honestly felt invincible and could make it on determination alone. Then within the hour, the pain took away my resolve. After swallowing two pain pills, it only took minutes for my eyes to grow heavy and my words to slur. "Bill, will you put the CLOSED sign up and as soon as those customers leave, lock up, and turn off the lights? I cannot stand up for one more second." Heavy medication was the only force powerful enough to slap me down.

Bill practically carried me to the cabin and tucked me into bed. "Thanks, honey. I'm sure I can work a full day tomorrow. I won't take any of those damn pain pills—they just make me sleepy," I whispered.

"Good night, Annie." He covered me and dropped a tender kiss on my lips.

Even though the ghastly sound of the alarm going off at five o'clock the following morning irritated me, I, nonetheless, obeyed its order and even managed to get myself dressed. By the time Myra arrived at the restaurant, the grill was hot and the OPEN sign displayed. The expression on Myra's face told me I looked like death— and I felt as bad as I looked. *Thank God Gentleman Joe and Bill will be in soon,* I thought.

Both hands hurt—one because it had had surgery and the other because it hadn't. With unthinkable willpower, I reassured Myra, "Don't worry, I can do this. But I'll be using my left hand, and since I'm not left-handed, don't be surprised if it takes a little longer to get orders out."

With my right arm in a sling, I stared down at the grill and my mind shouted, *How in the hell are you going to pull this one off, Ann?* No more than five seconds had passed before the first order was up on the wheel. Without hesitation, I whipped into action and a breakfast special was ready to be served. The order had been for eggs over easy, but I got no complaint from the customer when the eggs arrived a little more on the scrambled side. Myra had a way with her customers.

In the weeks that followed, both Gentleman Joe and Bill helped cook and chop vegetables for the soup pot, and after school, Lisa and Mike chipped in more than usual. Myra worked long hours and never complained, only commenting happily, "I need the money, and I like the tips!"

What would I do without everyone? I thought.

The cast on my right arm extended from my fingers to my elbow. However, once the swelling subsided, I discovered I could proficiently use my fingertips that protruded from the stiff plaster. Each day grew a little easier, and the spatula grew less heavy and awkward.

Four weeks later, Dr. Kinsman removed the cast. "You know, the average patient takes six to twelve weeks off work to heal from this procedure," he said in his most pleasant voice.

Certainly, the food-stained cast, visibly announced that I wasn't listening. If he only knew—that I was flipping burgers within an hour of leaving the recovery room. I thanked him and reminded him of the surgery for my left wrist in four days. He left the small room, holding my medical chart and shaking his head.

Sherm offered to go through the all-day hospital ritual with me again. "Thanks, Dad, but Bill wants to do it this time. Not sure why, but he does."

"That's good. But if for any reason he can't, just let me know."

Myra, a blessing as always, promised to oversee the crew from opening to closing on surgery day. I could go straight to bed upon arriving home.

Early Monday morning, I checked in at the hospital admission desk and soon regretted my decision to let my husband take me in. Bill, under the pretense of being my chauffeur and ally, had taken it upon himself to turn into a stand-up comedian and was using the patients in the crowded waiting room as his audience.

I sat alone at the desk where a sophisticated, stylish receptionist asked me routine questions concerning my pending surgical procedure. "After your surgery, you'll be in the recovery room for an hour or so. Do you have somebody to drive you home?" she asked.

"Yes, my husband," I answered.

"He needs to sign this paper."

I waved over at Bill to join me at the desk. Looking at Bill, she recited, "Anna won't be able to drive, operate heavy equipment, or make any important decisions until tomorrow." Not realizing that she was dealing with a comedian wannabe, the woman handed Bill a form and a pen. "You need to sign this, please."

"What? She won't be able to operate the backhoe this afternoon?" he announced loudly. The people in the waiting room burst into laughter, which only encouraged Bill to continue. Under different circumstances, I might've enjoyed Bill's quick-witted comic relief, but not today.

Still not catching on that she might best manage Bill by loosening up a bit, the receptionist asked, "And will you be in the waiting room while she is undergoing surgery? If you'll be elsewhere, we'll need a phone number to reach you."

Deadpan, Bill replied in full volume, "Well, I'm not sure... It depends... Are they serving cocktails in the waiting room?" Once again, everyone roared with laughter, and I sank further into my chair, eagerly anticipating my forthcoming shot of joy-juice.

It seemed like in no time at all. I was sleeping undisturbed from the hospital parking lot to the cabin door. Bill tucked me into bed with a glass of water and two pain pills. "Bill, please tell Myra and everyone thanks for their help."

When the morning alarm buzzed me to consciousness, I was ready, now a pro.

Chapter Twenty-Nine

JUSTIFIABLE AMENDS

With Mother's Day only two weeks out, we added three new waitresses to our workforce. Myra and Lisa were confident they'd have the new staff trained and ready in time for our busiest day of the year. Frank's Meats was set to deliver seventy-five pounds of choice, boneless prime rib. I had everything prearranged, except for just one hitch—the plaster encasing my left arm and hand. Even though I begged—Dr. Kinsman stayed adamant. "Sorry, but the cast will not come off in time for Mother's Day."

True to his word, Marty completed the deck by the first of May, and Mike and Tim were hired to do the staining. For three straight hours, the boys danced around with long poles attached to rollers. The boom box blared, and their shirtless bodies soaked up the chilly springtime sun. Excited, they called everyone out to admire their efforts. The deck was even more spectacular than I'd imagined. I pictured the twelve round tables and seventy-two stackable chairs that would be set up on the freshly stained deck and I realized what I had done—I'd just doubled my workload. But was I worried? Not a bit!

The day before Mother's Day was crazy-busy, giving us a taste of what was headed our way for the following day. Bill, his face tight and uncharacteristically grim, operated the dishwasher, played host, worked the till, bussed tables, made coffee, served beer, and sliced meat—practically all at the same time. Jodi and I were also doing our share of multitasking, but the grillwork required complete efficiency that was impossible with my cast. I knew what had to be done.

I went straight to my office area, retrieved a pair of heavy-duty scissors from the desk drawer, and clumsily cut away my impediment, then proceeded out the side door and tossed the cast into the dumpster. My plan, first thing Monday morning, I would call the doctor's office and cancel my next Wednesday's appointment. And my excuse would be simple, my cast got wet in the shower and fell apart, and if that explanation didn't fly, I'd come up with another one. I returned to the grill with a fresh attitude and a ridiculously scrawny left arm—where craggy dark hairs stood out against my pale skin. My arm worked great. "I'm ready to kick butt now," I said to Jodi. "Bring on tomorrow!" I laughed and pulled down two green order slips with my left hand. In the back, a buzzer went off, signaling that five trays of apple dumplings were ready to come out of the oven. The cinnamon aroma that wafted throughout the kitchen sustained my good mood and even improved Bill's.

By the end of Mother's Day, our customers had devoured seventy-five pounds of juicy prime rib. The handful of customers who braved the uncommonly cold weather to enjoy a meal on the deck were rewarded with front row seats to the show *Diehard Kayakers and Rafters Conquer the Ferocious Roaring Rapids of the Payette River*. Even with the cooler weather, the deck was an enormous attraction, and not a single customer ignored its splendor. Their *oohs* and *aahs* accompanied promises of "Can't wait for the weather to warm up. We'll be back."

Bill precariously balanced several baskets of fish n' chips on his hands and arms and scurried past me. *Evidently, I need to order extra serving trays*, I thought. Bill maintained a huge smile and called out to me as he continued en route, "Everyone loves how Marty built the deck around that big ponderosa pine."

"I told you! And if you think last summer was wild, hold on to your skivvies!"

I would've been thankful to reach the end of an exhausting day had it not been for the nagging thought of what lay ahead, like a history exam I hadn't studied for. It was to be my first catering job for

Woody's Rafting the following afternoon, which meant I had to pre-pare lunch for thirty-six rafting enthusiasts who didn't want to miss the excitement provided by the heavy spring runoff. *What were those people thinking when they signed up for that frigid water?* I wondered. *And what was I thinking on that quiet and gratifyingly boring winter day when I signed up to serve them a meal?*

During a conversation with Gentleman Joe, I casually men-tioned my catering concerns, and he jumped in with encouragement. "If anybody can do it, it's you, Miss Ann."

I believed him. Joe couldn't lie to Miss Ann—plus the slow sea-son was only six months away. "One catered meal at a time," I told myself.

It became more apparent every day that Joe was a crucial part of the Ponderosa team. Reliable and stable, he had a special way of sup-porting me. Something had occurred between us a few weeks earlier, on a bright Sunday morning before Jodi arrived, that would remain in my heart for life. The order wheel held its maximum capacity of green slips, and there was zero space on the food-covered grill for pancakes or hash browns. I panicked. The more I tried to focus, the more I fumbled, and the more overloaded the grill became the more overloaded I became. My mind went blank, my face flushed, and I crumpled to the floor like a rag mop. "*I cannot do this,*" I moaned to myself over and over. I wept softly, listening to the sizzling sounds coming from the grill top.

I don't know how long I sat on the floor before Joe, looking sharp in his wrinkle-free gray polyester suit, entered the kitchen, tot-ing a tub of dirty dishes. When he spotted me curled up on the floor in a ball of despair, his face showed alarm and compassion. Composure unbroken, he asked softly, "Are you all right, Miss Ann?"

"No. I *burned* the bacon!"

Calmly, Joe put down the oblong tub, walked over, and gently lifted me to my feet. "Miss Ann, this bacon isn't burnt, it's extra crispy. You can serve this food. Your food is always delicious, and people love it." His way and his words brought me to my senses, and I quickly regained control and began to kick out orders at a record pace. The hood-exhaust fan also kicked into full gear, sucking the smoke from the kitchen and piping it out into the early morning air. Travelers up and down the canyon surely caught the distinct smell of well-cooked bacon. Through the order window, I saw only happy faces enjoying their breakfasts, some with extra crispy bacon.

Thirty minutes later, Jodi moved into position at my side. The order wheel was still full, and the grill we faced was piled high with hash browns, sausage links, and omelets, but no sign of my meltdown remained.

With the catering business in full force, I needed ways to ease my workload. When I asked Myra if she might be interested in earning extra money by keeping the motel rooms clean, she jumped at the opportunity, cheerfully heading to the motel after her restaurant shift ended.

One afternoon, shortly after two o'clock, I heard Myra's voice coming from the side door and ricocheting off the walls. "Annie! Somebody stole the TV out of room 2!"

"You're kidding! I tried to make those twenty-five-dollar-a-night rooms a bit nicer, and this is the thanks I get. I'm so mad, I'm seriously considering removing the TV from the other room," I spewed.

I silently fumed until I noticed John Vander sitting at the counter. *Perfect!* "Boy, it's good to see you," I said. "You aren't going to believe what happened last night—someone stole a TV from one of the motel rooms." My sentences ran together.

John tilted his head to the left and responded in his familiar soft voice. "They did? Don't worry, Annie, I can fix it. I'll be back." He vanished through the side door like a magic trick.

A few hours passed before John reappeared at the counter. Looking rather smug, he calmly announced, "I've fixed your TV problem. Why don't you and Bill come take a look?"

"Lisa, take over the grill for a second," I said and quickly adding the word "please" when I noticed the look she gave me.

Bill and I followed John to the motel. "You guys stand here while I go inside and unplug the television set."

I'm not exactly sure how loud ninety decibels are, but if it's loud enough to rattle windows and vibrate roof shingles, then that's how loud this alarm was. Bill and I broke into wild laughter. John, obvi-

159

ously enjoying the loud commotion he had caused, took his sweet time to switch off the alarm. Bill shouted out, "You did it, John! Now, when some creep tries to swipe a TV, people will hear it for five miles."

"Yeah, and I'd love to see it happen! Just for kicks, it might be fun to replace the stolen TV with a really nice one," I said.

Like a kid demonstrating a project at a science fair, John pointed out how hidden wires passed through small holes drilled into the walls behind the beds. He then guided us into the laundry room behind the motel, where the sounds of our laughter could be heard over the rush of the river. There was an alarm box as large as the commercial clothes dryer next to it. Losing one used nineteen-inch black-and-white television set was a cheap ticket for this kind of amusement.

Chapter Thirty

THE SQUEAL OF TIRES AND SPEW OF GRAVEL

Three weeks post-Mother's Day brought pleasant, sunny weather. Traffic strung along the highway as close together as beads on a necklace—summer had officially arrived. Mike's '71 Ranchero was finally running, though making that happen had sucked his savings account dry. Lisa, on the other hand, had saved her money all winter and was ready to spend it. With her clothes closet crammed full, she decided to invest in a private phone line to her private bedroom. What followed taught her a lesson that enhanced her maturity far more effectively than anything Bill or I could have taught—monthly payments have due dates and months fly by quickly.

The side door swung open with unexpected vehemence. Bill looked over, paying more attention to the hole in the sheetrock that the doorknob had just enlarged than to the person who had entered. Mike, unaware of the force with which he had just presented himself, grinned at Bill and asked, "Hey, Dad, do you want to go for a ride?"

"For sure! Give me a few minutes to finish slicing roast beef for your mother," Bill answered. He tried to show Mike his excitement and, at the same time, to hide it from me. *Oh please,* I thought. Bill was as thrilled as one of Mike's seventeen-year-old school chums.

Mike gave the engine a few manly revs as his dad slid into the passenger seat. Then Mike backed the Ranchero out of the parking space and jockeyed it into position to enter the highway, revving the engine a few more times while he waited for an opening in traffic. The bursts of engine noise made it seem as though Mike was impatient to go, but I knew he was enjoying the pause and the opportunity to announce his grand departure. I hadn't yet grown accustomed to the revving noises when it was replaced with the sound of screeching tires. As Mike's car disappeared down the highway, I glanced at my watch.

After seven minutes and twelve seconds passed, and many promises to God on my part, Mike returned. He parked the car next to where I waited in the parking lot. Both doors swung open, and two men with identical grins sprung out. "Now, all I need are new tires and a paint job," Mike announced.

Not wanting to be a fun-killing, overly protective mother, I bit my tongue and pulled out a supportive response. "Good job, Mike. You got 'er running nicely."

"Thanks, Mom. I'll be back later. Tim wants to help install my stereo and speakers."

After a few more revs, followed by the screech of his tires, Mike joined the steady flow of traffic. I couldn't help but notice the Ranchero's back end slide out slightly to the right, off the roadway, flinging loose gravel. "I can't believe Mike just fishtailed, right in front of us. He wouldn't need new tires if he wasn't leaving rubber all over the road," I said to Bill.

Bill laughed, hand-combing his windblown hair.

"Bill, you're not fooling me. You think the sounds coming from Mike's car are some of the coolest sounds ever made. Am I right?"

Bill laughed again but didn't answer my question.

A dozen or so customers had formed a line on the deck, patiently waiting for tables to become available. Bill, not as calm as the customers, rushed into the kitchen, balancing a serving tray of dirty plates, glasses, silverware, scraps, and used napkins, and announced, "We should've built the deck larger!"

"Is he kidding? We can't handle one more order. Where are all of these people coming from?" I asked Jodi. She started to respond but was interrupted by the sound of a loud crash and a scream coming from the restaurant.

"What happened?" I asked Myra, who spun the order wheel around, looking for an empty clip. Her lips barely moving, Myra answered, "Melissa just dropped a tray loaded with milkshakes."

How Bill was able to hear Myra's quiet words is a mystery, but he did. "Dammit all to hell! She just dropped five milkshakes on the carpet?" Bill bellowed as he flipped up both his arms to send a *That does it, I've had it* message.

I felt terrible for Melissa. She had spent nearly ten minutes making the shakes, one at a time, from scratch. Now, on top of her embarrassment, she had to clean up the mess and remake them. The last thing she needed was a pissed-off boss. "Honey, it's okay, Melissa will deal with it. How about helping her out by delivering her food order—it's ready."

Several minutes later, I scanned the area to see what had become of Melissa's mess. That's when I noticed Myra stuck at the cash register, tending to a line of customers eager to pay and be on their way. I didn't have a chance to look away before Myra, a sickened expression on her face, shouted, "Ann, come here, quick."

"Good grief, now what?" I asked Jodi.

From the till area, Myra had a direct view of the well-stocked pop, beer, and wine cooler and of the front door. "Ann, a guy and gal just stole a bottle of wine and a can of beer and ran out!"

Without thinking or planning the safest way to handle the situation, I flew out the kitchen side door like a blow torch, my apron flapping and my blood pumping so hard, my eyeballs felt like they were pulsating. "This is another one of those bullshit situations," I ranted even though no one could hear me. "I'm working my butt off, and two assholes steal from me. *No way!*" The parking lot was jam-packed, but there was one moving vehicle, making the thieves easy to spot. The car did a quick one-stop turning maneuver toward the highway. When I yelled, "Stop!" it did. It took me a few seconds to realize that my command had had nothing to do with bringing the car to a halt. The highway's traffic had done the job for me, and I seized the opportunity, approached the car, and boldly confronted the driver through his rolled down car window. The guy was rough and scary but young—in his late teens. I speculated that his glare was intended to make me nervous as a Chihuahua about to be attacked by a Pit Bull, but it had the opposite effect on me. I was sick of thieves, and no shoplifter, not even one as strong as Rocky Balboa, would be a match for my rage. Instead of backing off, I stuck my head through his car window and saw his front seat passenger, a young female wearing a halter top that exposed her large breasts and a dragon tattoo, attempting to kick a bottle of Riesling and a sixteen-ounce can of Budweiser under her seat.

"You stole from me. I can see it on the floor of your car."

Both teenagers turned to watch the busy highway, ready to pounce at the slightest opening. While taking a small step back from the car, I shouted, "You'd better not leave!" I knew standing in front of the vehicle would be suicidal, so I remained at the driver's window, my face just inches from the pimply skin of the driver.

Then suddenly, the thieves luck turned, and the driver pushed the pedal to the metal in perfect coordination with a slight break in traffic. Gravel exploded and his tires screeched, and I screeched back, "I've got your license plate number and I'm calling the cops!"

As I walked back to the restaurant, picking rubber out of my teeth and wiping dust from my eyes, I imagined Bill watching me through the small window next to the dishwasher. I envisioned him shaking his head, saying, *Ann, what the hell are you doing? They could have a weapon.* I suppose they could've clonked me over the head with the wine bottle and dumped beer on me.

When I shouldered open the side door, Bill didn't say anything, pretending to wash dishes. It was Lisa who spoke. "Mom, you didn't get the beer and wine back."

"No, but I got something even better." I smiled and said, "*Their plate number!*"

Lisa gave me a puzzled stare. "What good is that going to do?"

"Those two delinquents are scared to death. They'll be looking in their rearview mirror for a police car for the next hundred miles. I hope they don't enjoy a single sip."

I walked over to the grill, dropped in a basket of curly fries, and felt my anger fizzle away. I said to Jodi, "It won't do any good to call Deputy Buck about this one—the evidence won't last long."

Just as the excitement was settling down, Woody stopped by with a list of the week's rafting trips. "Great, I only have to prepare food for twenty-one rafting trips," I said to Jodi.

"How many people is that?" she asked.

Quickly counting it up in my head, I answered, "Three hundred and forty-nine people. Oh, no wait, it's *four* hundred and forty-nine."

I smiled. Catering had become just another part of my routine.

Chapter Thirty-One

LIFE JACKET LEFT BEHIND

Several months prior, Mike and his drama class had been given the opportunity to show off their outgoing personalities by performing a skit at Garden Valley High's talent show. Rachel, a schoolmate and good friend to Lisa and Mike, had also participated in the contest. When Rachel, a petite dark-haired girl with snappy hazel eyes and a spunky personality, picked up the microphone and sang with a voice that resonated like Patsy Cline's, the audience was blown away. I turned to Bill, my mouth hanging open. "How can such a big voice come out of that little girl?" I asked.

Rachel received the loudest applause and the most votes. At sixteen, she was already a polished and dynamic performer. Rachel's parents, Larry and Debbie, were also in the crowd. Bill and Larry discussed his daughter singing at our restaurant, and soon an hour-long concert was scheduled for the middle of July. Larry would set up speakers and an amplifier with a microphone on the Ponderosa's deck, and Rachel would sing her heart out for our dining guests.

"Mom, they're here!" Lisa yelled.

I'd just stepped out from the walk-in fridge and only caught Lisa's last word: *here*. "*Who's* here?" I asked in what I thought was a fairly pleasant tone of voice.

Lisa shot me a pissed off look and snapped back, "Rachel is here with her dad." Lisa's typically sweet disposition had been tested for the last five minutes by the condition of the large table she was bussing. A group of four adults and three small children had dined at that table and had left behind a high chair and a booster seat soaked in a mess of spilled milk and cracker crumbs. Milk soaked napkins covered the table, and scattered french fries were smashed into the carpet. And they hadn't even left a tip! I knew Lisa's work ethic well enough to know the customers had been served well. It was surely an oversight on their part, but Lisa wasn't convinced and hung on to her frustration in spite of my efforts to soothe her.

"Super! Thanks, honey, tell them I'm coming!" I said, hoping my cheery voice might give Lisa's attitude a boost.

The middle Saturday of July was here and so was my Songbird, as Rachel was nicknamed. Her singing debut at the Ponderosa had been highly anticipated—and she didn't disappoint a single person. When she broke into song and captivated her audience, customers put down their silverware and derailed their conversations. For most of the concert, I was stuck in the kitchen, but thankfully, I was there to hear her last song. We'd all heard the song a hundred times, but Rachel evoked new emotion with her rendition of "Wind Beneath My Wings." Dinner guests used napkins to wipe their eyes and discreetly blow their noses. She would've made Bette Midler proud. At the end of the evening, my little Songbird got paid and hired for a second performance for the following month.

Rachel's performance gave the weekend an uplifted beat and left all of us, even Lisa, in a good mood. Things got even better on Monday when Gentleman Joe came into the kitchen and announced, "Miss Ann, your father's here."

Dad must have ESP, I thought. I'd been thinking about him a lot, worrying about him. Plus after such a busy weekend, the Ponderosa needed its favorite money-bag man to make our bank deposit.

I scanned the restaurant, looking for my dad's table, not spotting him at first because instead of sitting alone as I had expected, he sat across from a man I didn't recognize. Joe served each of them a cup of coffee and took their lunch order. I sat down next to Dad and he introduced me to his friend.

"Annie, this is Fred. I've been telling him about the Ponderosa," Sherm said.

"It's so nice to meet you, Fred," I said, smiling and reaching across the table to shake his hand. Fred nodded and extended an enormous calloused hand across the table to shake mine. His skin felt like a Brillo pad, but his grip was gentle and kind. I liked him instantly.

The three of us had only chatted for a short time, when Dad decided to break the news. "I hate to tell you this, but it looks like Ed and Connie are splitting up."

"Oh no, I can't believe it!" I said.

"Well, it's not a huge surprise—they've been having some trouble. Still, I'd hoped they'd make it work."

I sighed and shook my head. "I'll call them and see if there's anything they need. The least I can do is offer a listening ear."

Joe approached the table, balancing a round serving tray. He placed two plates on the table, and I couldn't help but scrutinize the presentation. The grilled tuna sandwiches looked delicious—Jodi had done an excellent job.

"Well, I suppose I should get back to work. You two enjoy your lunch. We'll talk before you leave." Hearing the news about Ed and Connie zapped my energy. The distraction of my kitchen would help.

Bill got the bank deposit ready for Sherm—he knew I didn't enjoy the task. "I don't like counting money," I'd told him repeatedly. I had plenty of my own everyday bookwork, so Bill willingly handled deposit duty.

After lunch, I walked Dad and Fred to Sherm's tin can of a car, passed the money bag to Dad, and gave him a big hug. "It was nice to meet you, Fred," I said, smiling over at him in the passenger seat, which had all but disappeared beneath his huge body. I laughed aloud as I watched the toaster on wheels pull out onto the highway. There wasn't a need for it to be armored—no one would ever expect someone to be transporting money in that car.

Tuesday's hot weather convinced Mike, Tim, and two other school chums to float the Payette River in an effort to cool off. The four teens gathered inner tubes and made plans to launch about three miles north of the Ponderosa. They would float south to Horseshoe Bend, then hitch a ride back to the restaurant with a friend.

Mike hustled out the door wearing a T-shirt, shorts, Tevas, and stylish new sunglasses. He yelled, "Bye! Make sure you watch us float by."

"Have fun! We'll watch from the deck. Be sure to wear a life-jacket and look out for KYBR!" I said, showing my uneven dimples.

Lisa desperately wanted to go, but it was her shift at the restaurant. Due to a loaded grill, I missed the fun of seeing the boys float by. "Too bad, Lisa. You and I missed out," I said, feeling sorry for us both.

"I'm going for sure next time," Lisa grumbled.

"Mom! Mike's back. And he doesn't look so good!" Lisa shouted.

When I came out the kitchen, there stood Mike, shirtless, barefoot, pale, and coughing uncontrollably. Tim stood beside him looking scared. "Mike, what happened?" I asked.

"Mom, you were right about wearing a life jacket."

"You mean you didn't?" I shot him an angry look, telling myself to stay calm and listen. Mike's eyes were bloodshot and wild, and the cough made it difficult for him to speak.

"Mom, you know where they put in the new bridge?"

"Yeah," I replied, trying to find a thimbleful of sympathy to cover my anger at him for not having worn a life jacket.

"Well, they just let part of the old bridge fall into the river, and it caused a huge, dangerous rapid. Tim floated through the rapid with no problem, so I thought the coast was clear, but I got caught in the current and couldn't get out. Then the rapid pulled me underwater about five feet and wouldn't let me come up. The whirlpool tore off my shirt and Tevas. I even lost my new Ray-Ban sunglasses, which cost me sixty bucks."

Tim finally spoke. "Yeah, before I floated around the bend, I noticed Mike had disappeared. When I couldn't see him anywhere, I knew he was in a shit sandwich."

"Shit sandwich is right," said Mike. "I kept kicking, and after a few minutes, I sort of passed out. It felt like I could have died. But when I stopped fighting, somehow the current floated me to the top. I'll never float that river again without a life jacket."

I bit my lip out of anxiety and to stop myself from saying, *I told you so.*

Chapter Thirty-Two

COMINGS AND GOINGS

Bill and I were about to lose our composure, and five waitresses, holding back tears, were about ready to walk off the job, Myra included. A charter bus sat empty in the parking lot, while no less than sixty senior citizens, dressed up for a tea party, filed into the restaurant. A portion of the group politely found their seats, while the majority lined up for the restrooms.

I struggled to hear or understand the bus driver's words through the high volume of happy chatter. "Didn't Jessie, the event coordinator, call you and set this up?" (I must have looked surprised.) "It's our field trip today, and this is our first stop on the way to McCall."

For a second, I stood there, wide-eyed and speechless, but after taking in a deep breath of perfumed air, I spoke with sudden calmness. "Actually, nobody called ahead, but welcome to the Ponderosa. We'll do our best."

I watched Myra as she dished up the last slice of cherry pie and dropped a scoop of vanilla ice cream on top. When she looked at my direction, it wasn't her strained expression that got me giggling—it was her words. "There are more raisins out there than in a box of Raisin Bran!" she mumbled, with a perfectly straight face. As usual, Myra's sense of humor could make even a frazzled cook laugh.

Lisa was at her most charming self, waiting on a table of women wearing heavy rouge and red lipstick, and I watched with amusement as they each tried to convince her to call them Grandma. An hour later, there wasn't a single unhappy person boarding the bus to McCall. "Bye, Grandma," Lisa yelled to the departing bus, making us all laugh until we spotted Woody running fast toward us from his rented building.

Woody approached, out of breath and on the verge of collapse. "My toilet won't flush," he said, panicked beyond belief.

For the second time in an hour, I didn't know how to respond. Laugh, cry, or run away were the first things that came to mind, but I did none of these. "Woody, is this an emergency, or do I have time to get Bill?" I asked and ascertained that it was the latter before entering the bar area to scope out the unsuspecting soon-to-be plumber.

Woody explained the problematic toilet in detail, then waited for Bill's response. But it wasn't Bill who jumped into the discussion with a solution; it was PeeWee, a bar patron who had been enjoying the senior citizen takeover of the restaurant. PeeWee, who had the stature of a twelve-year-old and the age of the exiting patrons, leaned against the bar and said, "Maybe I can help out, where is this backed-up toilet?"

We all proceeded to the last cabin, Bill swinging the toilet plunger around like a baton. Once we determined that the culprit was a plugged sewer line, we all huddled around, staring at the PVC pipe protruding from the ground.

"Now what do we do?" Bill asked quietly. At first, nobody moved or spoke. We waited, but the sewer fairies weren't flying in to save the day.

Pee Wee stepped forward, rolled up the right sleeve of his shirt, and got down on his knee, and his entire arm disappeared. Still, no one moved, except to restrain our gag reflexes. Our eyeballs were as large as the black plastic pipe. In no time, Pee Wee held up an old rusty pop can he had retrieved from a space only made for little people with big courage. In my eyes, PeeWee had earned the respect owed to a king.

It wasn't long after that that PeeWee's single-wide mobile home sat in the RV spot next to the PVC pipe he had cleaned out. He needed a place to live, and I needed a person with stamina and guts!

Whenever the restaurant's parking lot would fill up, PeeWee would appear at the bar from out of nowhere, wanting to be served. I knew he watched over the place from his trailer's front room window. To him, lots of vehicles in the parking lot meant lots of free entertainment. From that day forward, the Ponderosa employees never had to guess if they could label the restaurant chaos as a lunch or dinner rush—they only had to glance over to see if PeeWee was propped up against the bar, nursing a can of Hamm's.

PeeWee, who had emphysema, also had periodic emergencies. Next to his couch and across from the television, an oxygen tank waited for such occasions. One afternoon, PeeWee showed up beside me at the grill, not looking capable of flipping a burger—more like I ought to flip him into the nearest hospital bed. In a slurred voice, he asked me to call him an ambulance and said he'd be waiting at his trailer.

After calling for the ambulance (they knew exactly where to go as they had been there several times over the last couple of months), I went straight to PeeWee's trailer. I wasn't surprised to see him sitting on the sofa waiting for his ride to the hospital, but I was surprised to see him puffing away on a cigarette.

"PeeWee, what are you doing?" I asked, even more alarmed by the oxygen tank inches away than by the fact that he couldn't breathe.

He tried to explain. "Well, as soon as those paramedics get here, they won't let me smoke, and it's a long trip to Boise."

I sat down next to my friend with nicotine addiction, and we waited for the EMTs' arrival. The instant the ambulance stopped at his doorstep, PeeWee snuffed his cigarette in the overflowing ashtray, concealed it behind a stack of magazines and turned on the oxygen flow.

Several months would pass before PeeWee's daughter insisted on moving his trailer to Boise, closer to her and medical care. It was difficult to say goodbye to PeeWee. During his stay at Lower Banks, no matter where he was or where I was going, when our paths crossed, I would always stop to talk to PeeWee, if only for a moment.

Word about our new deck spread like wildfire, and soon the Ponderosa gained popularity as a great place to enjoy a good meal with a view. With the exhausting days of summer numbered and another school year approaching, Bill and I opted to close the restaurant every Tuesday during the winter months. On Monday evenings, after the restaurant closed, we planned to drive to Boise, spend the night, and enjoy all Tuesday doing whatever it is that people do on their days off. The idea of a weekly twenty-four hours free from serving people helped us get through the last of summer's busy days.

As we assessed the fall schedule, Lisa reminded us, "Don't forget. After school starts, I want two full days off each week." Bill and I never came right out and said it, but we enjoyed Lisa's days off as much as she did because she always made the most of her time. She usually came up with something unexpected—like the time she lugged a large cardboard box into the restaurant.

"Look what my friend Ashlee gave me!" she squealed.

I raced over to peek inside the oversize box, and stood stiff as a fence post, shocked to see two solid black kittens so young, their eyes weren't completely open. "Oh, aren't they cute. What are you going to do with them?" I asked, very afraid to hear the answer.

Lisa squatted down beside the box, picked up one of the tiny fluff balls, and cradled it to her neck. Her face lit up as she explained, "Ashlee's Dad found them behind their barn. Can you believe they're actually *giving them away*?"

"Oh, so they're outdoor kitties," I said.

"No, Mom, they're too young… I'll have to put them in my bedroom," Lisa said as she reached for the second ball of meowing black fur.

"Are you sure you're able to take care of two kittens—including taking care of their litter box?" I asked, hoping she'd say something like, "Well, now that you mention it, *I don't think I'm ready for that level of responsibility.*"

Instead, she jumped up, still holding her little darlin's, hugged me, and cried out, "Oh, thank you, Mom! I promise to take really good care of them."

"Okay, Lisa, we'll give it a try, honey." My jaw tightened. I wasn't as happy as Lisa—but didn't have the heart to spoil her joy.

A full month passed before the predictable happened, and I did my best not to react when hearing Lisa's new, really good idea.

"Mom, I think the cats are a little wild and want to be outside cats."

I'd been good about withholding complaints when the kittens climbed curtains and used the couch as a scratching post but was unable to hold back my distaste for the disgusting odor of a perpetually dirty litter box. Besides Bill and me, even Mike constantly hammered at Lisa to clean the litter box. After all, the cabin's interior being so small, a used toothpick could be offensive.

"Lisa, that's a wonderful idea! They'll love being outdoors." I felt worried that two kittens living next to a busy highway might have a sad ending but wasn't worried enough to suggest keeping them indoors.

I recalled our conversation when Lisa first acquired the cuddly pair. "Mom, what should I name them?"

"Honey, they're your kittens. I know you'll come up with good names for them."

"But, Mom, I can't think of anything good. I want to know what you'd name them!"

"Well, with the highway so close, I'd call one Audi and the other Ohse."

"Oh, Mom," Lisa groaned.

Several days later, I heard her calling for "Audi."

I hoped the kitten's names would keep them safe, in the same way that "A Boy Named Sue" made a kid tough.

Mike proudly showed off the Ranchero, ecstatic about its new paint job. I walked around the vehicle, inspecting it and silently praying he wouldn't offer me a ride. "I really like the color. What do you call it?" I asked.

"It's called *Bright Aqua Glow Metallic*. There were lots of different colors to pick from, but this was the best!"

Mike's car continued to be a big financial black hole, but he didn't care—he owned one of the coolest vehicles in all of Boise County. Everyone paid attention to his Bright Aqua Glow Metallic Ranchero—especially Deputy Buck.

As fall progressed, the traffic slowed, and so did business. Audi and Ohse loved their freedom outside the cabin walls as much as Bill and I loved our freedom on Tuesdays. For our Monday night sleepover in Boise, we had chosen a quiet Boise hotel with a lobby about as stylish as a Laundromat. But the location was convenient, the rooms large and clean, and the staff friendly. The best thing about it—there was no 5:00 a.m. alarm. Tuesday morning's routine was as laid-back as going to a musical at the theater. We would sleep in past seven o'clock, other people served us breakfast, then off to Kuna for a visit with Sherm, and lastly, stopping in to see Beth at the bank.

Tuffy hadn't changed—at each visit, she barked as if we were burglars in her master's home. Sherm hadn't changed either, always welcoming us as if we were the two most important people in his life, although we knew Tuffy came first. "So don't kick the dog," I'd remind Bill as we entered the city limits of Kuna, and we'd laugh. The mobile home's door would crack open, and we'd call out, "Hi, Dad!" We loved his grin, our leisurely visits, and even hearing the same old drawn-out stories. Tuesdays were unbeatable.

When winter season arrived, there were few enough customers that we could save a corner table on which to lay out an enormous jigsaw puzzle. While Myra and I sorted the nonedge pieces into piles of blue sky, white clouds, yellow wheat, and red barn, we planned our annual family Thanksgiving Day meal. "Tuesday, I'll pick up the biggest turkey I can get," I said.

"I'll bring a ham to put in the other oven," Myra offered.

"Everyone else can bring salads and desserts, so other than the meat, all we need to prepare is twenty pounds of mashed potatoes," I added. "Bill and Mike can get the tables arranged in the usual circular pattern. Did I tell you John Vander's joining us this year?"

"Good. He'll love it," Myra answered.

"It'll be fun to have him," I said. "And when I invited him last week, he nearly cried with happiness. Also, on Wednesday, Joe is leaving for Lewiston to spend a few days with Flora. He says she's doing well," I added.

Just then, a moving figure caught the corner of my eye. "Did you see that?" I asked Myra.

"No, I didn't, what is it?" Myra answered. Her round eyes grew larger as she jumped up out of her chair.

Although the restaurant was open for business, Myra and I were alone and had become so engrossed in our own private conversation that I was startled by the interruption and jumped out of my chair as Myra had done. We both stood perfectly still. Then in unison, we slowly crept toward the mysterious movement—and were nearly scared out of our shoes when a teenager came out of the restroom. Before anyone had a chance to say anything, a second teenager appeared. Myra and I stood face to face with a girl of about sixteen years old and a tall, skinny boy who couldn't have been much older.

"Can I help you?" I asked.

The boy was wearing baggy pants that made him seem even thinner than he actually was. He politely asked, "Do you happen to have any work for us?"

My heart rate slowed when I realized all they wanted were jobs. I took in a deep breath and answered. "Well, this is a slow time of year, so I don't have anything at the present. I'm sorry. Where're you from?"

The girl, a short blonde with a wide purple streak in her long hair, pulled her sweater down over her chubby hips and answered nervously, "We're just passing through, on our way to Boise to visit my grandma."

"Wish I could help you guys out," I said, and I really meant it.

The skinny boy replied, "Thanks anyway."

When the twosome left, Myra and I ran to the small viewing window by the dishwasher to watch them. "They don't have a car… they're walking to Boise," Myra whispered as if they could hear us from the parking lot.

"Myra, hurry up. Go tell them to come back."

While Myra called back the teens, I quickly put together two jumbo sandwiches, wrapping each one separately and placing them in a bag with a couple of oranges. The young couple waited patiently at the counter, not knowing why.

"Just in case you're hungry, here's something to eat," I said, holding out the sack.

I couldn't tell if they wanted to cry or hug me. They both reached for the brown bag. "Thank you!" they exclaimed.

"You're very welcome."

As they disappeared from sight, I sighed. "I wonder if Grandma knows they're coming."

"I hope somebody gives them a ride," Myra said.

"Me too," I replied. "Maybe this kind gesture makes up for the customer we pissed off last week when we served him fries instead of potato salad." We both giggled and returned to the puzzle table and our tranquility.

Chapter Thirty-Three

BUTTERFLY TOUCHES

On Thanksgiving Day, the Ponderosa looked anything but closed. Vehicles filled the parking lot and family and friends filled the interior. Neither Buddy Lee nor Michelle had outgrown their personal thirty-six-inch wide dance floor on top of the jukebox, and they hadn't forgotten the words to "Louie, Louie" either. We all missed Connie—but were overjoyed to see Ed's positive attitude, something we hadn't seen in a long time. Ed's new post-divorce life was in Gardena, in a mobile home nestled among the towering cottonwood trees that lined the Payette River. Ed told us that his tiring, thirty-mile, five-day-a-week commute to Boise was a cheap price to pay for the opportunity to live where our grandparents had lived, the place he'd loved as a child. Once again, the old bridge was part of Eddie's life.

At times, the noise escalated to such a level that I wondered if the outside traffic passing by the restaurant could hear us. As soon as everyone piled food onto plates, a peaceful silence fell over the crowd. Soon after the meal, John Vander slid his chair away from the table and quietly stated, "The food was delicious. Thank you, everyone." I don't know if anyone else heard him. The children resumed their play, leaving the adults to visit and lightheartedly complain about overeating. Later, I scanned the dining room and noticed that John wasn't in sight. "He's rather bashful—maybe the crowd was too much, and he decided to leave," I murmured to Dad.

When I entered the kitchen, balancing a lopsided stack of dirty plates, I saw a tall figure bending over the sink. It was John, elbow-deep in water and suds. "John, what are you doing?" I asked. *Now, that's a dumb question, especially to John,* my inner voice told me.

"Well, I think I'm washing dishes."

We both laughed, and I joined John at the sink, where heaps of dirty pots and pans spilled onto the stainless-steel counter.

That night, the parking lot emptied as quickly as it had filled. "Hey, Dad. We'll see you next Tuesday," I said, giving him a hearty hug. Sherm was always the last to drive away.

The following week brought snowy weather. "Mom, you want the Christmas tree in the same place as last year?" Mike shouted.

I glanced up to see Mike and Tim dragging a gargantuan fir tree through the doorway. Pictures fell off the walls and crashed to the floor, and when several chairs fell over, they laughed hysterically.

"Do you really think that tree is going to fit in here?" I asked, wanting to be a part of their fun.

"Hey, Mike, I think it's about eight feet too tall." Tim snickered.

"Yeah, dude, I think you're right," Mike answered. "I'll get the chain saw!"

"Well, boys, I have three tables and twelve chairs that don't have a home," I said. But Bill came to our rescue with a hitherto unknown talent for organizing extra furniture.

In December, as usual, the weather turned icy cold. On the first Monday of the month, the roads were so dangerously slick Bill decided we should cancel our evening trip to Boise. But to our surprise, we awoke Tuesday morning to a clear blue sky with a temperature above freezing. While we waited for the ice on the highway to melt, Bill got the bank deposit ready, and by ten o'clock, we were en route to Kuna.

"We'll pass through Boise in time for an early lunch. How 'bout we stop at that place on State Street—what's it called, the Jade Dragon?" asked Bill.

"Sounds good! I love that place, and we haven't been there for ages."

Because the traffic on Highway 55 was scanty, we quickly caught up to a large semitruck that set a comfortable pace making our drive relaxing. But not long after we passed the old Gardena bridge, the semi's brake lights went on unexpectedly, rousing Bill from his zoned-out state. When the semi came to a complete stop in the middle of the highway, Bill slammed on his brakes to avoid a rear-end collision. The truck driver jumped from the high cab, and Bill and I followed his lead. The fear consuming me made my legs seem like they weren't moving at all.

We made our way around the semi, then stopped abruptly and stared at the jagged steel of a small silver sedan smashed against the guardrail bordering the outside edge of the horseshoe curve. The truck driver raced back to his truck, presumably to call for help. I peered inside the crumpled piece of steel and broken glass, and my heart stopped beating. There were three young adults inside, silent and still.

When I focused on the girl closest to me, keenly aware of her body slumped forward and her auburn hair draped over her face, I imagined my Leecee in that car. Instantly, my gut wrenched. Compelled to touch her, I reached through the broken window of the car's back door and softly stroked her hair. My hand trembled, my heart pounded, and tears formed in my eyes. I placed my mouth close to her ear, which was covered by her long hair. "Help will be here soon. You have to hold on, honey." She took a shallow breath, and my heart filled with hope. I continued my butterfly touches and soothing words. With the faint sound of approaching sirens, I prayed. *"Hurry! Please hurry!"*

The girl took another short gasp for air, and I held my own breath, waiting for another to follow. "Please, somebody move or say something," I moaned. My arm stretched out as far as it would reach to a young man sitting beside the girl with the shiny hair, but only my fingertips touched the side of his wrist. I wished my arms were longer. "I'm so sorry," I whispered.

When the paramedics arrived, I wasn't prepared to move away. *Please don't make me leave her—I just heard her take a breath. How can I possibly get in my car, ride to Boise, and eat fried rice now?* When

I glanced around and noticed that the paramedics and most of the policemen were all familiar to me, a man placed a hand on my shoulder and said, "Ann, we'll take over now." (A polite way of telling me to step back and let them do their jobs.) I looked up and recognized Kevin, the coroner.

Reluctantly, I backed away from the silver car encasing someone's children, someone's babies.

"Bill, I need to go home," I said.

"That's just where we're going," Bill replied.

Bill maneuvered our car around several emergency vehicles, their flashing lights vividly announcing the grisly scene only steps away. In minutes, my sobs began. Bill, do you think any of those kids will live? Maybe they were just unconscious. Please tell me they will be all right."

"Honey, I'm sure Doug or Kevin will update us on all the details."

"Bill, I should've done more, if I could have got her out of the car, CPR might have helped. Do you think she could hear my voice?"

Bill, still white as rice himself, did his best to console me. "Annie, there was no way you could have gotten her or anyone else out of that vehicle without specialized tools. You did all you could."

I dropped my head, my chin touching my chest. "I'd make a lousy paramedic."

When I slipped into bed that evening, I knew it would be a night of tears and misgivings. But no matter how difficult the experience was for me, it was nothing compared to what it must be for the families of those teenagers. Before falling to sleep, I took a minute to ask God to help those families and then thanked him again for letting Bill survive his accident.

The following morning, I anxiously awaited Doug's arrival.

"What happened? How are those kids?" I asked when Doug came through the side door at six fifteen. I didn't want to know but had to know—and no doubt Doug would have the particulars.

Doug looked away, and without his usual grin, he answered, "Ann, there was one survivor. That's a dangerous, sharp curve—there have been accidents there before. Apparently, a large rock had fallen from the hillside and landed in the roadway. I'm not sure if their car hit the rock before it slammed into the hillside, rebounded off the hill, and ended up against the guardrail. I towed the wreckage into my garage and locked it up late yesterday."

The doorknob jiggled, and Kevin entered, holding his empty coffee mug. Without saying a word, he filled his twenty-ounce cup—and put the empty pot back on the hot burner. But I couldn't have cared less.

"Kevin, do you know anything about those three teenagers?" I asked, hoping his answer would be different than Doug's.

Kevin's eyes narrowed, and his brow creased. He appeared confused. "How many kids did you see in that car?" he asked.

"Three."

"Annie, I'm sorry to tell you, but there were four. That car was so crushed—it was difficult to see the young girl under the front seat."

I put both hands over my mouth, groaned loudly, turned, and headed for the kitchen, which was my safe haven—burnt bacon, chef salads, and all.

For nearly a week, the residents of Lower Banks remained solemn, and I began to wonder if the dark cloud hanging over us would ever dissipate. One afternoon, a group of five adults came into the restaurant. Bill whispered to me that he had seen them at Doug's station earlier, inspecting the wrecked vehicle. They slid into a booth overlooking the river but clearly weren't interested in the view or the five cups of coffee they had ordered.

Troubled, I watched them from the kitchen. Ninety-nine percent of me wanted to approach their table and give my condolences, but the remaining 1 percent resisted. What could I say to help them? And how do I say it without falling into a billion pieces? So I observed the group from a safe distance, unable to take my eyes off them. When they gathered their jackets and prepared to leave the table, somehow that 1 percent hesitation dissolved. I removed my apron, tossed it onto the counter, and began my approach, telling myself, *Stay composed, Ann.* My jaw clenched, and my mind cried out in pain, and instead of going to their table, I walked to the restroom.

That evening, after closing the restaurant and turning off the lights, I listened to the dissonant stillness of the empty building. I slid into the corner booth, folded my arms on the table, closed my eyes, and buried my face in my arms.

Chapter Thirty-Four

AN AMBULANCE FOR JOHNNY

T he dirty grill and unmopped floor could wait until I was ready to leave my corner booth and my memories.

It had been eleven years since my eighteen-year-old brother, Johnny, had died. I thought about Sherm—how does a parent survive losing a child? And how did I survive losing a younger brother, who, because of a wide age difference, was more like my child? I was thirty years old when Johnny, a new high school graduate, had his life ripped away. Then I thought about my mom, Marie, and how terrified she had been at the sound of the siren. My mind surged with empathy as I recalled my mom's depiction of what had happened on that hot July day back in 1978 (the prologue's conclusion). And also, an entire family's anguish at the deepest magnitude imaginable.

After exiting the Kuna Sav-On on that Sunday afternoon, Marie traveled the rural roads in the direction of her home. For a brief moment, she thought about the pork roast she wanted to have in the oven by two o'clock, until the distant sound of the siren had her heart racing, speculating that Norma, her aging neighbor and close friend, might've had a medical emergency. Three miles later, Marie was passing the chicken farmer's smelly acreage, when she spotted the flashing blue and red lights. Mercifully, the high-pitched sound had gone silent. She had wanted the horrible noise to cease—but not in her own driveway. Momma Marie tried to account for her family's whereabouts. Her home, which had once housed ten occupants, nowadays housed only four. On this particular

Sunday, Sherm had left the house at sunrise to help paint a nearby barn, while Beth, her youngest child, was out of town for the Fourth of July weekend. Marie's mind froze as she recalled that her youngest son, Johnny, had still been asleep when she had left the house a few hours earlier. Her eyes rapidly swept the area before fixating on a crumpled motorcycle lying alongside the road, and the air froze in her lungs. Her jaw clenched, and she couldn't swallow. Mom's arms and legs felt like heavy rubber, ready to melt away. When she slammed on the brakes, the abrupt stop threw up a plume of dust. Marie sprang from the vehicle, loose papers falling to the ground, and then with wobbly legs, she raced to the back of the ambulance just as the doors closed. Marie knew the answer already but asked anyway, "Who's in there?" She didn't wait for a response.

"Is Johnny in there?"

Marie locked eyes with the paramedic, who clutched John's wallet in one hand and student ID in the other. His complexion paled a shade, and he asked, "Are you John's mother?" Though he must have already known. He continued, "Yes, ma'am, John will be transported to Saint Alphonsus Hospital. You and your family should get there as quickly as possible." The ambulance sped off, its sound viciously assaulting the heart of a mother.

Marie understood the paramedic's tone and expression completely. This wasn't a skinned knee or simple bump on the head—this was new territory. She trembled, and tears flowed to the corners of her mouth and off her chin. Only eighteen years earlier, her five-pound, eight-ounce baby boy had been born, with dark eyes and a full head of black hair. Sherm and Marie had been as ecstatic over the birth of their seventh child as if he had been their first. They named him John Samuel and proudly took him home to join his three older sisters and three older brothers, each one eager to lay claim to the newest family member.

Thoughts racing and emotions colliding, Marie somehow managed to reach Sherm, and they drove to the hospital. Shortly after their arrival, they were told that John had died on the operating table. Neither of my parents had the opportunity to touch their eighteen-year-old son, tell him goodbye or how much he was loved.

Soon after Johnny's death, Mom and Dad were escorted to a secluded room. The space, small and stark, offered a sofa, an end table decorated with a silk flower arrangement, a black phone, a lamp, and a box of tissues. Under the phone lay a thick telephone directory with curled corners that suggested heavy use. In this room, Marie began the heart-wrenching task of notifying John's brothers and sisters. Mom called upon her strength and faith to enable her to explain the worst news imaginable seven times.

On that early Sunday afternoon in July, John had kick-started his newly purchased Kawasaki motorcycle and pulled out of the family driveway onto the two-lane country road. No one but John knew what his intended destination had been. Did he just not see the approaching car, or did he miscalculate the distance between it and himself? The car struck John's motorcycle at sixty miles per hour, tossing him into the air like a bull throws its rider. The helmet, knocked from his head, was later found far from Johnny's body. Nearly severed in half, his body lay motionless, partially hidden among tall thistles, next to the irrigation canal.

I remembered the day after Johnny's accident when all my brothers and sisters and I had gathered at our parents' home. Struggling with shock and grief, we congregated in the basement family room and stuck close to each other. Friends brought food, but no one could eat. When nighttime came, we crawled into our sleeping bags atop the gold shag carpeting, but no one could sleep—we were afraid another one of us might vanish into a dark unknown space.

We listened to each other's pain—unmanageable sobs that started low in the gut and refused to be contained. Eventually, our sobs subsided, but the whimpers and moans remained. I thought my tears would never stop and doubted any of us could ever feel carefree or normal again.

Before daylight that next morning, I had an overwhelming urge to stand up and move. After finding my equilibrium, I slowly climbed the narrow carpeted stairway, gripping the handrail. An unknown power moved my legs forward. As I passed through the kitchen, my eyes landed on the centerpiece of the dining table—a gift I'd given my mom on Mother's Day. A potted plant, its bright-orange flowers still vibrant. I moved toward the patio door, slipped into a pair of Mom's rubber thongs, opened the slider, and stepped outside.

I wasn't sure what I expected to find, but it seemed to me that I heard Johnny calling out, "Over here, Annie." I proceeded down the driveway, only the moon illuminating my way, to the centerline of the *highway. Loose gravel crunched under my thongs. I whispered into the shadows, "Johnny, I'm here." I stopped and stood immobile, listening intently for John. A lone cricket chirped its presence and went silent. Several moments passed before I continued walking. The slap of my flip-flops hitting my heels was the only sound. Then suddenly, a white object caught my attention—a wrapper for the gauze that had been used to bandage John. I picked up the discarded packaging and moaned, "I'm here with you, Johnny." The words were scarcely out of my mouth when it hit me that I didn't have to actually see Johnny—I just needed to feel his presence. I visualized his dark eyes and handsome face and remembered his innocence and his quirky sense of humor, and I cried out, "You weren't supposed to die. You're my little brother. You're my baby and I couldn't protect you." Consumed with anguish and powerlessness, I sat on the ditch bank, leaned over, curled my knees up to my chest, and pressed my cheek to the earth. A shooting star blazed across the sky and disappeared—it was gone forever as if it had never existed. I closed my eyes, and when I opened them sometime later, I observed the sky growing lighter. A small sparrow flew overhead, tweeting loudly. I knew I had survived the first night.*

Suddenly, a light went on in the Ponderosa, dispelling the darkness, and a deep voice interrupted my thoughts—Bill had entered the restaurant. "Annie, are you in here?" he asked, loud enough to awaken a comatose person.

When I spotted him, I sat up straight and waved at him from across the room. Bill walked over to my booth, slid in next to me, and put his arms around me. I leaned into him, rested my head on his shoulder, and cried. My chest felt as if it had been punched by a heavyweight boxer. "Oh, Bill, I'm devastated that all I did was touch that young girl. Maybe I could have saved her. Wouldn't a normal person have *tried* to pull her from the car and perform CPR? Did I let that girl die?"

Chapter Thirty-Five

DON'T EAT THE MUSHROOMS

Winter ended, spring flew by, and summer moved in. Once again, life moved into overdrive at the Ponderosa. Mike and Lisa, though happy to be free from school, weren't too pleased with the prospect of a summer of nonstop restaurant work. Though Lisa was resigned to another summer at the Ponderosa, Mike decided he'd had enough food service and gas station labor to last a lifetime. So when an offer for a new job surfaced, he was elated. Silver Creek Plunge, a busy resort with rustic cabins and a geothermal pool, needed a handyman. It was the ultimate job for Mike—outdoors in nature! But there were a few drawbacks. Situated high in the mountains north of Garden Valley, it was a dicey two-hour drive from the Ponderosa, and the phone service, like a CB radio with the reception often poor, could only be used for outgoing calls or emergencies.

The owner of the resort, Jerry, a Grizzly Adams kind of guy, would often stop at the restaurant on his weekly trips to Boise. Jerry had seen Mike on many occasions, working at the restaurant and at Doug's gas station, and had obviously noticed Mike's work ethic. And this summer, Jerry needed an employee, so he offered Mike the job. At seventeen, Mike felt grown-up and ready for a new life adventure. We'd all miss Mike and his wittiness, but he promised, "Don't worry, Mom. I'll be home on my days off."

"For crying out loud, Mike, take the job. Just don't grow a beard or make friends with a black bear," I said.

Hiring summer staff for the Ponderosa proved easy; everyone from the previous summer schedule was rehired and Myra helped me decide on three new hires, including one named Claire.

"Who hired Methuselah?" Bill asked, rubbing his right temple and shaking his head, so he almost appeared to be having a petit mal seizure.

"Methuselah! Who do you mean?" I asked, after determining that he was not, in fact, having a seizure.

Bill moved his right index finger from his temple to point at Claire, my adorable new hire.

"Oh, that's Claire! Isn't she the cutest thing?" I gave Bill a don't-mess-with-my-employees look, and he didn't say another word. My husband could have low tolerance for those who moved at a slower pace than him.

After only two weeks, however, it became clear that Bill had called it right. *(Slow)* Methuselah overrode Claire, and Claire's hours slowly declined until, by the end of the week, she stayed home and Speedy Shirley swiftly took her place. Again, the Ponderosa was back in full swing. "All I need now is another cook to fill in for Jodi and me," I told Bill. Cooks were definitely more difficult to unearth.

"Hi, Mom and Dad," Mike hollered. His dirty laundry bag dropped to the kitchen floor.

"Hi, Mike." It had only been a week since I'd seen him, but he looked older and taller—and I was pleased to see, clean-shaven and free of any bear scratches. "Are you hungry?" In my world, everyone was *always* starving.

Mike chuckled and replied, "How about one of those chicken booby sandwiches?" which was his way of telling me how much he'd missed home.

"One chicken *booby* sandwich coming up!" I said the word *booby* in a hushed tone. I didn't like saying these words within hearing range of customers, but this time I chose embarrassment over a missed opportunity to reiterate our private joke. Mike saw my joy at having him home and grinned back.

That night, Mike eagerly gave Bill and me the details of his first week away from home and presented an invitation he knew would make us both happy. "You guys need to drive up to the resort for a day and pick wild mushrooms. There are tons of them around."

Mike remembered how, in Oregon, the four of us had loved our annual family outing. We'd spend an entire day mushroom gathering, usually in the cold rain. We often fought our way through thick, overgrown brush, but nothing was more electrifying than discovering a patch of bright-yellow chanterelles poking out of the rich soil among pine and fir needles.

"Sounds fun," I replied. "Maybe Monday. I'll talk to Myra tomorrow and see if she'll help Jodi at the grill. It's Shirley's day off, but I'll bet she'll come in if I ask her."

"Sooooo…how's the Ranchero?" Bill asked.

"Pretty good, but the dirt roads are making it hard to keep clean," Mike said.

Mike's two-day visit passed too quickly for all of us. While Bill and I stood with Mike in the parking lot next to his newly washed and polished Ranchero—he seemed torn between anxious-to-leave and hesitant-to-leave. It reminded me of how his grandpa Sherm behaved when he found it time to leave Lower Banks. Bill and I always loved and encouraged lingering goodbyes, but finally, Mike piled his freshly laundered clothes into the passenger seat, along with a cooler containing some eggs, cheese, and milk. "I'll see you guys at the resort tomorrow about noon-ish," Mike said, sliding behind the steering wheel. We watched Mike drive away.

Under a cloudless morning sky, Bill tossed several empty pickle buckets into the bed of Ol' Blue. What could be better than a day off and the chance to see Mike again?

"Go have fun—don't worry about anything," Lisa said, trying to be a good sport about being left behind.

I could tell she really wanted to go, and I hugged her tightly. "We'll be home before dark with your mushroom treat."

Bill waved his arm out the window when it should have been on the steering wheel. "Watch the road!" I shouted.

Watching grown-up Mike converse with his customers without being coached gave me goose bumps. He was on the payroll and visiting with his parents wasn't a part of his job description, but he did take the time to point us to a prime mushroom location. Thinking there wasn't a better place to be than outdoors in nature, we traipsed up and down hillsides, happy as kids at a carnival. By late afternoon, we had loaded and bungee-corded three overflowing buckets into the pickup bed.

"Mike told me about a guy in Boise who buys morels by the pound," Bill said.

"We aren't gathering wild mushrooms for cash, are we? My plan is to eat them, and if there're any left, I might think about serving them," I lied, aware they weren't FDA inspected.

"Well, just remember, that's hard cash you're giving up!" Bill laughed.

By the time we said goodbye to Mike, the wind had picked up dramatically. Eager to get home before dark, we drove away, leaving Mike to his pool-cleaning task. "I don't know about you, but I'm having mushrooms for dinner tonight," I told Bill. I hadn't eaten a wild morel in years—just thinking about the flavor got me salivating.

But when we arrived back at the cabin, I took a much-needed shower; its warmth helped to ease my sore muscles. And then instead of making dinner, I dropped into bed and my eyes closed immediately.

While dressing the next morning, I felt eyes upon me. Lisa had spotted me from the other room. "Mom, your ribs show," she said, her tone a combination of slight alarm and revulsion.

"I've been busy and haven't had much time to eat," I answered in an unconcerned voice. It was a lame excuse, but Lisa seemed to accept it. I'd noticed my weight decline over the past several months but hadn't worried me until now. The second Lisa left the cabin, I looked at myself in the full-length mirror. Lisa was right. Without a bathroom scale, I guessed my weight to be no more than a hundred and ten pounds—at five foot nine. I promised myself to start eating more than just M&Ms so Lisa wouldn't worry.

But my resolution was soon forgotten, having missed dinner the night before and now breakfast. By lunchtime, I was starved. All I could think about was a burger patty covered with a generous quantity of sautéed morels. Right after the lunch rush, I picked through a bucket of mushrooms and scrubbed clean about a dozen of the finest, then sliced and placed them on the grill with a glob of butter.

Thirty minutes hadn't gone by before my stomach churned. Standing beside Jodi at the grill, my heart began to race, and my skin grew clammy. While struggling to prepare two chef salads, I raved, "These salads are stupid! People shouldn't be allowed to order them—they take way too much time to make! This kitchen is too hot!"

I fought the sickness for as long as possible, but the monster tore away my resistance. "Jodi, I don't feel so well." I ran from the stifling kitchen and zoomed past Myra, almost knocking her over.

"Ann, what's wrong?" Myra asked, wide-eyed.

Not losing a moment in my dash toward the exit sign, I answered in my weakest voice, "I'm going to the cabin."

Thankfully, I made it to my bed before collapsing. First came the chills, and then, within minutes, my body froze up solid, like being paralyzed. Sprawled out on top of the bed covers, I realized this wasn't just any ordinary sickness—this was something major. I couldn't move a single muscle, no matter how I tried. Suddenly, Myra showed up, my blue-eyed angel to my rescue again. "Ann, I came to check on you. You don't look well."

"Myra I'm so cold, but I can't pull up the blankets, will you cover me?"

"Ann, do you want me to call an ambulance?" Myra asked in a panicked voice.

"Please no, I've seen way too many already. Just check on me now and again. If I get worse, then call for help." Though my teeth chattered, my legs and arms were numb. "Myra, I think I'm paralyzed from my mouth down."

Myra shot out the cabin like a rocket. "I'm going to get Bill."

The next thing I heard was the alarm clock buzzing loudly. My eyes popped open, and I reached for the off button and thought, *Oh, happy days! I'm alive! I can move!* I jumped out of bed and dressed in a flash without disturbing Bill. I couldn't believe my luck—not only had I survived but the only residual side-effects were some achy muscles, a slight headache, and a dry mouth.

Myra arrived at the restaurant a few minutes before her six o'clock shift and seemed surprised to see me in the kitchen. "Oh, Annie, you scared the gee-wheezes out of Bill and me last night. I didn't want to leave your side, but Bill promised he'd keep a close eye on you."

"I'm sorry I scared everyone—including myself. I'm doing all right this morning. And, Myra, thanks for covering me up last night." I poured Myra a cup of coffee and refilled mine.

"I think those mushrooms you ate were poisonous," Myra declared.

"I thought about that too," I admitted.

Myra locked eyes with me for a few seconds right before I entered the walk-in refrigerator and grabbed two heavy buckets of the fungus, packed them outside, and heaved their contents into the dumpster. After disposing of the third and final bucket, I stood back and stared at the beautiful morels that topped off the heap of rubbish. They looked like chopped nuts on a banana split.

"Where's Mike? Lisa asked. Isn't today his day off?" Lisa actually looked nervous about her older brother.

"Yes, it is. He should be driving in anytime now," I said. With every hour that passed with no sign of Mike, my worries increased. *Maybe he didn't get the day off after all,* I told myself. *No news is good news.* But by nightfall, when he still hadn't arrived, I told Bill, "Bill, I'm scared to death something has happened to Mike. There's no way to phone him, so we'll need to drive up tomorrow." Actually, I wanted to leave that instant.

"Yep, we'd better, but let's leave early," Bill replied.

The following morning, with the sun barely lighting the sky, we traveled north. Two hours later, we pulled into Mike's workplace. "Good sign—his Ranchero's here," I said. "Let's start here."

Bill gave the door of Mike's small camp trailer three short knocks, its doorframe rattled. There was no answer. We waited for one and a half seconds, almost too long for my nerves to bear, before I reached down and was surprised to find that the doorknob turned freely. We entered the space that served as his living room, kitchen, and bedroom. Nothing was hidden—not even Mike, who lay on the pulled-out sofa in a twisted-up sleeping bag. An old kettle turned vomit receptacle was placed close to his face.

Mike could speak but barely. "Hi, Mom, Dad. I've been sick, but I might be better today." Mike struggled to sit up, his eyes squinty and his skin pale. "This morning, I only have diarrhea. Yesterday, I puked and crapped mushrooms and other gross stuff," he added.

"Then you ate those damn mushrooms, huh?" Bill asked.

"Yeah, lots."

Bill gave Mike the details of my mushroom incident—concluding with the paralysis episode. We easily surmised that both Mike and I had suffered from fungus poisoning.

Once Mike was cleaned up and sitting outside on a tree stump carved into the shape of a chair, I handed him a bottle of water. "Thanks, Mom. Nobody deserves to be this sick. It feels like I've been kicked in the gut by a kickboxer."

"I know exactly how you feel, honey."

"Jerry stopped by a couple of times yesterday," Mike said. "He told me about the false morels, which can make a person pretty sick. He thinks some of the mushrooms I ate must've been false morels. I knew I wouldn't die, but at times I wanted to—it was awful. Sorry you got sick, too, Mom," he added quietly. "What did you do with all those mushrooms you and Dad picked?"

"Donated them to the dumpster!"

"Mom, you probably ate the only bad one in the bunch."

The fresh air outdoors had Mike strong enough to participate in a ten-minute discussion on how to distinguish a real morel from a false morel. I sent Bill to find two cans of 7-Up, while I scrambled an egg for Mike. "Here, eat this. There's a little cheese on it—that should help your diarrhea." Mike nibbled at his meal while the trailer aired out. I used an old T-shirt to wipe off a fifteen-inch table attached to the wall with one screw. "Where's the broom?" I asked.

"Don't have one."

"Well, how do you sweep your floor?"

"I just use my boot."

"Oh, Mike. If this room were larger, it would make a perfect spot for wildlife to bed down." This statement got Mike's eyes bulging, and his mullet ruffled. And nobody messes with a man's long clump of hair. Not even a mother.

"Mom, I really like this place."

"I'm joking with you, Mike. We can tell you're happy here. Sorry if I offended you. This is just a pretty rustic way to live." I took several minutes to scope out the surroundings and understood the reason for his fondness. "By the way, there's a can of chicken noodle soup on the table for another meal."

"Shoot! Mom, I won't be home for another week, because I wasted my days off puking and sleeping."

"We're just glad you're all right, Mike." I gave him a long hug.

With both hands on the wheel, Bill drove past smoky campfires, saggy tents, and dirty kids on tricycles and bikes. Before we lost sight of Mike, I yelled back to him from the car window, "Mike, don't eat the mushrooms!" Mike only waved back.

"Bill, watch out for that fisherman!" I squealed.

"I see him."

Chapter Thirty-Six

SNOWPLOWS AND SNOWMOBILES

After the mental and physical stress of summer, poisonous mushrooms, a near drowning, meltdowns behind the grill, a surplus of catering, and a fatal car accident—fall transitioned into a slow-paced winter season, with Tuesdays off.

Bill stomped his snow-covered boots on the rubber doormat. "It's so crappy outside. Bet it'll snow all day…again," he reported.

A channel 7 meteorologist he is not, I thought. "How much do you think is out there?" I asked.

"I'd say at least four feet." He shed his heavy coat and gave it a shake, oblivious to the snow clumps landing everywhere but the mat.

I stoked the woodstove and looked up to see Ben coming through the door, cheeks red, and the white-fluff-covered stocking hat looked like a giant snowball on the top of his head. "Good morning, Ben. How's it going?" I asked.

"Okay," he answered with typical Ben shyness. Myra used her left arm to give her seven-year-old son a quick hug, while her right hand reached over and grabbed the stocking hat from his head.

It was Saturday, so Lisa and Mike would be sleeping until noon. Because of treacherous road conditions, there were few customers, so Myra and I expected a leisure day.

"The snowplows can't keep up," I said to Myra. "Doug has spent hours plowing out our parking areas for the few die-hard travelers who stop in." Though I was talking to his mother, my attention was on the blond-haired boy sitting patiently at the restaurant counter. I could feel him peering over at me with big eyes and a small smile that opened my heart. It was time for our pancake ritual. I winked at Myra and whispered, "I'll let him sit there a few more moments before asking the million-dollar question. He's so adorable—I have to stretch this out." Myra smiled back at me. She enjoyed watching this dance between her son and her friend.

Finally, I asked, "Hey, Ben, are you hungry?" We both knew the answer.

"Yeah, I guess so."

I followed the script precisely. "Well, if you're hungry, how about I make you a *big* pancake? You remember what you need to do, don't you?"

"Yep. I have to eat *all* of it, or I'll have to pay for it," he answered. I picked up the pitcher of pancake batter and poured a generous amount onto the sizzling grill. Ben's pancakes were so large they could be difficult to flip. About 25 percent of the time, the flipping turned into a huge mess, but if that happened, I'd just start again. Seeing Ben's face light up when I set the plate in front of him made the ordeal worth it. Before he spread the butter or poured on the syrup, he'd take a few moments to stare at the enormous pancake hanging over the plate's edge. A small fruit cup was included with every breakfast served at the Ponderosa. Ben regarded the fruit cup as dessert, always setting it off to the side, saving it for last. Or maybe it was a smart reserve tactic, as our deal didn't include payment for the fruit cup if he couldn't eat it. Ben and I loved our pancake routine—it was our special connection. And in all the time I served him, no matter how large the pancake, Ben never called my bluff about having to pay for uneaten food.

Thanks to the steady snow accumulation, our day off was spent in Lower Banks. "I'm not interested in driving anywhere on these roads," Bill announced.

"I agree. We can stay home. The restaurant's closed, and we have no to-dos," I said.

Shortly after lunchtime, I glanced over at Bill and said, "It's our day off…how about pouring three cold mugs of beer?" An hour earlier, Myra, bored and knowing we were snowed in for the day, had come by for a visit.

Three of the Ponderosa's hardest workers cozied up to the wood-stove and enjoyed a few beers. By the time Mike, Lisa, and Ben got off the school bus, they found their parents singing to the jukebox, and the beer tap dialed to the easy flow position. "Hi, kids. Did you have a good day?" Myra asked loudly, and we laughed like it was the funniest joke we'd ever heard. The kids stared at us for a minute in disgust, then headed to the kitchen for a snack.

Being a school night, the party soon came to an end for Myra and Ben. "Be careful, you two. Don't get lost in that snowbank," I yelled from the restaurant's open door, loud enough for Doug's family to hear me. I chuckled, thinking, *What a fun day.* Then Bill took my hand and we ambled—a tad unsteady—to our cabin.

Mike and Lisa's daily after-school job of shoveling a path from the side door of the restaurant to our cabin went from boring to motivating when enough snow had accumulated to turn the pathway into Herbie the Hamster's Habitrail. With Ben's help, they spent hours designing the impressive passageway.

"Mom, do you want to know how deep the snow tunnel is?" Lisa asked. She held a wet, soon-to-be-rusty tape measure in her gloved hand and exclaimed, "It's almost six feet tall!"

It was both eerie and peaceful, passing through the snow burrow, surrounded by nothing but white silence.

The snow continued to accumulate, so much so that the only functional vehicles around were the county's snowplows and Doug's snowmobiles. For over a week, Lower Banks residents frolicked in the deep snow, made snowmen, and rode snowmobiles around the local properties. We all agreed that playing outside was better than cooking, waiting tables, or pumping gas.

"This is probably the most snow Lower Banks has ever seen. At least in all the years, I've been here," Doug said.

Each morning and evening, Doug plowed both parking lots, creating a two-story-high snow berm that stretched the length of both properties. When Doug ran out of places to pile the snow, he would push it over the bank and into the river.

I felt it essential to stay in close touch with Sherm, who relied on me for winter weather reports. "Do you want to know how much snow we have now?" I would ask him, snickering. Dad would laugh and say, "Annie, this is Idaho. You'll probably get another couple of feet before it's done." Each time we talked, I ended our sometimes-lengthy conversations by saying, "Not sure when I'll see you next—probably summer."

Another Tuesday rolled around, and again we decided to remain at home. In an attempt to make the day special, I decided to prepare a conventional family meal. I put meatloaf and potatoes into the newly cleaned oven and invited Gentleman Joe to join us for dinner. Joe, worried about his aging mother, looked forward to his monthly visits with her but had been unable to visit her this month because of the wintry road conditions. Also, his diminishing scotch supply added to his concerns.

"Mike, would you make a salad? And, Lisa, will you set the table with an extra place for Joe?" Lisa liked choosing from the entire lot of empty booths and tables.

As I removed the meatloaf from the oven, Gentleman Joe arrived, freshly showered and shaved, with a hefty splash of fresh cologne. Behind Joe's back, Mike pinched his nose and pretended to choke and gag. "Stop that," I mouthed to Mike when Joe turned around to carefully hang his unstylish but valued overcoat on a hook in the entryway.

"Is everybody hungry?" I asked, carrying meatloaf and spuds to Lisa's chosen location, a table in the distant corner. Mike followed close behind with his salad. "Your table looks nice, honey," I said as Lisa helped place the large platter in the center of the table.

Mike ate everything on his plate in less than ten minutes—record time. Then having had enough of the old peoples' dialogue, he announced, "I've got a lot of homework," knowing that excuse would reliably set him free.

"You may be excused," I said, though not before giving him a look that said, "I'll be talking to you later and be *afraid*." Smiling, he pumped his fist, knowing I was blowing smoke.

The three adults lingered, enjoying a nice conversation at the table, when Lisa impressed us by jumping up and clearing the table without being asked.

After an hour, Joe stood up, moved to the foyer, and put on his overcoat. "Thanks for the delicious dinner, Miss Ann."

I gave him a gentle hug, noticing as I did, that his body seemed slighter than the last time I'd hugged him. "You're very welcome, Joe. I'm so glad you came." He opened the door and disappeared into the cold night air.

I was wiggling into my winter coat when the side door reopened, and Joe stood in the doorway, cradling his left arm close to his chest, face ashen. "I might've broken my arm, Miss Ann."

"Oh no, Joe, what happened?" I helped him to the closest chair.

"I slipped on some ice walking to my room," Joe said in a shaky voice.

"I'm so sorry, Joe. Bill, we need to call an ambulance." Mike had shoveled a trail to the motel and applied rock salt, but with single-digit temperatures at night, it created a sheet of ice over the path. "Dammit! I should have walked Joe to his room," I fretted aloud to Bill.

"No, you shouldn't have. There'd be two people with broken bones. I should've been the one," Bill said.

No matter how we argued about the situation, it was too late to change anything. Our job now was to figure out the best way to help Joe, who couldn't hide his pain. It moved me to tears to see this gentle man suffer.

"Joe isn't going to the hospital alone. I'm driving to Boise," I said. "Joe, I'll be back in a sec." Quickly, but carefully, keeping my steps close together, I picked my way along the narrow pathway—the width of a shovel—and entered Joe's room. I grabbed the down comforter, two feather pillows from his bed, and a nearly empty bottle of scotch from the dresser.

Bill helped load Joe into the car, and I gingerly propped up his head with one pillow and his arm with the other. The large, fluffy comforter was way too big for the situation, but I tucked it around Joe anyway.

"There's enough in here for a little snort," I said, handing Joe the scotch bottle. "We'll be in Boise before you know it."

"Thanks, Miss Ann."

The emergency room doctor put Joe's left arm in a cast, and in four hours, we were back on the road. Joe, heavily dosed with pain medication, fell asleep.

When Joe was secure in his motel room, I paused for a moment in front of my cabin. "Damn this snow," I said aloud. Angry and frustrated, I kicked a mound of snow, which painfully turned out to be a solid chunk of ice—letting out a rigorous, "Ouch!" Grateful to climb into bed but concerned that the clock read two fifteen, I curled up under heavy quilts.

"How's Joe?" Bill asked, eyes still closed.

"His arm's in a cast, but he's okay, thank God," I said, punching my pillow to give it some bulk. At first, Bill seemed too sleepy for a detailed discussion—but I was wrong.

"Well, he wears those highly polished slick shoes with no tread on them," Bill said, his voice gravelly.

I started to snap back with a mean comment but decided to squelch my temper. The last thing I wanted was a spat. "It's not entirely his fault. Somebody should've walked him to his room. I've got to get to sleep." I retrieved my share of bed covers by giving the blankets a firm tug and rolled over.

Chapter Thirty-Seven

MIKE'S NEW CAREER

S pring brought warm weather, which melted the snow and created lots of mud. Bill, who got a kick out of watching Ben tramp around the properties wearing tall rubber boots and jumping into every puddle, gave Ben the moniker 'Muck Luck.' Whenever Ben heard 'Muck Luck' called, he would come running.

Myra and Jodi convinced Bill and me to take a short vacation before the summer rush. Someone mentioned Hawaii, and soon the idea took on a life of its own. The winter puzzle was stored away, and dozens of travel brochures took its place. Notes scratched on green order slips multiplied as customers made suggestions about where to go and what to see. "If the actual vacation is half as fun as the planning, we've got a winner," I told Bill.

Lisa and Mike weren't happy about being left behind, but they promised to be on their best behavior.

"Maybe next time we can all go," I said, mostly to make myself feel less guilty.

Bill and I excitedly boarded the plane headed for Seattle. There we were scheduled to connect with another flight destined for the Big Island. The only problem—my anxiety about leaving behind two teenagers and a restaurant was as great as my excitement.

"Annie, we're on our way, and you can't waste the whole week worrying. Mike and Lisa will be fine. Mike's almost nineteen, and

Lisa thinks she's twenty-five. They're responsible kids, and Myra can manage the restaurant as well as us," Bill said.

Once the plane reached cruising altitude, Bill ordered two cans of beer from the flight attendant. Bill knew words alone wouldn't distract me from my unease, so when the beverages arrived, he reached into his carry-on bag and pulled out a tank top and Hawaiian lei made of silk orchids. He put the lei around my neck, took a swig of beer, and said, "Baby, it's time to *hang loose!*"

"What are you doing?" I asked with a laugh, hoping he wasn't going to put the tank top on just yet.

"Cheers," he said, banging his beer can against mine.

After that, my guilt about our one-week vacation eased. Myra never called with a problem or question, and the days passed quickly, as vacation days always do. We enjoyed warm ocean swims, sunbathing by the pool, breathtaking sunsets, fresh fish, and fruity drinks. When we arrived back in Idaho, suntanned, cheerful, and restored, Bill happily announced, "Hit the reboot button and bring in summertime!"

Once Myra filled us in on all that happened during the week, I told Bill, "I'm so impressed with Myra. She did a great job of managing the restaurant. There weren't any dramatic rescues, fires, or broken backs or arms. She has better luck than we do. Maybe we can take another vacation next year, hopefully with the kids."

Mike and Lisa had done a good job of proving they could manage their lives for a week without parental supervision but seemed to be keeping a secret. Hoping that whatever clogged their minds would break loose, I didn't probe. But the mystery lingered for another week, becoming, in fact, more transparent. One evening, while the two sat at the bar doing homework, I interrupted them. "You two have been pretty quiet since we got back from Hawaii. What's up?"

Lisa looked at Mike. Mike looked at Lisa. Neither of them looked at me.

"Come on, kids, spill the beans," I said lightheartedly, though my words resonated concern.

Mike swept the deserted restaurant with his gaze. "Where's Dad? He needs to be here."

As if he'd been summoned, Bill walked out from the kitchen, carrying a platter of nachos. I called in his direction, "Bill, come here."

We all gathered at the table, waiting for the details from Mike. "Don't be mad…but…" Mike paused for five seconds and then continued, "While you guys were in Hawaii, I joined the Army."

It was one of those rare occasions on which I had no response. Mike's face flushed, his leg bounced nervously, but his eyes showed confidence.

"Mike, is this something you want to do, or did someone talk you into it?" I asked, surprised that my voice worked and wanting to blame someone else for Mike's rash decision.

"Army recruiters came to our school," Mike answered honestly. "It sounds like a good job with a lot of benefits, and they promised me an incentive package when I sign up."

"When are you planning to enlist?" Bill asked casually, as though he were asking, "Have you brushed your teeth?"

"Of course, I have to graduate first. I'll probably leave for boot camp at the end of this year."

I didn't oppose his decision, but neither could I rally a ticker-tape parade. I hugged my son and somehow found the words he wanted to hear. "If this is something you want, you go for it, Mike."

Bill forced out the same amount of support. "We're proud of you, son, and we stand with you."

Now that the news became public, Mike and Lisa seemed to have returned to their former selves and plowed into their dad's plate of nachos. Bill didn't eat a bite. Neither did I.

That night, I crawled into bed tending a splintered heart. "Bill, why can't Mike go to college and become a veterinarian, or something less dangerous?" I buried my face in my pillow.

As the weeks passed, Bill and I avoided any mention of the Army, hoping Mike would have a change of heart and choose a different direction, but instead, Mike grew more passionate about his new career.

The day after Mike received his high school diploma, he cheerfully announced, "I'll be taking the summer off from work."

This time, Bill didn't try to hide his lack of enthusiasm. "Just what do you intend to do all day?" he asked.

"Oh, just hang out. I have to sign the Army's paperwork next week," Mike said as if he thought this would satisfy our worry about his lack of ambition.

"Wow, that's a huge commitment—it might even take, oh, as much as a couple of hours," Bill said sarcastically. "Just don't become a damn couch potato," which would be difficult, as there wasn't a television in our cabin. "And you'd better stay out of trouble. The Army won't take you if you get into any scrapes with the law."

"I know, Dad. They mentioned all that stuff."

Bill and I looked at each other, thinking the same thing: *Hold on…our son plans to get in enough partying to make up for eight horrible weeks of boot camp.*

Later that evening, I noticed Bill sitting on the edge of our bed, resting his forehead in both hands. Sensing my approach, he sat up straight. I'd planned to console him, but before I could speak, Bill's words poured out. "Annie, Mike will turn nineteen in a couple of months. He's old enough to make his own choices and I believe in him—but I must confess—letting go of Mike is much more difficult than I could have imagined." Bill leaned over and his head rested in my lap. Together we prayed.

Chapter Thirty-Eight

LISA'S SPORTS CAR

When summer kicked into high gear, Lisa began waitressing full-time. By the third weekend of June, Lisa discovered that her extra cash was collecting dust—clearly a cause for panic. She convinced her friend Jenny to drive her to Boise to spend it. Later that same afternoon, Lisa burst into the kitchen, nearly hyperventilating. "Lisa, what's wrong? Do you need an ambulance?" I asked jokingly.

"No, Mom. I found the perfect car! They're holding it for me until tomorrow. You and Dad have to cosign for me," she squealed.

With a full grill and an even fuller order wheel, there wasn't time for a car buying discussion. "Lisa, I can't talk right now," I said and squinted to read Melissa's order ticket. "Jodi, what does this say? Sometimes I can't read her writing." Jodi must've felt the pressure building in me because she jumped in to prevent my meltdown.

"I think it says two roast beef sands, hold the mayo on one," Jodi answered.

Just then, Myra called in a gigantic order for a large group of customers who were relaxing on the deck, enjoying the view, completely insulated from the behind-the-scene strain. "Four Ponderosa burgers, one with tots, one with potato salad, barbeque beef san, fish and chips, BLT, chef salad, hold the ham and add more turkey," she recited like an auctioneer.

Did she really say chef salad? Wouldn't you know somebody just had to order a chef salad? Sadly, I gave Myra a look that told her I was about to come apart, and she whispered, "I'm sorry."

Bill dashed by the grill, dirty dishes exploding from the tub he carried. "Woody is here to pick up lunch for forty-six rafters."

"Okay. Tell him I'll bring it out. Jodi, I'll be right back." I raced to the walk-in cooler. The heavy door of the giant refrigerator closed behind me, shutting out the chaos and wrapping me in cool air—a relief from the roasting heat of the grill. Besides being ripped to shreds by excessive work, I jostled with the thought of Lisa driving on these roads. I wanted to stay hidden in the coolness forever and cry but knew that wasn't feasible. I lingered another minute, then gathered Woody's food and left.

Lisa held off until late evening to explain the car situation, though I was certain it had bugged her all day. This time she stayed cool and charming when she asked Bill and me to make a trip with her to the dealership.

"Lisa, if you can get Mike to help Jodi cook for half a day tomorrow, I'm in," I promised.

"Me too," said Bill.

Since Mike was committed to taking the summer off, Lisa had to plead with him. "Come on, Mike. Pleeeease! I'll clean your bedroom."

I laughed and said, "Oh no, you're going to clean his room? Lisa, are you sure about that? Maybe you need to rethink this. Lisa, if you are so willing to clean, how about sprucing up the cabin? It'll take less than two hours, not two days."

"Oh, Mom, why bother? It just gets dirty again."

"Yeah, suppose you're right. Maybe we should add a few extra letters to the reader board: VACUUM 4 SALE. TOILET BRUSH INCLUDED."

Mike finally gave in, promising to work the grill, but not without giving Lisa a playful smack on the arm and calling her "a big cry-baby puke."

Bill and I were about to face something we had intentionally avoided over the years—being schmoozed by a car salesman.

Lisa guided us to a sporty, nearly-new, two-door automobile. "This is it, Mom. What do you think?" Her face flushed, and her eyes danced around the car lot, looking for *her* salesman. She must've detected my disappointment when I saw that she hadn't chosen a safe big tuna boat—like an Oldsmobile or Buick. Without waiting for my answer, she blurted out, "Don't worry, I'm a good driver. I'll be careful, and don't worry about being my cosigner either. I'll make all the monthly payments, I promise. I've got to have *this* car!"

After an intense discussion over price and warranties, all of us, including the salesman, judging by the look on his face, was glad to move on to the paper-signing part of the deal. Lisa beamed at the teal racing stripes on her new, white Geo Storm. She climbed into the driver's seat, buckled her seat belt, and got herself comfy, the dimples on each side of her smile deepening.

"Mom and I will follow you home," Bill told Lisa.

"You look pretty darn cute in your car. Drive careful honey," I said, trying to hide my worries about having another child behind a steering wheel.

"Goodness, Bill, our daughter's not even seventeen, and she's driving a sporty little car. How'd that happen? At least it's too small to haul around a load of her friends."

Bill stared straight ahead at the small white vehicle in front of him, not taking his eyes off it even to blink, and asked, "What's next?"

Chapter Thirty-Nine

CLASS V RAPIDS

At every opportunity, Bill and I peeked out the restaurant's windows, checking the parking lot for the arrival of Bob and Louie, two of our close friends from Oregon. Eager to entertain them with fun and unique Idaho experiences, we had planned a float trip for our first activity, provided by Woody's Rafting.

"Bill, I'm not so sure about whitewater rafting. Did you forget I don't know how to swim? I cannot go through Class V rapids!" I protested.

"Bob and Louie will be disappointed if you don't go," Bill retorted.

"I don't care! Read my lips—I can't swim! How would you feel if I drowned? Who would cook?"

Bill got Woody involved, and together they tried to convince me of the safety of a trip on a large raft, with a guide, a wet suit, a helmet, and a life jacket.

"That's all nice and dandy, but you didn't mention a personal lifeguard," I said to Woody. I was joking—but I liked the idea so much, I decided to ask Mike to be my lifeguard.

Mike was tinkering with the brakes on his Ranchero when I approached him with my proposal. "Hey, Mike, how'd you like to go whitewater rafting down the South Fork of the Payette—for *free*?"

He pulled his head out from under the vehicle, looked up at me, and said, "Of course I would. It's like fifty bucks, isn't it?"

"Well, yes, it is, but there is a small catch. You'll be there to protect me. No matter what happens, your only job will be to *save* your mother." I'd selected the perfect person for the task. Mike, a strong swimmer, had spent several years on his school's swim team in Oregon. And after learning firsthand the power of the river (from the no-life-jacket episode), he wouldn't take the job lightly. Mike was thrilled, and I was a little less fearful.

Bob, Louie, Bill, Mike, and I, along with two other guests, carried the heavy raft to the river's edge—and then put on skintight wet suits (which made me look even bonier), life preservers, and helmets. Our guide gave us instructions on what to do and what not to do under different circumstances. Mike, sensing my distress about trying to assimilate all the details, cinched up my life jacket and promised he'd make sure I stayed safe. Acting professional, he positioned me in front of him on the raft's edge, which confused me—why weren't we sitting *in* the raft? One big bump and surely all of us would bounce into the river.

"Mike, please don't let me fly out of this piece of rubber," I pleaded—scared stiff. The raft left the shallow water and began to float lazily down the river. "Weee-hoooo, this is kind of fun," I said as our raft meandered through the canyon slowly and gently.

Then I heard the guide yell out, "Okay, folks, paddle forward, *hard!*"

Straight ahead was a rapid called Staircase, but with its churning, frothy water, it looked (and sounded) more like Niagara Falls than a staircase. Moments before the raft hit the apex of the rapid, it dipped abruptly, causing my rear end to come off the raft. Mike quickly grabbed the strap of my life preserver and snapped me into the boat, and I instantly realized why passengers don't sit *in* the raft—a person curled up and holding her breath on the bottom of a boat is unable to help with the necessary paddling. I was no help on the first rapid or any other rapids for that matter, including a big one called Bronco Billy, which bucked Bill overboard. Louie and the guide quickly rescued him, and everyone laughed. Everyone, that is, except me. For me, the day was a blur from the moment I hit the first rapid until our landing on a sandy beach, where I got to watch people enjoy the food prepared by Woody's catering queen.

At the end of the day, I gave Mike a well-deserved bear hug. "Thanks for taking good care of me today. You'll be happy to know it's the last time you'll ever need to safeguard your mom in a boat."

A few weeks after our Oregon guests left, Doug and Adelle came in for dinner. Doug described the latest vehicle he had towed. "The trailer is in great condition with one exception—it can't be pulled anymore because of a bent axle. It had been used only a few times before the owner jackknifed it. But the cost to make it mobile again is more than its worth, so the insurance company is auctioning it off to the highest bidder. Someone will get it for a prayer," Doug explained.

Within the week, Bill and I were the proud owners of a twelve-foot travel trailer that couldn't travel. Doug towed it over and placed it in the RV spot facing the river. "Sure has a nice view," Doug said, working the winch. Once John Vander connected the sewer and water lines, the trailer became a permanent addition.

Chapter Forty

ALICE'S NEW HOME

An unforeseen circumstance unfolded, when a middle-aged woman stopped by the restaurant inquiring about a job. "I'm Alice," she said politely. Alice, presumably destitute, made an awkward first impression. To me, she seemed troubled and a little unmotivated, and I felt a tinge of uneasiness about her but scolded myself for judging her character based on appearance alone. If I gave her a chance and taught her to cook, she could give Jodi and me some much-needed relief. Was it her outgoing personality or my desperation for a cook that manipulated my thought process? "All right, Alice, how about I teach you to cook? Your pay will be minimum wage but will include a place to live. If you're interested, you can start right away. I'll show you where you'll be living." Alice, ecstatic about her new *im*mobile home on the river, swore she wouldn't let me down.

"Your first shift will start tomorrow morning at seven o'clock. See you then," I told her. As I walked away, I heard loud screams coming from KYBR—or perhaps it was the sound of my conscience scolding me for this unconventional hire. Sometimes people just need someone to believe in them, I told myself. I spent the next ten minutes trying to convince myself that I hadn't made a huge mistake.

Alice arrived for work five minutes early the following morning—a promising sign. She was clean, enthusiastic, and attentive to my directions, and by the end of her four-hour shift, I felt some ease with my newest employee. "Good job today, Alice. Go ahead, fix yourself something to eat," I said. I turned to the counter, picked up a large knife, and began to chop a yellow onion, destined for the monstrous soup pot.

"What are you making?" Alice asked, eager to learn everything about cooking—which gained her even more points.

"Clam chowder, and wow, this onion is really strong," I answered, wiping my watery eyes on my shirt sleeve.

Alice untied her apron and carefully folded it. "Annie, you are the best teacher. You didn't yell at me once."

I smiled at her and replied, "Thanks, Alice. You were a good student."

"Hey, Mom, do you want to meet him?" Lisa asked nervously.

Lisa never blushes, I thought. "Meet who?" I asked.

Lisa came to where I stood at the grill. "Flip those burgers while you stand there please," I said, handing her a greasy spatula. "Who do you want me to meet?" I asked again as I topped the hamburger buns.

"Sam! Remember, I told you about him last week," she answered, somewhat irritably. "Sam and his dad came in for lunch. They're in the small booth." I started to turn around to peek at the twosome. "Mom, *stop*! Don't look at them," she whispered.

I smiled at my bashful fireball. "Okay, let me know when it's okay to look."

Awhile later, Lisa introduced us all. "Mom, this is Sam and his dad, Dave," Lisa said, as sophisticated as the speaker of the house would be announcing the president of the United States. "Glad to meet you both," I said politely. We shook hands, exchanged a few words, and I returned to the kitchen.

"Well, what do you think?" Lisa asked quietly through the order window.

"They're both very nice. And very quiet," I answered softly and honestly.

Lisa pulled down two plates holding bacon cheeseburgers, leaving a handful of curly fires on the ledge. "Not everybody is a loud family like we are," she said and ran off to deliver the order to her new favorite customers.

Chapter Forty-One

CONSEQUENCES

After weeks of listening to Mike's Ranchero tear out of the parking lot with tires squealing and stereo thumping, I finally confronted him. "Mike, what are you thinking?" I asked, hoping for an answer that contained the phrase "maybe I should get a job."

"I'm just making the most of my last few months of freedom," Mike answered and walked away, leaving me standing alone in the kitchen.

Two minutes later, when Bill entered my work zone, I asked him point-blank, "Bill, don't you think Mike might have too much liberty?"

"Probably," is all Bill would say.

"Did he tell you what happened yesterday?" I asked, hoping to enroll Bill in my concern.

"No, what happened?"

"Well, I'm glad you asked. He told me that a state trooper pulled his sorry ass over—him and Tim actually. Apparently, they were driving on the highway to Kuna, testing out the Ranchero's speed on a straight stretch, when a cooler lid and a lawn chair flew out of the back."

"Oh yeah?" Bill said, finally looking at me.

"After the trooper took Mike's driver's license back to his patrol car, Mike said he and Tim were pretty nervous because they both had been drinking a little. I wonder how they define *a little*? Anyway, I guess they sat there, scared to death, until the police officer handed Mike his license and said something like, "Happy nineteenth birthday. You and I share the same birthday, and I'm giving you a present—a *warning*. So secure your load, turn this vehicle around, go home, and drive the speed limit!'"

A gruff expression on his face, Bill said, "If that kid's joining the Army, he needs to stay squeaky clean."

"Well, it seems Mike did tell the officer he enlisted with the Army, and I assume the trooper realized a citation could affect that outcome. Mike dodged a bullet last night, and hopefully learned a lesson."

Sam and Lisa were soon inseparable. After her previous boyfriend, who had had a reputation of being a well-rehearsed lady's man, Sam looked like a gift-filled Easter basket. Lisa's nonstop admiration was obvious. "Sam does this and Sam does that—"

"Okay, Lisa, we get it. You really like this guy." I laughed. "And so do we."

Sam, known as the guy who owned the coolest car in the area (we never told Mike), drove a bright-orange 1969 Chevy Camaro. He enjoyed extra torque and driving on the high side of the speed limit. Although his classic orange car worried me, I trusted he cared enough for Lisa to keep her safe.

August arrived. Mike would be home for several more months, but I was already fretting over his imminent departure and longed to get in family time. Family time in the summer had been as scarce as hen's teeth. After several weeks of working on a secret plan, I gathered Mike, Lisa, and Bill together and revealed my idea. "Before Mike leaves for boot camp, we'll go on a family ski trip to Canada. I've already discussed it with Myra, Alice, and Jodi, and they gave me the go-ahead. Business is slow in early December, and Lisa, you can miss school for a week, don't you think?"

"Sounds like fun to me," Bill said.

Mike, overjoyed with the news, jumped into the air like he was going up for a basketball dunk—his head just missing the ceiling fan. "Can Sam go too?" Lisa begged.

"Do you think his dad will let him go?"

Lisa raced across the room like Sea Biscuit on the home stretch of the Kentucky Derby. "I'll call him right now."

A few hours later, our plans were set. Sam would join our family and learn how to ski on the slopes in Fairmont, Canada. Over the next few months, the trip was a constant topic of conversation.

Summer duties, however, still had a grip on us. "Mike, I really need your help this Saturday. Jodi needs the day off because of a family crisis, and Alice is out of town until next week. I'll have to work in the kitchen alone. Would you be able to BBQ steaks on the deck for twenty-six rafters?"

"Oh, Mom, it's Horseshoe Bend Days, and I've made plans," he said.

"Please, Mike. Woody is bringing them in for lunch, probably around one o'clock. You don't have to show up until then, and I don't think it'll take you more than forty-five minutes to cook the steaks. You know I wouldn't ask if I didn't really need your help. Can I count on you?"

Unenthusiastically, Mike obliged. "Yeah, I guess."

Lisa sprinted into the kitchen. "Mom, Woody just arrived with the rafters."

"Run to the cabin and tell Mike to come get the steaks and salads," I told her.

"I already did, and he's not there."

"You're kidding, right?"

"Nope. I'm not."

"That boy is way too *Free Willy!*" I cried out in frustration.

A nightmare of epic proportions unfolded for the next hour. While Bill filled bar orders and stayed ahead of dirty dishes, all six waitresses were busy taking orders from nonrafting customers. When I returned to the kitchen with an empty steak platter, I actually cried when I saw the order wheel—or rather, when I didn't see the order wheel—it was hidden behind green slips.

By the time Mike's Ranchero pulled into the parking lot, the rafters had finished eating, and the order wheel was almost visible again. Unabashed, Mike sashayed into the kitchen and asked nonchalantly, "Hey, how's it going, Mom?"

I couldn't look at him, let alone speak to him. The anger made my hand clamp tight around the spatula's handle, and I rapped its edge on the grill with a resounding clank. Then without looking up, I pushed past him.

He came after me, trying to explain his tardiness. "Mom, they closed the highway. I couldn't get through."

"That's such a load of bull. You just didn't want to be here. And *you* know what it's like when we're busy and short-staffed. You don't even care about how horrible it was for us—all you care about is yourself." When I opened my mouth to continue, Mike turned to walk away, and I pursued him. I was about to release months of pent-up worry, frustration, and anger about everything—including the fact that he had joined the Army. "Stop, Mike. I'm not done talking to you," I began.

Mike interrupted, "Mom, you're not listening to me, so I'm leaving. I don't need this crap."

I followed him to the cabin and watched him pack a bag of belongings and toss it into his Ranchero. He laid rubber and disappeared around the bend.

"That's fine. He needs a dose of reality," I said to Bill, who had tagged along. "I've had about enough of his baloney."

Bill wrapped me in his arms, and I knew my angry, vengeful words were only an attempt to cover my broken heart.

Mike moved in with a school buddy, and fortunately for him, his decision to leave home coincided with the eruption of a large wildfire northeast of Horseshoe Bend, giving him a job as a firefighter.

Mike's friends would occasionally stop by the Ponderosa and release bits and pieces of information about Mike's new life. Though I was grateful for the stories, their words couldn't cure my sadness over Mike's leaving.

Mike had been gone almost four weeks when Deputy Buck mentioned the road closure hassle caused by *the accident near Horseshoe Bend three Saturdays ago.* I remembered Mike's words "They closed the road."

"Bill, damn it! I've made a horrible mistake with Mike," I admitted.

"Go talk to him, Annie."

I drove south toward the fire camp, thinking how good it would feel not to lie awake tonight, beating myself up for alienating my son. The miles passed quickly, and soon I entered the congested campsite, looking for someone to direct me. Learning that Mike was expected back shortly, I waited in my car, going over what I would say to him, and wondering what he would say to me. Was he still angry? Would he forgive me? After a long hour, a bus pulled into camp and stopped just short of the first row of droopy tents.

The twentieth person off the bus was Mike. He looked like a full-fledged firefighter in need of a shower and nap. When he caught sight of me, though, he perked up and headed toward me.

I reached out to give him a hug. "I'm so sorry, Mike."

"I'm sorry too, Mom."

He tolerated my long hug. "Mike, I should've known you had a good reason. I'm sorry I didn't listen. Mike, you can come home if you want."

"Thanks, Mom, I'll let you know. Right now, I've got to clean up for chow."

"Okay, let's stay in touch."

I watched Mike walk toward the row of tents; his long shadow stretched out behind him.

Three days later, while I absently prepared a Denver omelet and short stack, Mike unexpectedly walked into the kitchen. "Oh, Mike! It's great to see you. Are you here for a while?" I had to ask.

"Yep, I'm moving back home. The fire's been contained, and they don't need me anymore."

"Would you like some breakfast?"

"Sure, but I can fix it."

We stood side by side at the grill, just like old times, and when I tripped over his right foot, I smiled at him and squeezed his arm— not even the pope could have felt more blessed than me.

Chapter Forty-Two

YOUNG AND BRAVE

Hot summer gave way to cooler days, and the morning frost on Ol' Blue's windshield grew more common. Every detail of our ski trip seemed to be covered, from our lodging in Fairmont, Canada, to the van rental. As soon as we had "only two months to go," Lisa started her packing. "Keep it simple," I reminded her. "All five of us and our belongings have to fit into one minivan." But I was wasting my breath. Lisa would pack enough for two people, and Bill, of course, would find a place for it all.

When the first winter storm brought six inches of snow, it brought with it another Mike adventure. On a lazy Tuesday afternoon, Mike came through the unlocked side door, wet and red-checked. "Mike, what happened?" Bill asked, alarmed.

Mike poured a soda and found a chair, then spoke. "Well, you may not believe this, but about a mile before I got to Horseshoe Bend, I noticed vehicle tracks going off the highway toward the river—just like when Tim and I saw the ref's car tracks. I couldn't see over the bank from the road, so I pulled into the closest turnout and went back to check it out. When I looked over the bank, I saw a pickup truck on the sandbar next to the river with a lady standing beside it calling for help.

"What I saw when I got down there made me want to throw up. A chest freezer in the bed of their pickup had been thrown forward through the back window and into the cab of the truck. A little boy about four years old was pinned between the dashboard and the freezer. His upper body looked all right, but his legs were broken, and the bones stuck out through his skin. I tried to help the man move the heavy freezer, but it was wedged in too tight. When I remembered the blanket in my car, I ran up and got it for the little guy, who was shivering. Plus I thought if I covered up his legs, he wouldn't be so scared about how bad they looked. The weird thing is, he wasn't crying or screaming. He must've been in shock.

"He was so cute, with freckles all over his face, and he seemed to listen when I told him he'd be okay. I told him my name was Mike and asked him his name. He said, 'Jofes,' which I think meant Joseph, so I said, 'Hi, Joseph. You're the bravest dude in the world.' He even said, 'Thanks, mister,' when I took off my cap and put it on his head.

"Somebody must've stopped, saw the wreck, and called for an ambulance, because I could hear sirens. I talked with Joseph until the paramedics arrived, and then I watched them take him out of the truck—that's when Joseph started to cry. It made me cry, too, Mom."

We sat in silence for several moments. "Mike, it sounds like you kept Joseph calm because you stayed calm. It's a miracle you spotted those tracks in the snow. You were supposed to be there for that little boy."

"Wish I knew Joseph's last name so I could check on him," Mike said.

Mike received his official military orders in early November—he would be leaving from Boise on January 6. Though boot camp would last only eight weeks, Mike seemed sure it would feel like eight years. In an effort to take our minds off his impending departure, we all focused on our upcoming ski vacation.

The rental van was jammed so full, Mike and Sam had to slam the van's back door shut on the final suitcase.

"Nobody had better open this until we get to the hotel," Mike warned.

Lisa ran from the cabin, waving a small tote bag in the air. "Wait, I have one more bag!"

Mike rolled his eyes, grimaced, and shook his head. "Lisa, there's no more room. You'll have to hold it on your lap." When Lisa reached for the backdoor latch, Sam almost tackled her to the ground.

We traveled for nearly eight hours before stopping to spend the night on the Idaho–Canada border. By sunrise the next morning, we were up, reloaded, and traveling north.

"We should be arriving at the condo close to noon," Bill calculated.

The trip continued without incident until Mike, who was driving, got pulled over and was issued a speeding ticket.

"Mike, I can't believe you were ticketed for going seven miles over the speed limit," I said. But the unwarranted episode didn't dampen our spirits.

We arrived at noon, then unloaded the van, and by one o'clock, we were checking out the hot tub near the main lodge and searching for a place to have lunch.

Sam received his first ski lesson the next morning by watching others. "Doesn't Sam ski great for his first time?" Lisa gushed, her cheeks pink from the cold air, and her face glowing with a Sam-does-everything-perfectly look.

The week flew by, and as expected, leaving was difficult. But now, Mike had many good memories to take with him to boot camp, which was part of my plan all along.

The Ponderosa had fared well during our absence. "I'm so thankful for all your hard work," I told Myra and Jodi. "Take the next couple of days off. Bill and I are rested up and good to go."

Mike prepared himself for January 6 by partying every night. However, there was little I could do to prepare for my first child leaving home. On January 4, with two nights to go, I lay in bed, staring at the red numbers on the alarm clock, which seemed exceptionally bright in the darkness. When the numbers read 2:29 a.m., I started to get worried that Mike wasn't home. A few moments passed, and then I heard Mike's voice call out from a far distance. *"Mom! Mom! Mom!"* Then everything went as silent as death. I leaped out of bed and rushed to the front door. After looking around outside, something told me to check his bedroom. I switched on his bedroom light and saw Mike curled up, unmoving under the blankets. I didn't get it. Why was he calling out to me when he was asleep in bed? It took a few minutes to realize that I'd just had the most realistic nightmare of my life. I climbed back into bed, knowing that the next time he called my name, he wouldn't be in the next room safe among stacks of dirty laundry.

On the night of January 5, we took Mike out to dinner, savoring the last moments before his 9:00 p.m. check-in at the Holiday Inn, where all recruits stayed before flying off to camp. Bill and I would spend the night in Boise.

"Good night, Mike. We'll be at the airport by eight o'clock to say goodbye," I said, trying to hide my agony.

The indescribable sadness I felt after Mike boarded his plane left me speechless during the drive back to Lower Banks.

"Mike will be home for a couple of weeks when training is over. Annie, he'll be okay, I promise."

I looked over at Bill and noticed the twitching muscle in his jaw.

That first week in February, as soon as there was a break in the weather and the roads cleared for travel, Gentleman Joe packed up his belongings. A setback in Flora's health had Joe eager to spend the remainder of the winter months in Lewiston. Joe carefully laid several suits across the back seat of his brown sedan. *His arm has healed nicely,* I thought to myself.

"Stay as long as necessary, Joe."

"I'll be back early spring, Miss Ann," he replied.

Amazingly, the following weeks passed quickly as Mike's homecoming drew closer. The winter's snowfall was minimal compared to previous years, so the restaurant business stayed steady.

"Hurry up, Lisa, we have to leave," Bill yelled up the steep stairway. We were getting ready to pick up Mike at the airport.

"I'm coming, Dad," she hollered from her bedroom.

The three of us entered the airport carrying a cluster of helium balloons, and Lisa's large homemade sign, which read, WELCOME HOME MIKE!

"Do you think Mike will look different?" Lisa asked. She'd be the last to admit it, but nobody had missed Mike more than Lisa.

"Oh, he'll look different all right." Bill snickered. Twenty-five years had passed, but Bill still remembered his own leave after military training.

Lisa was the first to identify Mike in the string of recruits coming off the plane and began waving her sign.

"He must see us because he's smiling," Lisa said.

Lisa pressed through a herd of people, rushing toward Mike. Bill and I followed close behind, the balloons whipping through the air behind us. There were tears, laughter, and hugs. Mike was home!

Even though it had only been eight weeks, Mike, tight-muscled half man, half boy, looked a whole lot different. The descriptive word Mike preferred was "buffed." Although Mike was the one who'd done the hard work, all of us were as proud as if we'd won an Olympic gold medal.

"Let's get out of here," Mike suggested.

The three of us stared at him in shock. His voice had also changed—grown much deeper and more mature. We burst into laughter and headed toward baggage claim, where Mike gathered up his duffel bag and threw it over his shoulder. Then we drove to his Aunt Beth's house, where she was throwing a small homecoming celebration in Mike's honor.

Back at the Ponderosa, Mike headed straight for his bedroom, proclaiming, "It feels great to be home. My bedroom is exactly how I remember it."

"It's good to have you home, Mike. Everybody missed you. Get a good night's sleep—you probably haven't had one in months. We'll catch up tomorrow."

I climbed into bed next to a snoring Bill. Once again, the small cabin contained the entire family—just the way I preferred it. Mike quickly settled into a completely different schedule than the rest of the family. While Mike slept through the daylight hours, Bill, Lisa, and I worked. And at night, while Bill, Lisa, and I slept, Mike entertained his old school chums.

Too soon, however, Mike prepared to head out again. He stuffed clean skivvies and socks into his military duffel bag.

"Looks like I won't be home for a while," Mike said.

"Yeah, when you're stationed in Germany, it isn't so easy to come home on the weekends," Bill teased.

Mike tossed the overstuffed green bag into the back seat of the car. "Maybe you and Mom can come and visit me," he replied.

"I don't know about that, Mike, but would you do me a favor? Write lots of letters to your mom. She's going to miss you, and she'll be hard to live with."

"I hate writing letters, but I'll write to you and Mom, I swear."

At the airport, we met up with fellow recruits of Mike's. When it was time to say our final farewells, I hugged Mike for what felt like an hour—though even that wasn't long enough. I forced myself not to cry until he turned his back and boarded the plane. To me, Mike seemed just as young and brave as that freckle-faced little boy he had told us about several months back.

"Well, here we go again, honey," I said to Bill. "Why does this have to hurt so badly? He'll always be my baby. I can still remember bottle-feeding him for the first eleven months of his life."

Bill gave me a confused look and asked, "Didn't you *breastfeed* Mike?"

"Well, yes…I just wanted to see if you were paying any attention to me."

We both laughed and talked about the easy winter days ahead and our Tuesdays off. On our way out of town, to my surprise, Bill stopped at the Jade Dragon.

Chapter Forty-Three

LOVE STORY

"So what do you think?" I asked Bill.

Bill gave me a quick wink and said, "Why are you asking me? Go ask them!"

Sam and Lisa sat at the far corner booth, snacking on popcorn, and supposedly doing homework. I practically catapulted to their table, excited about my news. "Hey, what do you two say about going to Maui with Dad and me over spring break?"

Their mouths dropped open, and Lisa screeched, "Sam, will your dad let you go?"

"He'd better!"

Next, I consulted Myra about the help she'd need if Lisa, Bill, and I were gone for a week at the end of March.

"If I have Jodi, Alice, and Joe's help, there shouldn't be a problem. Go make your plans!" Myra said, radiating confidence. I trusted Myra entirely and hoped she knew the extent of my appreciation.

Lisa's anticipation of her upcoming high school graduation was suddenly replaced by her excitement over spending spring break on Maui's beaches with Sam.

"Lisa, you're aware that you and Sam will have separate bedrooms, right?" I asked.

"Mom, of course we know that." Lisa barked back. She shrugged her shoulders and was unable to hide a fleeting look of mortification.

Sam and Lisa were in love. I knew it, Bill knew it, of course Lisa knew it, and we all thought Sam should have known it too. One afternoon, Lisa shared a story with me: "Mom, last Friday night, I told Sam I loved him, but he didn't say anything back to me—he just got really quiet and brought me home."

"Oh, honey, I'm sorry. That must've felt awful. He probably needs time for it to sink in." I knew, though, it wasn't *my* words that would heal Lisa's broken heart. Only Sam could take care of that.

A few days later, Lisa burst into the kitchen, her face glowing. "At school today, I found out from my friend what Sam did after he dropped me off last Friday night. On the way back to his house, he rolled down his car window, banged on the outside of the car door with his hand, and shouted, "*Whooopeeee! Lisa loves me! Wooohooo!*"

Sam's response was so characteristically Sam, it made us both laugh. His shyness was one of his most endearing qualities. We all knew in time, he would be able to tell Lisa directly how much he loved her.

Lisa and I hugged, and happy tears formed in Lisa's eyes. "Leecee, I'm thrilled for you, honey. Sam is a super guy!"

"Alice hasn't come in yet, has she?" I asked.

Joe answered, "No, Miss Ann. I haven't seen her."

For the tenth time, I glanced at the clock on the microwave. "She should've been at work twenty-two minutes ago," I grumbled.

Ben had just finished his biggest pancake to date. "Hey, Muck Luck, would you do me a big favor and go check on Alice?"

"Sure," Ben answered. Right away, he got up from the counter and carried his plate to the dishwasher.

"I don't think we need to wash that plate, it looks pretty darn clean to me," I snickered.

"Thanks for the pancake!" Ben said and ran out the side door.

Within minutes, Ben was back in the kitchen with an Alice update. "She's in bed, but she got up when I knocked on the door. She might have the flu."

"Thanks for your help, Ben. Oh yeah, before I forget, Bill would like you to pull weeds around the motel and RV spots, either today or tomorrow. Do you need a couple of bucks in your pocket?" I asked. Ben promptly ran off to locate Bill.

Forty-eight minutes late for work, Alice entered the kitchen, looking even worse than Ben had described. *Flu, my ass,* I thought.

"Sorry, Annie, but my boyfriend, Marcus, showed up late last night from California, and we overslept. He's looking for a job, and we're thinking he could help Bill at the bar." Alice's eye contact was direct and bold, though her baggy bloodshot eyes, smudged with old mascara, smacked of a wild night spent on the trailer's pullout bed.

Who do you think you are, and why am I putting up with this? I thought. I considered firing her on the spot but knew Myra would need her help while we were in Maui—even a little help at the grill is better than none. For now, I bit my lip, kept quiet, and let her talk.

"Marcus is coming up later to meet you guys. He wants to talk to Bill."

In my most sarcastic voice, I said, "It's nice that you and Marcus could sleep in this morning." I could tell by the look on her face, however, that my sarcasm was lost on her. "Alice, you appear to be hungover, and I don't think you'd be much help in the kitchen today. Go back, tell Marcus we don't need his help and that he can't live in that small trailer with you. Your shift starts tomorrow morning at eight o'clock sharp. If you are here one minute after eight, you will not have a job!"

Myra and Bill were eavesdropping, and they, like me, expected Alice to get upset, but she turned without comment, wobbled to the side door, and left, banging her left shoulder on the doorjamb on her way out.

"Wow, you told her." Myra chuckled.

"I think she's happy to be able to spend the day in bed with Marcus," Bill added.

I shook my head. "I don't understand how she can waltz in here an hour late, hungover, and act like nothing's wrong. She looked like *hell.* She didn't even comb her hair!"

Alice's best month at the grill had been her first one. After that, her attention had dulled. I'd hoped she'd catch on eventually, but in my heart, I'd known the truth for a while—she didn't have a future as a cook. She didn't have a future as an *anything* if she kept spending all her earnings on beer and wine.

A few hours later, Myra announced through the open food window, "Annie, Alice and her boyfriend are here." Myra grinned.

Bill, busy slicing tomatoes, heard Myra's proclamation. "This ought to be good," he muttered.

Marcus looked worse than I'd expected. His hair looked as bad as his girlfriend's—like a rat's nest but longer—and his teeth were brownish gray. After I'd told him several times that the bar didn't need an employee, he grudgingly accepted it. But the topic of his uninvited presence on the property was harder to address.

"Marcus, this is how it is…Alice lives there as part of her wages. That trailer is scarcely big enough for one person to live in. You cannot stay there."

"Look, I'm having a hard go of it right now," he said. "I sure would appreciate your help. Can I just stay until I find a job and another place to live?"

I wasn't sure why, but I softened, shrugged, and said, "You can stay until the end of the week, Marvin. Oh, I mean Marcus." I hurried off, feeling sick about my mute ridicule and then giving him permission to stay. Why hadn't I just kicked him off the property? Maybe I felt sorry for him, or maybe I naively hoped the problem would disappear.

"Myra, I hope Alice doesn't cause problems for you next week while we're gone. You'll need her help, or she would've been canned. I'll talk to her again tomorrow when she comes to work. That is, *if* she shows up."

The next morning, at 7:56 a.m., Alice stood at my side with a fresh apron—her hair clean, combed back, and held securely with a red rubber band—smiling as if nothing had happened.

On Friday evening, Sam and his dad stopped in for dinner and to discuss the particulars of our departure early the next morning.

"We'll have to leave here no later than 5:00 a.m. Sam, are you packed and ready?" I asked.

Lisa chimed in before Sam could answer, "I'm packed."

"Honey, you've been packed for a month."

Since it was spring break for most of the area schools, the airports were crowded and hectic. But after our long wait at the Maui airport, baggage claim, and car rental, we were finally admiring our quiet condo—overlooking the Pacific Ocean. In record time, we were unpacked and frolicking in the warm ocean.

On our first day of vacation, we learned the consequences of too much sun (like most nonlocals did their first time in Hawaii). That night, Lisa eyeballed her sunburn and suggested we spend our second day touring the island.

Late the following morning, Sam and Lisa excitedly jumped into the back seat of our rented convertible. Bill pulled onto the highway and stepped hard on the gas pedal.

"Put the top up!" Lisa screamed.

"No, we aren't putting the top up. What's the point in having a convertible if the top isn't down?"

To Lisa's distress, her long hair, which she had spent the entire morning making look suitable for a shampoo commercial, was tangling in the wind. We let her rant and rave. In fact, the sight of Lisa's hair blowing uncontrollably about her face was part of the day's entertainment. Bill only gave in when it began to rain.

"Bill, you can put the top up now. *My* hair is getting wet," I said, smiling.

"You guys are cold-blooded!" Lisa said. We could see her brown eyes, amused and bright, through a tiny peephole in the mass of snarls.

When the rain ceased and a rainbow appeared, we pulled to the side of the road so Sam could snap a picture.

While Lisa and Sam snorkeled, boogie-boarded, and shopped, Bill and I relaxed poolside. Toward the end of the week, I mentioned to Bill, "Did you notice Sam smiling even after Lisa took him on an all-day shopping trip? Looks like Lisa might have found her soul mate."

Chapter Forty-Four

BENDERS VERSUS LIFE

During the wait at Maui's airport and the long flight home, I worried about the restaurant—and about Mike in Germany. How had Moriah fared? Had Alice shown up for her shifts? Had Marcus moved off the property?

When we arrived home, Bill and the kids unloaded the baggage, and I went directly to the restaurant. Myra, who was helping a customer at the cash register, looked drained.

"Hey, Myra, we're back."

"Hi, Annie. You're a sight for sore eyes. Did you have a good time?"

"We did," I said, purposely keeping my voice low and unexcited. "How'd it go here?"

"Everything is all right, but it's been a long week. Alice was only late for work once, but she came in hungover almost every day, and Marcus is still living with her. They're trying to be real sneaky about it, but they must think I'm stupid because I can see his car parked over there. Oh yeah, and your sister Tootie called yesterday, which is when she thought you guys were getting home. She said it's not an emergency, but it's important, and she wants you to call her."

"Thanks, Myra. You did a great job as usual. I'll nip the Alice and Marcus situation in the *butt* today."

The expression on Myra's face told me there was more. I took a deep breath and asked, "Anything else happen?"

She nervously tugged at her apron and said, "Well, there's been a problem—I think there is some missing food, including some steaks, and several half-cases of Coors. My guess is that it's all going down to the little trailer."

"That wouldn't surprise me. I'm sorry you had to babysit Alice and her boyfriend all week. I'll bet they don't realize we took a red-eye flight and we're home this early. They're in for a big surprise."

Coping with exhaustion and a throbbing head, I decided to fortify myself before going head-to-toe with Alice and Marcus—calling Tootie would be easier. I dialed her number and left a quick message. I stayed at the grill long enough to prepare a couple of breakfast specials, giving Myra a much-needed break, and then headed to the small trailer.

"What the hell happened around here?" I grumbled to myself, surveying the area that surrounded the trailer. Marcus's rust bucket, an old Chrysler, was parked at an angle, its bumper pressed against a pine tree. "Did Marcus have a collision with a tree?" I wondered aloud. There were two plastic lawn chairs, a Styrofoam cooler, and dozens of empty Coors cans strewn around. "What a disgusting mess. This is ridiculous."

I knocked loudly, stepped back, and waited for the door to open. *How can two people live in there?* I wondered.

I was about to open the door myself when it cracked open, and Alice peeked through a five-inch opening and spoke in a gravelly voice as innocent as a child. "Oh, hi, Annie. You're back from Hawaii. What's going on?"

My frown should have said it all, but apparently Alice needed it spelled out. "I have to talk to both you and Marcus. Get dressed and come to the restaurant. Now!"

"What's the soup of the day, Miss Ann?" Joe asked.

Without looking up from the grill, I answered, "Vegetable Beef."

"Alice and Marcus just walked in," Joe revealed.

"Joe, can you please tell them to have a seat at the far corner table?"

I approached them, reminding myself not to overreact or accuse them of stealing without proof. My words were forceful yet controlled. "Alice, I'm sorry, but this job didn't work out for you. You'll both need to vacate the property by noon tomorrow." I knew I should shut up, but I couldn't. "And I don't appreciate your disregard for my property. The place looks like a junkyard. And Marcus, you were supposed to be off the property last week."

When Marcus opened his mouth to speak, I cut him off. "This is not a two-way discussion, and I won't say this again. Both of you will be gone by noon tomorrow, and you'd better have the trailer and property cleaned up," I said, handing Alice her final paycheck.

"Tootie's on the phone," Bill reported.

"I'm coming. Myra, can you work the grill for a few minutes?"

"Sure, Annie," Myra said and scooped up the spatula's handle.

"Hi, Tootie. How are you?"

"I'm okay. I didn't want to bother you in Hawaii but want you to know about Dad. When's the last time you saw him?"

"It's probably been about a month since we've seen him at the Ponderosa. Why?"

"Well, he's been on one of his benders for nearly three weeks now. Ed's been checking on him and says he's not looking too good."

"What do you think we should do?" I asked.

"I don't know. Do you have any new ideas?"

Dad's drinking was nothing out of the ordinary. My siblings and I had lived with his binges all our lives, and after forty years, we were hard-pressed to find any new ideas on how to intervene. In the past, we had tried everything from forcing him into a recovery facility to taking away his car keys—only to find out he had extra car keys hidden away. On one desperate occasion, we even supplied the booze so he wouldn't drive drunk. For the past decade, we'd come to the conclusion that it worked best to ignore the binges, check in on him, and let Sherm work out things on his own.

"Ed's been trying to get Dad to taper off the alcohol and start eating. Annie, this one's lasted longer than usual, and Ed seems extra worried. He told me, 'Dad better get himself turned around or he won't pull through this time.'"

"Thanks for the update, Tootie. I'll try to call him right now," I said.

"You can try. But when he's like this, he doesn't usually answer his phone," Tootie reminded me.

"Do you think I should drive to Kuna?" I asked.

"Well…try calling him. Who knows, maybe he'll answer. If not, call me or Ed tomorrow, and we'll figure something out."

After saying our goodbyes, I trudged back to the grill, retrieved the spatula from Myra, scraped its edge several times on the side of the grill and tossed on a pair of beef patties.

In the two days that followed, I stayed in contact with Tootie and Eddie, and on the third day, Ed called with the news that Dad made the turnaround and begun to drink hot tea and nibble on crackers. "His skin is yellow, and he looks worse than I've ever seen him. Honestly, I don't think he can survive many more of these binges," Ed reported. "I took over a dish of baked chicken last night and I'll check tonight to see if it's gone. Hopefully, he didn't feed it to Tuffy."

"I know, Eddie. Would you tell Dad I love him, and I'll see him when I can get away from the restaurant? It's hard to ask Myra to handle the grill by herself when she's still burned out from our vacation. I'll keep trying to call him, I promise. And thanks for taking such good care of Dad."

In late May, Lisa graduated from Garden Valley High with excellent grades and a plan to start her *own* business. When Lisa received her diploma, Bill and I applauded loudly, but it was Sam who whistled and cheered the most, outdoing everyone in the gym. It was Lisa's big night, and she soaked up the moment.

After the ceremony, I hugged my daughter, who had grown into a beautiful woman with all her splendor. "Congratulations, Leecee. I love you and couldn't be prouder of you," I whispered in her ear, not wanting to let her go. "Have fun tonight, and please be safe," I added as an afterthought.

Lisa and Sam were known around school and the community as the couple most likely to get married. Each time I heard these rumblings, I wanted to shout, "Wait, Lisa's just a kid! She won't be eighteen for another couple of months."

As I watched Sam and Lisa leave the gymnasium, hand in hand, tears welled up in my eyes. Bill reached for my arm. "Annie, don't you cry," he said. The parking lot's outdoor floodlight caught a wet sparkle in Bill's eyes too.

Chapter Forty-Five

CATERING

That May, an early summer catering job kick-started the busy season. "Myra, this coming Friday, Woody expects me to cater a meal on the river's sandbar for *a hundred and six* rafters."

"Annie, that's absurd. Is it even possible?"

"It's crazy, but I'm going to go for it. And of course, Woody doesn't want simple, easy hamburgers. He's chosen the barbeque chicken menu. So in addition to all the side dishes, I'll be cooking fifty-three whole chickens."

On Saturday morning, while sitting at my office desk taking notes on the merchandise order, I heard Jodi call out, "Annie, I need your help at the grill." Leaving my desk stacked high with order sheets, scheduling notes for fourteen employees, unpaid bills, state taxes to record, and payroll hours to calculate, I joined Jodi at a grill as cluttered as my desk.

"I knew you had office work to do, Annie, so didn't want to bother you. I really thought I could manage, but I've fallen way behind," Jodi said.

My first reaction was to think—*no kidding!* But understanding the overwhelming feeling of drowning in tickets, I said instead, "I'm sorry, I should've noticed you were swamped and gotten here sooner."

Nearly every slot on the order wheel was taken, and judging by how full the restaurant looked, there were probably many more green slips to come. With every table occupied, Bill began placing chairs in the foyer for the growing line of waiting customers.

"*Holy cow*, where did all these people come from?" I asked Jodi, forcing myself to sound upbeat.

Bill, who couldn't fake cheeriness, high-tailed it past Jodi and me carrying a tub heaped so full of dirty dishes that two plates and several glasses went crashing to the floor with a terribly familiar shattering sound. "Why don't these sonsabitches stay home and eat?" Bill exclaimed.

Jodi and I froze. "Bill is handling the stress very well today, don't you think?" Jodi whispered, giggling nervously as she rolled sausage links on the grill.

I cringed, praying the restaurant commotion was loud enough that it had drowned out Bill's outburst. Peering out into the congested dining area and seeing no one looking in the direction of the kitchen or the EXIT sign, I relaxed a little. And once I had pointed out several enjoyable regulars, Bill calmed his nerves and winked at me.

Click, snapped the order wheel. Joe's eyes were bugging out, and perspiration dotted his forehead as he hung the green ticket and proclaimed, "One Denver omelet, order of biscuits and gravy, a short stack with a side of bacon, not too crisp." Joe wasn't smiling.

Glancing at Jodi, I murmured, "I'll bet Joe wishes he could run to unit 3 about now for a shot of scotch and a shower."

Myra clicked her order slip into the only spot left on the wheel and announced, "Two Spanish omelets with extra salsa, one bowl of oatmeal, number 2, eggs over easy, and an extra plate."

"How big do they think our grill is?" Jodi said, pulling down two more orders. She scrutinized one of the slips and asked, "We don't have dark rye bread, do we? Dark rye toast is on Brenda's order."

"Let me see that!" I snatched the green slip from Jodi's fingers. "What *is* it with that girl? I've told her we don't have dark rye. We didn't have it yesterday, we don't have it today, and we won't have it next week. Who eats dark rye anyway?"

"Here's some burnt whole-wheat toast," said Jodi, laughing. "That'll pass for dark rye, don't you think?"

Jodi and I did our best to keep the mood light through the breakfast, lunch, and dinner rushes. Each meal might've been a new show for the customers but was an exhausting repeat performance for the Ponderosa employees.

"Is this what summer is going to be like?" I asked Bill. He didn't answer me—he had dropped into bed and fallen asleep.

On Monday, Sherm showed up at the restaurant, pale and in need of a haircut. He said he'd been "fighting some sort of flu bug." When I hugged him, his shoulders felt narrow, and his chest boney, and he squeezed out a grin that made his facial features appear even gaunter. *Oh, Dad, how can I help you?* I thought. This question had surfaced many times throughout my life, and I still didn't have an answer. Although I hated my father's binges, they evoked in me more compassion and love than anger.

"Annie, Pacific Wholesale and Frank's Meats are waiting for your order," Bill called.

"I'm coming!" I looked across the table at Dad and said, "I'll be back in a few minutes." When Myra placed a bowl of ham and bean soup in front of Sherm, I could see him thinking, *I didn't order this.* But I knew ham and bean was Dad's favorite, so I took it upon myself to place the order. I couldn't help but laugh at his reaction when Myra followed the soup bowl with a grilled tuna sandwich.

I tackled Frank's Meats first. Quickly but carefully, I went over my order list: "I'll need an extra fifty eight-ounce steaks—oh, just make it an even two hundred. Also sixty chickens—if you could have them cut in half, I'd appreciate it." Jim, an easygoing man with a shiny bald head, clean-shaven face, and a bush of curly chest hair pushing out of the open collar of his white dress shirt, commented, "I sell more sirloin steaks to you than anyone else on my route."

Half smiling, I replied, "Not sure if that makes me happy or want to cry. Oh yes, I need the usual four boxes of extra thick bacon. That should do it for this week, and thanks, Jim. See you next week."

I spun around to face the Pacific Wholesale distributor, Tom, who'd been waiting patiently. "Hi, Tom. This week, I came close to running out of eggs and curly fries, so let's double last week's order. By the way, those mushrooms delivered last Thursday were at the end of their shelf life. Would you write down on my order that I prefer *fresh* produce?" When I noticed him blushing, and his hesitation, due perhaps to an uncertainty about where or maybe *how* to write my special request, I was slightly embarrassed that I might've embarrassed him, so I quickly added, "It's not your fault," and pointed out a good place on his order sheet to write down my request for "fresh."

I turned and walked back to Dad's table, hoping to get in at least a short visit. When it came to handling pressure and responsibility, Dad and I had a lot in common—we could swap stories even in the face of an impending nervous breakdown. Myra cleared the table of an empty bowl and plate and refilled Dad's coffee cup. Dad looked better already. I sat down across the table from a six-foot-tall man who must've weighed no more than a hundred and twenty pounds. "Dad, we worry about you."

On Wednesday, I called Mike's friend, Tim, and asked if he would help haul a BBQ grill to the sandbar on Friday.

"Sure I can. Do you need any help cooking or serving food?" he asked.

"Actually yes, Tim, I could really use your help. Are you available for the entire day?"

"You bet," he answered.

I spent most of Thursday preparing side dishes and precooking the chicken so that it would be easy to just reheat on the barbeque. In case Woody's count was off or a plate got dropped in the sand, I prepared an extra four servings. With Tim's assistance, a veritable feast was on its way.

On Friday morning, Tim helped carry coolers and supplies to the river's edge. Making a flat surface in the sand to set up the BBQ was tricky, but with a little ingenuity, we figured it out. In spite of a scary moment when the front leg of the grill slipped off the jimmy-rigged pile of rocks, the catering event went smoothly.

Back at the Ponderosa after the barbeque was over, we spent another hour toting empty coolers and heavy bags of rubbish. And then, with pleasure, I handed Tim a big, fat check. "Thanks for all your help today. I couldn't have done this without you. Don't be a stranger—we've missed you, and Mike does too. Every time he calls, he asks us to be sure to tell you hi."

"How's Germany treating him?" Tim inquired.

"He says he's fine, but it's obvious he's a little homesick. Well, I'd better get back to the kitchen. Would you be interested in helping again if I get another big job?"

"Of course!"

Having Tim around made me feel like Mike wasn't quite so far away.

Chapter Forty-Six

FIGHTING THE FIRE

The heat of summer persisted, and when the *Idaho Statesman* featured a story about the Ponderosa with photos of people enjoying food on a picturesque deck, it brought many new customers. Simply put, the publicity was fantastic for business but terrible for our sanity. I identified with the Ponderosa's air conditioner, struggling in a near-futile attempt to beat the heat.

Late one Friday afternoon in July, instead of prepping food for the dinner rush—which is what I should've been doing—I sat at my desk, unproductively shuffling invoices and creating a to-do list. Sick of kitchen work and inexplicably preoccupied with thoughts of Sherm, I scratched on the list *Monday, call Dad*, which made me feel a little better. Then suddenly, an uncanny silence descended on the building. The hums, rattles, and buzz from the overhead lights, hood exhaust fan, and air conditioner all stopped simultaneously. It took me a moment to realize the building had lost power.

More out of instinct than anything, I bounced out of my chair and dashed out the side door. Once outside, I blinked several times, trying to make sense of the scene before me. Directly across the highway from the Ponderosa, giant flames licked at the mountainside. I looked north and then south, astonished to see hopscotching flames lining the east side of the highway in both directions. I raced back inside, my heart pounding like a jackhammer, grabbed the phone, and dialed the fire department. "There's a fire! Banks II is on *fire*! Hurry! We need help *fast!*" I screamed into the receiver.

The dispatcher calmly reported, "Help is on the way." When I started to speak again, she cut me off. "Ma'am, the fire covers six miles of roadway. Firefighters should be arriving shortly."

"Please, they have to hurry. It looks like the cabins across the highway are on fire, and people live in those cabins! Oh, I hear a helicopter." I hung up the phone and ran outside to the parking lot, where a group of customers and local residents had congregated. We all gazed up, expecting to spot a helicopter overhead—but only smoke and flames filled the air. Perplexed, I scanned the area, and then it hit me. The noise filling the canyon was not the reverberation of revolving helicopter blades—it was the loud whoosh of fire raging up the mountainside.

In dazed disbelief, the group watched the wall of flames surround five cabins, small and defenseless against nature's destruction. The first to take action was Doug. He ran across the highway and began spraying his home and the surrounding area with a puny garden hose, while the rest of us stood and watched as if paralyzed. Then someone yelled, "C'mon, let's fill buckets!"

Bill scrambled through the restaurant's storage area, dug out some pails, and distributed them. "I knew I washed and hoarded mayo and pickle buckets for a reason," Bill said. Everyone took turns at the two outdoor spigots, filling the five-gallon containers and hauling them across the highway. Though preposterous, our attempts gave us an illusion of being useful—and an outlet for our nerves. I watched Lisa struggle with a bucket that weighed almost as much as she did.

"This is a friggin' wildfire, and we're fighting it with buckets of water," Bill shouted. Perhaps Bill's words triggered a realization, like a hard slap in the face, of the futility of our actions, because people put down their buckets and again assembled in front of the restaurant to gawk at the raging inferno swirling high into the sky. Suddenly, without warning, Bill took off in a sprint down the highway. Instantly, I knew where he was headed and whom he was thinking about...Ned and Thelma, the retired couple who rarely left the trailer house they rented at the south end of Lower Banks.

As I watched Bill disappear into the smoke cloud, it occurred to me I too should check on someone—I'd promised Myra, who had gone to Boise for a dentist appointment, that I'd be available for Ben if he needed anything.

"Has anyone seen Ben?" I screamed.

"He's at the service station with Adelle," Jodi and Lisa answered in chorus.

"Good," I said, letting out a deep breath. "That's the best place for him."

By the time the two helicopters, with dangling water buckets, appeared over the ridge, our customers had scattered like fleas on a dog's belly. Soon the parking lot filled with fire trucks, firefighters, water tankers, and police cars. In the midst of mayhem, an ambulance with doors open waited for patients.

When it became clear that all five cabins had survived the flames, we relaxed a little. But we still did not know if Ned and Thelma were okay, for the thick, black smoke made it difficult to see their trailer. I looked repeatedly south and eventually spotted a figure coming toward us. I recognized Bill, then noticed he held something large and restless in his arms. Thelma and Ned's old hound dog, Homer. Bill, who was carrying Homer as if he weighed no more than a rake, was still choking from the smoke as he tried to rattle off everything at once. Thelma and Ned weren't home, the firemen had the cabin protected, and old Homer, arthritic and confused, needed a friend. As Bill talked and coughed, two paramedics approached him and suggested he go to the ambulance, which he agreed to—but not before making sure old Homer was resting in a quiet place beside our cabin with a bucket of fresh water close by. When Bill got to the ambulance, the paramedics promptly adorned him with an oxygen mask.

Suddenly, a police officer announced with authority, "Anyone who doesn't reside at Banks II must leave immediately—the highway is being closed." I assured the officer that all the restaurant patrons and employees had left.

Deputy Buck joined our group and reported, "The highway's been completely shut down for at least fifteen miles. The only vehicles getting through are for emergency and fire."

"Buck, what the hell started this fire?" asked Bill, who'd just been released by the medical team. After twenty minutes of sucking oxygen, Bill sounded pretty peppy.

We'd never seen Buck exhibit distress in the face of any crisis, but this time his face was rosy, and his voice cracked as he spoke, "At this point all we know is that a motor home was the culprit. We don't have any other specific details…we're still collecting stories, trying to piece it all together. We do know the entire canyon is burning, but the focus is to protect Lower Banks—so you don't need to worry. They're installing a large holding pool between your parking lot and Doug's, and they'll pump water straight up from the river to keep the tank full."

I looked where Buck pointed and saw what looked like an oversize swimming pool being assembled. A collection of fire hoses stretched from the pool, across the highway to the cabins, and up the mountainside behind them.

"That mountain burned a couple of years back—can't believe there is anything left to burn," Bill commented.

"Oh, there's plenty left to burn," Buck answered.

I wanted to continue the conversation, but just then, I saw the paramedics loading Ben into the ambulance. *Dammit anyway, I should've checked on him myself.* I poked my head through the open ambulance doors and saw Ben, his nose and mouth covered by an oxygen mask.

"What happened?"

"Just a little too much smoke, but he should be okay in few minutes," the paramedic reported calmly.

For Ben's sake, I stayed composed. "Hey, Muck Luck, I told your mom I'd take care of you. She's fine, but can't get home because of the road closure, so you'll stay with us. What do you think about sleeping in Mike's bed tonight?"

Ben's blue eyes lit up, and he smiled behind the plastic mask.

The paramedic told me that she'd caught sight of Ben venturing across the highway. I assumed he must've wanted to inspect his mom's cabin. "Ben, I'm sorry you're scared, but promise me you'll stay close to Lisa, Bill, or me, okay?"

Ben shook his head up and down.

"You'll be all right, Ben. Don't forget, stick close."

If Woody happened to be looking out his sloping bedroom's window then, he would've found he had front row seats to watch the two helicopters taking turns dipping their buckets in and out of the river. When a tanker plane appeared to drop red powdery flame retardant over the mountain, and a smaller plane, called a spotter, joined the air space overhead, they created a deafening noise. The entire day was one long déjà vu for the residents of Lower Banks, right down to the firefighters' concern over the aboveground gas tank on Doug's property. Bill counted a dozen firefighters canvassing the gas tank scene, which held our full attention until we overheard a fireman telling Buck, "The fire has crossed the highway one mile south of here." Now that the fire was on the Ponderosa side of the highway, everyone's sense of fortification began to unravel.

Returning to the dark, abandoned restaurant, I picked up the phone to call Sherm. Of course, I shouldn't have been surprised that the phone line was dead. But I was—actually, more frightened than surprised. The realization that we were cut off from the world scared me as much as the fire crossing the highway. Thankfully, just then, Lisa ran inside and distracted me. When she reached for the phone, I gave her the bad news.

"Sam will be worried about me...I mean *us*," Lisa said.

"Don't worry, Lisa, Sam will find a way to get information."

"Bill, go find a big cooler," I said loudly, morphing again into Bossy Priscilla. "I've got an idea."

Bill and I lugged a heavy igloo filled with water bottles and sodas into the crowd and announced, "Everyone, please help yourselves to beverages."

A man holding a clipboard of maps was the first to grab a water bottle. He took a long gulp, reached out to shake my hand, and spoke in a deep voice. "Is this your restaurant?"

"Yes, it is. My name is Ann."

He took one step back and said, "It's nice to meet you, Ann. I'm Ozzie. Thanks for the cooler of drinks. I have a question for you—would you be interested in supplying beverages and possibly feeding a fire crew?"

With the highway closed, the restaurant customers and Woody's rafters were cut off, I'd have plenty of free time. "I can help with whatever you need," I said.

Ozzie explained, "I'll have to get authorization, but that won't be a problem. You'll need to keep records of the food you provide. At the end of services, you can submit the final invoice to the State of Idaho for reimbursement. Would you be able to wait for the payment?"

I nodded yes.

"That's good. A fire crew of approximately fifty will need an early sit-down breakfast. Also, they'll each need two sack lunches with a meat sandwich, fruit, dessert, and a beverage. Are you still interested?" Ozzie asked.

"I can handle that."

A man approached the two of us, seeming anxious to attract Ozzie's attention. Ozzie gave him a quick nod and turned his attention back to me. "Ann, for now just keep the cooler full. We'll talk later."

Then Ozzie turned to the man trying to catch his attention, who said, "The fire jumped the river and is coming around the back side."

Ozzie must have noticed my eyes widening to the size of the fire hose. He kindly explained, "Ann, there is no need for alarm. At this point, the fire is not threatening lives or personal property."

Bill and I stayed busy restocking the cooler and keeping a watchful eye for flames that might jump the river again and sneak up behind the restaurant. "Our new deck can't burn down!" I whined to Bill.

"What? I can't hear you. It sounds like a war zone." The noise nearly drowned out Bill's words.

Soon, Ozzie appeared at my side with a food update. "Day after tomorrow, a crew of forty-eight will need food service—beginning with breakfast at four o'clock. They'll each need the two sack lunches we talked about." He stared at me as if expecting me to have second thoughts about my commitment.

"I'll have the restaurant open at 4:00 a.m. with breakfast ready and their sack lunches too." I calculated that I'd have to get up no later than two o'clock on Sunday morning. Hopefully, by then, the power would be restored. If not, the crew would eat by candlelight and I'd cook with Bill's flashlight hanging over the gas grill.

The sun tucked itself behind the mountain, and the sky darkened, forcing the helicopters and plane to retire for the evening. As darkness descended further, Ben, Lisa, Bill, and I gathered inside the restaurant, where we lit candles and ate ham sandwiches, chips, and bowls of chocolate ice cream.

"This has been a stressful day. Let's hit the hay early," I suggested. "Ben, I bet you'll be able to call your mom in the morning." I winked at him and added, "Mike will be tickled when he hears you stayed in his room."

We locked up the restaurant, marched to the cabin, and ignored the sparks and glow of red flames on the mountain. Each of us petted old Homer, who lay on the doormat.

Within the hour, Ben was tucked into Mike's bed and Lisa asleep up in her bedroom—likely dreaming of Sam. Once in bed, I tried to thread together all my duties for the following day. The first task was to inventory my food supply. Since there wouldn't be deliveries, the crew's meals would be limited to what was on hand. *What if I spoke too soon, telling Ozzie yes without checking provisions?* I wondered.

When Bill crawled in beside me, my anxiety over the fire resumed. "Honey, they wouldn't let us sleep here tonight if our cabin was in danger, would they?"

"I would hope not," Bill said, pulling my back into his chest.

Chapter Forty-Seven

THE HEAT GOES ON

The sound of a helicopter abruptly awakened the cabin's sleeping inhabitants, and the flashing numbers on the digital alarm clock told us the power had been restored.

"Ben, let's go call your mom," Lisa said, and she and Ben were out the door in a flash. Sam, of course, would be second on the call list. In less than five minutes, however, they returned with long faces—the power had been restored, but the phone lines were still down.

The smoke peeled back, and there was enough light for us to make out a swarm of firefighters, like ants on the distant mountainside. A couple of men remained on guard at Doug's gas tank, though there were no flames nearby. The morning sunrise, unaffected by the chaos, pierced the smoke on the horizon and created a kaleidoscope of light.

Doug entered the restaurant holding his empty coffee mug.

"Good morning, Doug. Coffee's ready—help yourself. What's the latest?"

Doug poured himself the first cup from the freshly brewed pot before giving us the update. "The word is, they've set up a fire camp in Gardena and are bringing in crews from all over the state, possibly from other states as well. The hot weather and dry conditions are making the fire move fast, and it's getting worse by the hour. I've heard there are trees, rocks, and burning debris all over the roadway, covering more than fifteen miles, so it doesn't look promising for getting the highway reopened anytime soon."

"Well, at least the power's back on. Have you heard when the phone lines might be?"

"No, I know nothing about the phone, but I do know what started the fire. And honestly, I can't figure out how somebody could be so unaware. The fire is being blamed on an out-of-state couple who was driving a motor home and towing a car with a flat tire. They drove for fifteen miles before noticing the car's wheel rim, sparking against the asphalt and igniting the roadside grass. And by that time, it was too late—the entire canyon was in flames."

Our conversation was interrupted by a loud bang, startling us. We bolted outside to locate its source. Seeing anything through the multitude of people and equipment was difficult, but then another explosion ripped through the sky. The sound, flames, and a spiral of black smoke drew our eyes to the property directly behind Doug's home.

"What the hell is exploding?" Bill yelled. "I thought they had your gas tank guarded."

"It's not my gas tank," Doug said with an undisturbed expression. "It's my junkyard of vehicles."

The explosions were loud and continuous.

"Just how many vehicles are going to blow up?" I asked with an uneasy laugh.

"Oh, probably close to...well..." Doug closed his eyes and tilted his head sideways as he calculated. "Maybe a hundred or so."

For the remainder of the morning, we drank coffee and listened to a late Fourth of July fireworks display. I wondered but didn't ask if Doug's scrap metal yard, now being consumed one old heap after another, was insured.

Once the pyrotechnics dwindled, I got busy assessing the food supply. Without the usual barrage of weekend customers, there would be enough food and beverage to feed the firefighters for at least five days.

Bill helped push two long tables together, as if preparing for our family's Thanksgiving meal. Afterward, I opened ninety-six brown paper sacks, placing them in perfect rows—then like an assembly line worker, went down the row, placing a can of soda, a candy bar, an orange, and a potato chip bag into each sack. The real work, however, would begin at two o'clock the following morning with the preparation of ninety-six turkey sandwiches, which would be stuffed into each bag with a napkin. The image of rugged firemen with smoke smudged faces delicately patting their lips with a paper napkin made me giggle. "Maybe they can save it in their pocket and use it for toilet paper instead," I mused.

Mentally, I went over every detail of tomorrow's massive breakfast of scrambled eggs, sausage links, and biscuits and gravy. Lisa and Bill were essential to my plan, and I dreaded giving them the news that they'd have to report for work at three thirty the following morning.

By late afternoon that day, the phone was working. Lisa called Sam, Ben called his mom, and I called Sherm. Life gradually improved and things were getting back to some resemblance of normality.

That night during dinner, a television news broadcast captured our attention. We were surprised to see that the fire had made national news.

Bill's wide eyes, fixed on the television, seemed to say, *"Wow, this fire is massive!"*

"It's so bizarre that we can only see what's happening right here at Lower Banks, where it seems as though things have simmered down, but in actuality the whole canyon is still burning. But I can't worry about it now. I'm going to bed." I retreated toward the door and then added, "Remember, three thirty sharp."

"Do you need my help?" Ben's voice was big, and his eyes were even bigger.

"That would be nice, Ben. I could use all the help I can get. I'd love it. Thanks a lot, Muck Luck."

By the second day, we had the feeding routine down to a science. As the fire retreated, the helicopters moved farther into the mountains, and the smoke gratefully eased up. The highway remained closed, but thankfully, an emergency vehicle escorted Myra through the canyon. Myra gave us a full report on the nine miles of devastation she had observed during her drive from Gardena. She looked like she had just finished watching a Freddy Krueger horror movie.

"You wouldn't believe how bad it is! There are rocks and burnt trees all over the highway. No wonder they closed the road," Myra said. Her voice sounded high and nervous. She wrapped her thin arms tightly around Ben, who snuggled into his mom.

When the phone rang an hour later, Lisa shot across the room like a pebble from a slingshot. "She thinks it's Sam," I said, laughing.

In a loud and happy voice, she yelled, "Mom, it's Mike!"

Now it was my turn to jump up and fly across the room, moving as fast as a pit-crew at a NASCAR race. "Hi, Mike!" I spoke loudly into the receiver as if it were necessary to shout in order for him to hear me in Germany.

His voice full of alarm, Mike rattled off a string of questions: "Mom, what's going on? Is Dad all right? Is the Ponderosa still there?"

I interrupted him, "Honey, everything is okay, and everybody's fine."

"But I just saw Dad in an ambulance getting oxygen. He was on TV."

"Mike, your Dad's fine—there is no need to worry. Wait, what did you say? Are you joking? You saw the *Ponderosa* and *Dad* on TV *in Germany?*" I couldn't help but giggle, which seemed to relax Mike.

We chatted for the usual five minutes, and then Bill got his turn, reassuring Mike all was well.

We said goodbye to Mike and looked at each other and shook our heads. "Can you believe what Mike said? So happens that he and an Army buddy were watching the Armed Forces Network Channel when he spotted you on the television. Apparently, a news reporter's coverage on a large wildfire burning out of control in Idaho got his attention. Then it showed a helicopter dropping water onto the flames, and when they scanned the area, Mike recognized it. They showed the Ponderosa, the swimming pool full of water, and then the camera went directly to the ambulance and zoomed in on *you*. That's when Mike started screaming at his buddy, 'That's my dad! That's where I live!'"

On the sixth day after the fire started, the bottlenecked high-way reopened, and sightseers arrived in droves. Air quality improved and the parking lots were reclaimed for customer use. Old Homer, reunited with Ned and Thelma, were allowed to move back into their partially blackened trailer house. On Monday, a Boise TV station sent a reporter and camera crew to the restaurant for an interview. For another week and a half, we sustained our routine of early morning breakfasts and preparing ninety-six sack lunches along with our regular restaurant duties. Our normal sixteen-hour workdays had turned into nineteen-hours. At every opportunity, even if only for a few minutes, I'd lie down on the cool concrete floor next to my desk, put my head on a pillow, and curl up like a cat.

Chapter Forty-Eight

WINNERS

Most every morning around ten o'clock, I'd remove four freshly baked pies from the oven, allow them to cool just long enough to make the restaurant smell like a bakery, then shelf them in the walk-in cooler.

Lisa skipped off toward a booth where a well-dressed couple sat. While Lisa wrote on her order slip, Myra kept a watchful eye. I watched the sequence of events unfold and chuckled to myself. I always told the waitresses, "Remember, the higher the customer's tab, the bigger the tip. And I'll raise the stakes even more—the waitress who sells the most desserts during the next pay period will receive a fifty-dollar bonus on her paycheck." I wanted to sell more of my pies, but more importantly, the girls were having a blast.

"We have dutch apple, peach, cherry, strawberry-rhubarb, and apple dumplings," Lisa said to the man. Then with a broad smile, Lisa went to the cooler, dished up a generous slice of strawberry-rhubarb pie, zapped it in the microwave for thirty seconds, and delivered it to the man.

A few minutes passed before the man called out to Lisa, "Waitress!" He motioned for her to come to his table.

Still smiling, Lisa approached his booth. "Is everything all right?" she asked.

"No, it's not. This pie is *way* too sour. Tell your baker it needs more sugar." He rudely emphasized his distaste by screwing up his face in displeasure.

"I'm sorry," Lisa replied. Her smile faded as she continued, "No one has ever complained before. Would you like to try another kind?"

"No. I had my heart set on strawberry-rhubarb, but it's not edible."

"Sir, we don't make the pies here. We buy them, and my mom just bakes them," Lisa added with a slight smile, knowing that smiles, even when a little forced, had a way of softening people.

"I'm telling you, this pie is *awful*." His face flushed as did the face of the woman with him. "Of course, I don't expect to pay for it," the man added vehemently, gesturing to signal he wanted the pie removed from his sight.

"No, sir, you won't be charged," Lisa replied, her face getting as red as those of her two customers. Suppressing tears, she turned away, pie plate in hand.

Lisa came into the kitchen carrying the slice of pie, missing a single bite.

"What's the matter, honey?" I asked, though I'd been eavesdropping from the kitchen and had gotten the gist of their conversation. My voice triggered full-on tears from Lisa, and since Lisa wasn't usually so sensitive to customers' behavior, I inferred the man must've been over-the-top rude. *To heck with the "customer is always right." Who needs these kinds of customers anyway?* I thought and stormed from the kitchen.

Lisa watched from the food service window. She looked slightly embarrassed, not knowing if she was humiliated about being overly sensitive, or embarrassed that her mom had to stick up for her as if she was a little girl. As I stood at the booth, tall and confident, discussing the situation with the man, Lisa's embarrassment was replaced with satisfaction.

When I returned to the kitchen, Lisa gave me a squeeze and said, "Thanks, Mom. What did you say to him?"

"I told him that our pie is not nearly as sour as his disposition."

Lisa giggled and said, "I probably don't get credit for selling that dessert…or do I?"

"Only if you want to pay for it."

Myra, thrilled to see the $50 bonus added to her paycheck, asked, "Can we have another contest?"

"Of course. Let's start one this weekend. It'll be orange juice. Whoever can sell the most orange juice will receive $25."

Myra smiled broadly, knowing she had this one in the bag because her shift covered the breakfast rush.

It was the end of October and our first Tuesday off since the previous spring. Both Bill and I were more than ready for the break that naturally came with the fall and winter months. That day we drove to Boise and were shocked by how the fire had changed the landscape. The devastation continued for miles. Instead of beautiful fall foliage, we gazed at charred ground and burnt remnants.

"Fire is vicious. I remember the stories my dad told me when I was growing up about his experiences as a fireman. Looking at these black ruins makes those stories real," I said.

"It's horrible," Bill replied. "But thankfully, no lives were lost." Bill grinned and added, "The only good part was when you became a spokesperson for the news broadcast."

"Excuse me, what are you trying to tell me? Did I sound really stupid? That's why I didn't want to do the interview in the first place. At least I didn't run and hide, like you," I said, teasing him back.

It took a little over an hour to reach Sherm's mobile home. The plan, as usual, was to take him out to lunch and then on to visit Beth at the bank. We stood on Dad's front porch and knocked for the fifth time. Tuffy barked, but Dad didn't open the door.

"Maybe he's in the bathroom. Let's wait a couple more minutes before panicking," Bill suggested.

Since the sun-bleached curtains covered the living room windows and blocked our view, I stood on tiptoe, trying to peek through the kitchen window, which only had a valance, but it was too high to get a good look.

"Sherm knew we were coming, right?" asked Bill, watching me jump up and down in the flowerbed beneath the kitchen window.

"I might get lucky and catch a glimpse of Dad," I said, then answered his question. "Well...I think so...when we talked two weeks ago, he said, he'd mark it on his calendar. I got the impression he was looking forward to our visit."

Just then, we heard the squeak of the door opening and Sherm's inebriated voice, low and raspy, saying, "Hi. Come on in." Even in the dimly lit room, I could see his ashen complexion and his blood-shot yellow eyes. His shoulders slumped in the limp white T-shirt he wore, and his baggy jeans couldn't hide his skinny legs.

"Dad, are you all right?" *What a stupid question,* I thought. Of course he wasn't. Obviously, he was on another bender.

I tried to stay calm. "Dad, what can Bill and I do for you?"

"Nothin'."

"How about I fix you something to eat? Or maybe go out to lunch?"

"Nah," he mumbled.

"Dad, let us take you to the doctor. Please."

His answer was predictable. "No, I'm all right." He reached for a can of warm beer that sat on his side table, almost knocking it over. Everywhere we looked, beer cans decorated the mobile home's interior.

I filled Tuffy's empty food and water dishes, then bent over the back of his recliner and hugged my dad. He couldn't see the tears in my eyes.

"How's the Ponderosa?" he struggled to ask.

"It's doing well, Dad. You have to come up to see the fire damage through the canyon."

For the next hour, Bill and I sat with Dad, conversing and trying to engage Sherm, but he was either unwilling or unable to communicate. At times, he seemed to struggle to stay awake. He surprised us when he rose from his recliner, hoisted up his sagging pants, and moved to the backdoor to call out for Chester Boy, his cat. Dad's unrecognizable voice made my heartache in pain.

"Dad, you have to start eating. There's some saltines on the counter—can I get them for you?" When Sherm didn't answer, I spoke out, this time purposely changing the subject. "Dad, you can't imagine the devastation the fire caused, you'll be shocked." Again, bending over, I hugged him, kissed the top of his head, and touched his whiskered cheek. "Dad, I love you. And don't forget we'll be back next Tuesday to take you to lunch, any place you choose."

Bill and I slipped out the door and quietly pulled it shut. I stood on the porch and recalled how my heart had pounded with happiness five years earlier when I drove from Oregon, pulled into the driveway, and saw him standing right where I now stood.

Later that evening, I contacted Ed, who assured me he would keep a close eye on Dad.

"Ed, Dad loves when you visit him, he told me so."

Ed was quiet. I could tell talking about Dad bothered him, so I changed the topic. "How's your new place in Gardena coming along?"

"Great!" he answered with renewed energy.

I was proud of Eddie, who seemed to be handling his divorce quite well. He had stayed on track and started to build his new home in Gardena, facing the river just as he'd envisioned. "What an awesome place for you to live," I said.

"Thanks, Annie. I'm pretty happy about it."

"Hey, why don't you drop by the Ponderosa tomorrow night and play a game of pool with Bill? I'll fix you a famous Ponderosa steak and save you a motel room, so you won't have to drive home."

"Wow, that sounds fun. I'll see you guys tomorrow night," Ed said.

Chapter Forty-Nine

HELLOS AND GOODBYES

Ed showed up early the next evening and enjoyed a steak dinner and a cold mug of beer. Once the restaurant closed, Bill joined Ed at the bar, while, with Myra's help, I completed the end-of-the-day kitchen cleanup. I convinced Myra, who had worked a split shift that day, to stay an extra fifteen minutes to have a quick beer. She and I were sitting at our own table, chatting away, when Ben came through the unlocked side door, his round blue eyes searching the room for his mom.

"Mom, what's there to eat?" Ben asked.

Sam and Lisa were playing a game of pool, and the jukebox was taking quarters. Our private party was underway.

"Oh, you must be starved, Ben," I said.

He bashfully gave me his ravenous look.

"Lisa, would you fix Ben something to eat? Sam's probably hungry too."

"Okay, Mom. But can we finish this game first?" Lisa answered gruffly.

I placed two empty glasses on the bar. "Bill, how about a couple of refills for the girls?" Ed sat close by, his legs dangling from the barstool. I asked, "Ed, how about a game of pool when the kids get finished?"

"Sure!" Ed answered and then looked Myra's direction, obviously wondering if she planned to play pool too.

I carried two full mugs back to my table, and Ed followed close behind. Ed and Myra had met each other at our last Thanksgiving celebration, but it wasn't until tonight that they had seemed to really *notice* each other.

Our party continued until Sam, who had to work the next morning, departed, leaving behind a sulky Lisa. Ben happily took me up on my invitation to spend the night in Mike's empty bed.

"Bill, how about you and I retire for the evening?" I said, giving him a beguiling look. "Myra, lock up the door when you and Ed are done for the night," I said. The jukebox continued to boom, and they continued to dance, neither of them noticing as Ben, Bill, and I disappeared.

The following morning Myra wasn't on the schedule to work, but just before eight thirty, she floated in and poured herself a cup of black coffee. Although her glow said it all, she still couldn't wait to fess up. "Ed and I danced and talked until almost four o'clock, and now we even have our *own song*." She blushed. "Ann, you know the song 'When I'm Back on My Feet Again' by Michael Bolton? It's amazing that every single word in the lyrics rings true for *both* Ed and me. It's so perfect, and I can't believe we danced for six hours to the same song." Myra scoped out the restaurant's customers and added, "Ed must be sleeping in." Myra smiled.

Seeing Myra and Ed, two of my favorite people in the universe, connect as a couple warmed me to the core. Myra left the restaurant in a glow of happiness, looking pretty amazing for someone who'd had only four hours of sleep.

Minutes after Myra floated away, her feet hardly touching the floor, in came Gentleman Joe, shuffling his feet like bricks of cement, surrounded by a cloud of despair.

When I saw him, my first thought suggested that he must have gotten bad news about Flora. "Is your mother doing all right?" I asked, concerned.

"Yes, Miss Ann, Mother is doing fairly well."

Still puzzled, I pressed him for information. "How's everything else going, Joe?"

"Well, I've been putting off telling you this, but I've decided to move up to Lewiston," he said sadly.

"Joe, that's wonderful news. I've been expecting you to make this decision for months."

"But I hate to leave you and the Ponderosa. You've been wonderful to me, Miss Ann."

"Joe, you saved the day when Bill got hurt, and you came to help me at the restaurant. You've encouraged me and given me strength more often than you'll ever know. I owe you so much. Don't worry about the Ponderosa. We'll be okay, though we'll miss you, Joe."

"Thanks, Miss Ann. I'm not on the work schedule until next week. I know business is slow, and you just put me there for my sake, so if it's all right with you, I'll head north right away. I want to make sure I get situated before winter hits."

"That'll be fine. You don't need to worry about anything here."

The following morning, Joe had a small suitcase and two boxes neatly arranged in the back seat of his clean but aging Buick—several suits and shirts hung on hangers. I gave him a clinging hug to communicate my deep respect and gratitude. "If you ever need a place to stay or just a getaway, you're always welcome at the Ponderosa. Thank you again for all your hard work. Have a safe trip, give Flora my best, and promise to call once you arrive so I don't worry."

"I promise to call, Miss Ann. Tell Bill and everyone goodbye for me, if you would. I'm sure going to miss this place." Joe's voice quivered. His car door shut, and I watched him pull out of the parking space and waved until his car turned the corner, already missing the smell of his cologne.

Chapter Fifty

YOU STILL HAVE ME

Bill sat reading the daily newspaper in a chair he'd pushed up as close to the woodstove as was physically possible to do without getting burned. Even for a wintertime weekend, business was slow, but he didn't seem to mind the lack of customers. Confident they'd all return in the spring, he turned the page to the weather forecast.

"Well, honey, they say we're supposed to get another four to six inches of snow tonight," he said.

"Oh, so you're telling me we're in for another one of those *harsh* Idaho winters? Gee, what a surprise." I pumped a couple of logs into the woodstove and continued, this time without sarcasm. "But I have to say, it's great to have some peace and quiet around here."

Without looking up from his newspaper, he nodded, picked up his cup, and took a big swallow of coffee, burning his upper lip in the process. He hadn't noticed I'd poured him a hot refill.

I'd just pulled up a chair beside Bill and begun to read the "Daybreak" section, when the door swung open. In danced Sam and Lisa, grinning, holding hands, and swinging arms.

"Hey, you two, what's up?" Bill asked.

"Hi, Dad. Hi, Mom. Sam and I want to talk to you guys."

Blood rushed to my head, but still, I made an effort to appear unruffled. We all moved to the table closest to the warm stove and sat down. Deep down, I'd been expecting this conversation to take place and had been preparing myself for when Lisa would show off her engagement ring. My elbows dug into the tabletop, and I was aware of my own heartbeat pounding in my ears. When Lisa finally spoke, she and Sam were no longer grinning. She rubbed and twisted her hands together, and then in a straightforward manner, said, "Sam and I got jobs in Boise, and we don't want to commute from Lower Banks every day. Sam's mom says we can move in with her."

Bill and I stayed silent, staring blankly at the kids. After an awkward pause, Sam spoke timidly. "We'll each have our own room. Last year, my mom turned her garage into a bedroom for my sister, but now she's moved out."

Lisa quickly added, "I have car payments, you know. So I *have* to have a job!"

I thought, but did not say aloud, *What is she talking about? She's had a job since she was thirteen. That can't be the issue here.*

I was sure Lisa knew her protest was illogical but had decided that the job matter would be her best—most distracting defense. She was eighteen—there was no stopping her, I concluded.

"Congratulations," I said.

"I'm going to be a secretary and Sam will be a heavy equipment mechanic. Isn't that cool?" Lisa said, her feet dancing under the table.

"It is," said Bill.

"We start work Monday morning, so today we're packing."

As the two of them be-bopped out the door in a bubble of happiness and commitment, I fell back into the chair and let out an enormous sigh. "That was a close call!"

Bill interjected, "I know, I can't believe they didn't mention the M-word."

"Yeah, that, or the triple-Gs."

"Triple Gs? What does that mean?" Bill asked, puzzled.

"Grandpa...Grandma...Grandbaby!" Once we stopped laughing, however, I suddenly visualized Lisa's empty room but didn't say anything to Bill. It seemed better not to discuss it.

The following Saturday morning, Ed drove from Gardena to have breakfast. He said he had an update on Sherm, but I knew Myra was the real incentive.

"Annie, this is the best omelet I've ever tasted."

"Thanks," I said. "Isn't it funny how everything tastes so much better when you're in love?"

Ed took a swig of coffee and changed the subject. "Dad started eating again, so that's the good news. The bad news is that the drinking hasn't stopped completely. Its slowed down, but he needs to stop because he looks like death."

"Last week, I told Dad we were taking him out to lunch next Tuesday. Hopefully, he's planning on it. I've tried calling him, but he doesn't answer, which is generally a bad sign."

As we talked, Ed glanced frequently at the wall clock. "Well, I'd better get a move on," he said. "I have an appointment in Boise today at noon. When I stop by Dad's this afternoon, I'll mention you'll see him on Tuesday."

When Ed pulled out his wallet, I stepped forward. "No way, you aren't paying for that omelet. Especially after telling me it's the *best* you've ever had. The only thing I ask is that you tell me how you and Myra are doing."

"She's great!" Ed said, breaking into a grin. His brown eyes sparkled with the same shine I'd noticed in Myra's blue eyes. "I'm going to stop by her cabin and say hi before heading to Boise. We've talked on the phone every night. She's so easy to talk to." Ed hesitated and his cheeks turned pink. "We have our own song, so I guess that means something."

"Oh yeah, I've heard all about your song."

When Bill and I arrived the following Tuesday, Sherm was waiting and ready for our lunch date. We went out for his favorite meal of pork fried rice and egg foo young. His appearance had improved from the previous week, which was a tremendous relief, especially after hearing Ed's description. Years ago, my siblings and I had nicknamed him Miracle Man, and Dad continued to hold true to his nickname.

The winter months dragged on with more clouds than sunshine. But mercifully, we didn't get buried in snow—instead, we had weeks of gloomy rain and huge mud puddles, which froze solid every night. Mike's monthly phone calls from Germany, Sam and Lisa's weekend visits, and Lisa's frequent phone calls, however, were enough to keep depression at bay. At times, adapting to the stillness of the cabin was difficult, but we coped. When Bill sensed my loneliness, he'd embrace me and say something corny like, "Don't be sad, you still have me. And you'll never get rid of me, either." He knew how to get a laugh out of me.

Early spring brought the responsibility of rehiring and gearing up for another summer.

"Myra, do you realize it's impossible to replace Lisa and Gentleman Joe?"

"I sure do." Myra laughed. "We'll need to hire at least four people to fill their shoes."

"Hey, Myra, if we can get a competent work crew organized, do you think Bill and I could take a week off? It wouldn't be until after summer, probably in late fall."

Myra's eyes flashed like crystals. "Of course you can. Where're you going?"

"Are you kidding? There's only one place to go…Hawaii."

Mother's Day quickly approached, which meant it was time to order the prime rib. Myra took on the responsibility of training four new waitresses, and with typical efficiency and skill, in less than a week, she had them wearing aprons and taking orders. As always, Myra was a huge part of the Ponderosa's success.

On the Friday before the big day, Lisa phoned. "Mom, do you need any help on Mother's Day?"

"Sure, I can always use help on the busiest day of the year. It's so nice of you to offer."

"Sam and I'll help out with whatever you need us to do. Sam can do dishes," she added with a giggle.

"I'll have your apron ready, sweetie. It'll be wonderful to have you running around the tables again."

"Okay, Mom, we'll see you early Sunday morning."

When I hung up the phone, I couldn't help but laugh. Who does she think she's kidding? There are a lot of things Lisa might like to forget about waitressing, but the best tip day of the year wasn't one of them.

Mother's Day arrived with a bright blue sky. The exceptionally warm sun encouraged our guests to dine on the deck. Though it was too early to plant flowers in the outdoor pots, the freshly stained wooden planks, fast-moving river, and tall trees provided plenty of color and beauty.

"Good grief, where did all these people come from?" Jodi asked. It had become our favorite thing to say, especially if the timing and tone of voice were just right. We had orders on top of orders, but we'd become pros at keeping our spirits high. We knew the tension was only temporary, and that laughter provided a release far more productive than tears. Lightheartedness in the kitchen was as essential as the serving plates. One of the highlights this Mother's Day happened when Jodi spread mayo on a BLT sandwich so hastily a blob of it flew from the spatula and landed on my chin. Unaware, I continued to work like a maniac, but every time Jodi glanced at me and spotted the mayo, she cracked up.

At the end of the day, Sam and Lisa returned to Boise with a bucketload of tips and a Ponderosa check. They'd been amply rewarded for their long hours and hard work.

"I think this might've been the busiest Mother's Day so far. Are we ready for another summer?" Myra asked. She sat at the counter next to Ben, who sorted his mother's tips into piles as if it were a stash of Halloween candy.

Since we no longer had Tuesdays off, inviting Dad to the restaurant or asking for his help was essential. Dad stopped coming to the Ponderosa, but I didn't take it personally. He had stopped going anywhere, except occasionally to the Kuna grocery store. But I knew my father would likely respond to pleas for help, and after the epic Mother's Day, his Brinks service was indeed necessary. On Monday morning, I dialed Sherm's phone number, praying he would answer.

"Hello."

"Hi, Dad, how's it going?"

"Everything's fine. What's up?"

I explained my need for a bank deposit. "I could really use your help, Dad. I'll buy you a cup of coffee and a meal when you get here."

"How about I come up on Wednesday?" he asked.

"That's perfect. I'm looking forward to your visit. See you then, and thanks, Dad."

Late Wednesday morning, Dad arrived as scheduled. His chipper attitude thrilled me, and I loved listening to his take on the fire's destruction. "Dad, can Jodi fix you some eggs to go with that coffee?" I asked.

"No, I'm all right." His answer to my offer for food was always the same, like a recorded comment.

He and I held a lively thirty-minute debate about how somebody could drive for fifteen miles before realizing they'd started a large part of Idaho on fire. After a cup of coffee and a single refill, though, Dad was restless to get home.

"I appreciate you taking this to Beth," I said, handing off the bulging blue bag printed with cartoon characters. "I won't be getting to Kuna anytime soon, so you'll have to come back. Bring your friend, Fred, with you." I gave him a big hug. "I love you, Dad!" I watched his bitsy Yugo disappear around the bend with its muffler buzzing like a kid's kazoo.

Chapter Fifty-One

GETTING IT RIGHT

It seemed the Ponderosa's newest employee, Arlene, a stocky country girl, would work out just fine. At least I thought so. Long ago, I had learned to be patient about assessing new employees—but not too patient. It was a fine line.

"Arlene's a bit of a fireball, but I like her," I told Myra. "She shows up for work on time and listens well. I'll keep her on the schedule for a couple of weeks, but if you decide she isn't what the Ponderosa needs, just say the word. No use wasting her time or ours if it's not a good fit. Myra, I trust you 100 percent. You know that, right?"

"I sure do, Annie. And I promise to keep a close eye on her."

The special for Saturday night was a sirloin steak served with an Idaho potato, baked until its skin turned slightly crispy. A meal delicious enough it wouldn't end up in the garbage bin. I hated the waste of the uneaten bread crusts, twisted orange slices, lettuce, peas, french fries—all perfectly edible—that were scraped into the garbage every day.

Tonight, the eight-ounce sirloins were charbroiled to perfection, and Jodi and I kicked out orders in record time. I was completely absorbed in my work, when I sensed the presence of somebody standing quietly behind me. It was Arlene, holding a dinner plate with a juicy eight-ouncer.

"What's the matter, Arlene?" I asked.

She smiled at me, so I figured the problem wasn't major. "Well, this customer ordered a *rare* steak, but he says it's not done enough," she explained, handing over the plate with the sight of an untouched steak.

"No problem, I can easily fix that," I said, returning the perfectly done rare steak to the charbroiler.

"The customer must've meant *medium* rare," I said to Jodi, who had her own issues—two chef salads.

I retrieved a clean plate, decorated it with a new sprig of parsley and a spiced apple ring, and added the now medium-rare steak. I hit button number 9, the one assigned to Arlene, and the light on the waitress panel lit up.

"Here you go, Arlene, this should do it. Sometimes customers just aren't aware of how *rare* 'rare' is. You can apologize for me." I spoke softly from my side of the service window, feeling proud of my composure and pleased that I had the time and opportunity for a teaching moment.

A few minutes later, while working on a spaghetti order, I again felt a presence. It was Arlene.

"What's wrong?" I asked, unflustered.

"He said it's still not done enough." She handed back the plate.

"All-righty then, let's try *medium*. Maybe he's never ordered a steak before," I said, my eyebrows beginning to close in on each other. A new plate, a new sprig of parsley, and number 9 lit up once again. I tossed a couple of burger patties onto the broiler. Within minutes, I had company. I didn't have to look up. I recognized the shoes and thick ankles. They were Arlene's.

"What the hell's wrong now?" I asked under my breath.

Arlene stood like a soldier, holding the plate, on the verge of tears. She spoke with a quiver. "I'm sorry, it's still not done enough."

"Come over here, Arlene." I motioned her to a corner of the kitchen, hidden from everyone's view. "This is *not* your fault or mine. Apparently, this guy has never eaten a steak in his life. So we'll try it again, okay?" I gave her arm a squeeze and off she went.

"This is ludicrous," I mumbled to Jodi.

For the fourth time, I put the steak on the broiler, but this time I vehemently topped it with the heavy bacon press. "Now I'm cooking it *perfect*—absolutely no juices will remain!" I was trying to be funny in case it was all a big prank with a hidden camera on me.

"This guy isn't getting a new plate, sprig of parsley, or apple ring," I said to Jodi, right before I hit button number 9. "What do you bet the steak is returned because now it's tougher than shoe leather? And then he'll order a grilled cheese."

Minutes later, Arlene skipped back into the kitchen, wearing a colossal grin. "He loves it! It's perfect!"

"Where do *these* people come from? I can't take this anymore," I said to Jodi. Laughter replaced our stress.

"All I know is we'd better keep Arlene around. She has the four Ps it takes for the job," Jodi said.

"Four Ps?" I asked.

"Patience, persistence, perseverance, and pluck!"

I laughed, threw two more steaks onto the broiler, and gave the order of chicken strips in the fry basket a vigorous shake. Hot oil splattered onto my forearm. "Yep, Jodi, this is going to be a loooong and interesting summer."

Wednesday was inventory day, and Nick, the manager of the main food distributor for the Ponderosa, carefully wrote down my requests. He handed over the completed order form, and as I checked it over, I could feel his stare. I had liked Nick from the start—when he had patiently talked me through my very first order, years earlier. I remember his advice on my efforts to select just the right dishware and glassware. "If you serve a good size portion on this eleven-inch plate, you'll have a full plate and the customer will be impressed with your generosity. However, if you serve that same portion on a twelve-inch plate, that same customer might feel he's been gypped," Nick said.

Deciding that his serious expression reflected his high degree of knowledge, I ordered nine dozen eleven-inch dinner plates—which turned out not to be enough.

His large company had many sales reps, so Nick only stopped by a couple of times per year. I was always happy to see him. He and

I hadn't changed much over the years, other than he'd gained the twenty pounds I had lost. Today, though, when I handed the clipboard back to Nick, I could tell he wanted to say something.

"What's up, Nick?"

"Ann, I have a confession to make. When you gave me your first order—when was that—about five years ago? Anyway, I was shocked when you mentioned you'd never operated a restaurant before. And I had a hard time keeping a straight face when you ordered fry oil and asked me, 'how does one get the oil out of the deep fryer to clean it?' I liked you instantly but didn't think your business would last more than six months. Back at the office, we talked about placing wagers on whether or not you'd make it, but everyone wanted to bet the same way. I'm happy to say we're all walking around with egg on our faces now."

Nick's words caught me off guard, but after a few moments, I smiled at him and said, "Oh, really? Well, every summer, the jury is out on whether or not we'll make it, but it's not because of lack of business."

"That's evident by the size of your orders," Nick replied.

Nick went on to tell me about an article he'd filed away that discussed the factors and chances of a restaurant's success. He promised to look for it and bring it the next time he came.

Four days later, I was surprised when an envelope from Nick arrived in the mail. Enclosed were two sheets of paper. The first sheet was a copy of the article he'd mentioned, and the data I found there amazed me: "During the first year, a restaurant has a 90–95 percent chance of failure." The second piece of paper was even better, a page of motivational quotes with a notation in Nick's handwriting that read, "Way to Go!" I read the quote, highlighted in yellow, "Winning is about heart, not just legs. It's got to be in the right place.—Lance Armstrong." *Nick is a good person,* I thought.

I could hardly wait to share this information with Bill but wanted to wait for a special moment, not unlike the two times I had told him I was pregnant. After locking up and switching off the overhead lights for the seventeen hundredth time, I moved toward the bar area where Bill was gathering empty beer mugs and wiping down the bar top.

"Would you please pour us a couple of brewskis and come over and sit down with me?" I asked.

From the grin on Bill's face and the sparkle in his eyes, it appeared he hoped I wanted to get frisky at ten forty-five on a Monday night—at the bar.

I quickly steered him away from that interpretation. "I have some really neat information to share."

Bill clanked two mugs down on the table, and beer splashed out of one.

"This one is yours." I laughed and pushed the mug with the least amount of liquid over to his side of the table. I brought out the article from Nick, and read it verbatim, and then showed him the Lance Armstrong quote.

Bill sat quietly for a few moments, then raised his mug in a toast, "Baby, we did it. *We got it right.*"

"Nick said they all talked about placing bets on whether or not we'd make it. Guess we showed them. And we also showed Mike and Lisa that with hard work it's possible to turn a dilapidated building with zero clientele into a prosperous business. We had no idea what we were doing...we just figured it out as we went along. It wasn't pretty at times and still isn't. You probably aren't even aware of how many times I've wanted to give up, but something always happens that makes me realize the difficult times are temporary. Also, as horrible as it was, wouldn't you agree that your and Ed's accident was a turning point for us? I really thought you were going to die and, not having your help around here, forced me to acknowledge I couldn't do it alone. We couldn't have done it without Lisa and Mike, and all the other amazing people, especially Myra, who've helped us along the way."

Bill nodded in agreement. "Annie, I think it's the consistent quality of your food. Everybody knows they'll get a great meal every single time."

"Thanks, honey, that means a lot. The food is good, but be honest here, it's those five-star bathrooms that bring people in."

"You're right. We do have bathroom clientele that *never* order anything but keep coming back." Bill chuckled and rolled his eyes.

"And, Annie, I know you hate to admit it, but the harsh Idaho winters are our best friend. It gives us a break just when we're about to break."

Three beers later, we locked up the side door, strolled to our humble, quiet cabin on the roaring river, and dropped into bed. "Bill, I sure do love you."

"I love you too, sweetheart." Bill's arm moved under my head.

I reached over and flicked off the bedside lamp, sending a cloud of dust particles into flight.

Chapter Fifty-Two

MIRACLE MAN

From out of nowhere, a cheery voice sounded from across the room. "Ann, you'd better get your flight reservations made," Myra exclaimed.

Myra's command shifted me into high gear. Soon I was on the phone with a travel agent, scratching down some notes, and handing Myra a proposed itinerary. Bill and I would be leaving for Hawaii in late October.

"How does this look? Will it work for you?" I asked Myra.

"It looks good to me. Go show Bill."

She's as excited about this as I am. How I love this girl, I thought and raced off to find Bill.

Pulling the trigger to finalize our Hawaii plans put me in a good mood. While I prepared food for the last float trip of the season—a meager twenty-nine people—and daydreaming of Hawaii, Bill interrupted my salad making.

"Annie, Ed's on the phone," Bill said. He stepped in close and whispered, "I think something's happened. He doesn't sound good."

I wiped my hands and picked up the receiver. "Hi, Eddie," I said cheerily.

"Hi, Annie," Ed said in a deep voice that didn't sound anything like Ed. Ed was crying, I realized. My breath caught in my throat, and the receiver suddenly felt heavy in my hand. After what seemed like five minutes, Ed spoke again, "Annie, I'm over at Dad's house. I don't know how to tell you this, but when I got here, he didn't answer the door, so I let myself in. Annie, he's in his recliner with Tuffy on his lap. He's gray and has no pulse. Dad's not breathing. I called 911 first and then called you. I didn't know what else to do.

"Oh no! Oh my God, Eddie!"

Bill, standing close, heard my words. "Bill, Dad died," I cried.

Both Ed and I sobbed for what seemed like an hour, though it was likely only a few minutes. "Bill and I are leaving right now. Call Kat or Tootie. They'll call the others. Someone needs to be with you right now."

"Okay, Annie," Ed said, his voice still unrecognizable.

I hung up the phone. "I've been preparing myself for this day, but I'm not ready," I bawled. "Bill, how can my dad be dead? How can that be?"

Myra, who'd also come close when she heard my cries, embraced me tightly. "I'll take care of the restaurant. You guys leave right now and stay as long as you need to. Will you tell Ed I'm here for him?"

Sherm's seven children, with their spouses, and his grandchildren gathered quickly. We cried, laughed, and talked about all the ways in which Sherm had been a great father—and the ways in which Sherm had fallen short weren't discussed. Many decisions had to be made; the most immediate of which was what to do with Tuffy. After a difficult debate, we concluded the most humane option was to put Tuffy, who was one hundred and twelve in human years, to sleep. When Sherm's body had been removed from his trailer, Tuffy grew confused, refused to eat or drink, and wouldn't let anyone touch her. Clearly she wouldn't survive long without Sherm. After a unanimous vote, we concluded that a container holding Tuffy's ashes would be placed appropriately on Dad's lap.

At the vigil, held at a Boise funeral home, the first thing I noticed when approaching the open casket was Dad's mouth. His thin lips were relaxed and appeared to be smiling.

"Have you ever heard of anyone smiling in a casket? Leave it to Sherm," Tootie said, making everyone crack a smile. But I couldn't resist expanding on Tootie's comment and let out a soft "Tuffy yip," knowing that she shared the casket. Humor was a way of coping.

In my heart, I knew Dad was all right, and that I wouldn't need to worry about him any longer. He was with Mom and Johnny now. For the longest time, my family and I stood next to Dad's casket, holding hands and wiping away tears. When I leaned over and kissed my dad's cheek, I whispered, "I love you. Thanks for being my dad." And then, for the last time, as best I could, I gave him a hug.

Though I missed my dad and would've given anything for one more hug or to have him walk into the Ponderosa for a visit and a cup of coffee, I surrendered him to heaven to be with Mom and Teeto—the only way to heal the broken pieces of my heart.

But then, a little over a month after Sherm's funeral, Bill loaded luggage into the car, and my grief lightened a speck. It was time for our Hawaii vacation.

"Don't worry about anything. You guys go have a great time!" Myra said.

"We cannot thank you enough, Myra," Bill said.

"You guys need time away from here. Now get going, or you'll miss your flight."

Myra was right on as usual—Kona, Hawaii, was exactly the salve I needed for my broken heart. For a week, we relaxed and enjoyed perfect weather. Bill's all-day fishing trip yielded a good-sized marlin, which thrilled him to no end. As anticipated, the week flew by too fast, and before we knew it, we were sitting in the open-air terminal at the Kona airport waiting for our return flight to Idaho.

"We should just move here," I said to Bill.

"I know," Bill answered quickly.

"Seriously, someday we should!"

"Annie, I know you're serious. So am I."

"How could we ever pull it off?" I asked.

"Who the hell knows, but it doesn't hurt to dream," Bill replied.

Twelve hours later, Bill stopped the car in front of our cabin, turned off the ignition, and commented, "It feels kind of nice to be home."

"I guess so, but I like the climate much better in Hawaii."

Bill offered to unload the suitcases, knowing I liked going directly to the restaurant. It was late in the day, almost time to close the restaurant, when I called to Myra and waved to her from across the room. She looked up instantly, and an expression of relief washed across her face. She explained how busy the restaurant had been. "There must've been activities going on in Garden Valley or McCall because it was hectic all week long."

"I'm sorry. Who would've guessed October would be so busy?" I said.

Strangely, Myra started laughing. "Well, something good came from it. You won't believe who helped me out all week."

I looked at her puzzled and asked, "Who?"

With her curly hair framing her beaming face. "Ed!" she said. "He cooked, waited tables, did dishes, and made salad. We've had the best time together. I've never laughed so much in my entire life."

There wasn't a question about it—Myra was in love. I grabbed her, squeezed her for the second time, and asked, "So is the jukebox's A-10 button, 'When I'm Back on My Feet Again,' all worn-out?" I thought about her last statement, *I've never laughed so much in my entire life,'* and it sparked doubt—knowing that Moriah never stopped laughing.

Myra blushed, flashed a grin, and changed the subject. "There is more news. Let's go sit down."

"Oh no, now what?" I asked. "Should I be scared, or is this good news?"

"I'm not sure," Myra said as she settled into a comfortable position and began her story. "Somebody stopped by on Thursday and inquired about the restaurant, right after Art Linkletter came in for a sandwich."

Ignoring the presence of a famous television celebrity at my little ole café, I stared at her, wondering what she meant. "Myra, tell me about the people who stopped by!"

Myra continued, "Apparently, they're interested in buying the Ponderosa and said they'd come back."

"Seriously?"

When Bill came in, Myra waved him over and repeated what she'd told me. After hearing the story for the second time, I looked over at Bill. "Wow, I can't believe this—a whole lot can happen in a short week."

The following day, the only thing we could think about was Myra's news. Could there really be a prospective buyer for the Ponderosa? We'd never contemplated selling the place, the Ponderosa, was not on our radar.

Early the next afternoon, a group of three people entered the restaurant. Myra, in the kitchen with me, spotted them and said, "Look! Annie, it's them! That's the couple who stopped by. I'll go wait on them, and tell them you're back."

Myra took their order and gestured for Bill and me to come over. The couple introduced themselves as Archie and Juanita Paulkner. The third person held out her hand. "Hello, I'm Betty Rowe from Gem State Realty. It's a pleasure to meet you both."

The extremely friendly middle-aged couple told us about a restaurant they had owned in California and had sold six months earlier.

After finishing lunch, they asked, "Mind if we take a look around?"

"Go right ahead," replied Bill.

While Bill and I stayed in the kitchen, striving to appear busy and disinterested, they strolled about the restaurant and bar area, scrutinizing everything. Archie repeatedly returned to the window and stared out, seduced by the river.

"What's happening here?" I whispered to Bill.

"I think they're excited about buying the Ponderosa."

"Are we selling?"

When the tour ended, our three visitors took seats at the counter. Bill and I came from the kitchen and casually stood a few feet away. Bill offered them coffee.

"Oh, no thanks," all three replied.

"We absolutely love your restaurant—we've been looking for something like this for a long time," Archie said, smiling like he had just discovered his own personal paradise.

I thought to myself, *Wow, these buyers aren't much for playing it cool.* I had to slow them down. "Well, this is definitely something we need to talk about because honestly we haven't discussed selling the Ponderosa. However, if you'd like to make an offer, we'll consider it." I tried to keep the excitement out of my voice.

Juanita, Archie, and Betty reached out to shake our hands, not even trying to keep a lid on their enthusiasm. "We'll get back to you soon," Archie promised.

Both Bill and I spent the rest of the day obsessing about what had occurred, trying to decide if the potential sale was a pipe dream or a budding reality. "This is almost unbelievable. How can they make an offer without an appraisal or an examination of our books to see what the income is?" I asked.

"I don't know, and that's a darn good question. I guess they're judging it from the appearance alone."

"I bet their offer comes in far under what this place is worth. They probably think that they can pick it up for a song," I said, moving my head from side to side.

Two days later, Betty Rowe hand-delivered a written offer. "Mr. and Mrs. Paulkner are anxious for your reply and would like to hear something by tomorrow," Betty said. When Betty walked to the window and looked out at the river, we watched her well-dressed figure, hoping she wouldn't sit down for a meal. Thankfully, she was gone in minutes.

As soon as the door shut behind Betty, Bill and I quickly moved into a booth, dying of curiosity. Gently but briskly, we opened the white business envelope to find a straightforward offer with no contingencies. Astounded by their generous offer, I spoke out. "Bill, maybe Sherm is telling us to move on. We did what we came to do—rebuild the Ponderosa into a thriving business. And without Dad, how can we make our bank deposits? There are eager buyers who want to take over *yesterday*. Now is our time to sell. Hawaii, here we come!"

I jumped up, did a little victory dance, and continued, "The kids are gone, the kitchen is too small for the amount of business we get, and I'm sick and tired of watching the mountainside burn up every other year."

"I hear you, Annie! I'm ready too. I guess we should wait a little while before calling Betty."

An hour later, I phoned the Realtor. She gave me the details of her client's prior restaurant experience and added, "The Paulkners are preapproved for the loan and would love to be in the restaurant by the end of the year."

In my most professional tone, I said, "Tell them we accept their offer."

"Wonderful. I'll be at the Ponderosa tomorrow morning at nine o'clock to pick up the signed papers."

Chapter Fifty-Three

THE TRAIL'S END

The months that followed were not without some discontent. With our time at the Ponderosa dwindling fast, I said to Bill, "It'll be hard to leave. We've made so many friends and memories over the past years. Plus we've put our hearts and souls into this business. I can't believe I'm saying this, but I'll even miss all the impossible-to-please customers. They kept us entertained."

But every time I grew weepy, Bill interrupted, "Let somebody else make memories—we're headed to the beach."

"But we'll miss our traditional Thanksgiving Day with the family and John Vander. Oh, I don't even want to think about saying goodbye to him!"

When we revealed the news to a few favorite customers, they were thrilled for us. They'd become our friends...friends we'd likely never see again. Although Bill blustered on about leaving without mourning, I knew it was just a cover for the same emotions I was experiencing. The thought of walking away from the Ponderosa made us sad but knew we'd made the right decision.

As expected, it was most difficult to say goodbye to our employees. On my last day at the grill, standing beside Jodi, my words sliced through my emotions. "Thanks for every moment of your help and for the fun we've shared. You mentioned before you would like to go to college—maybe this is a good time to rethink that. You and your daughter deserve a great life."

Myra was noticeably worried about the new Ponderosa owners, fearing the unknown, and I wanted to promise her everything would turn out okay, but of course, I couldn't. Saying goodbye to Myra was impossible, so I didn't. The strong intuition that someday Myra and I would be related gave me little reason to say goodbye—we'd always be connected. She had become my sister the day she walked into the Ponderosa and blessed my life with her presence.

Doug and Adelle, the best neighbors anyone could ask for, were happy for us. "We're disappointed that you're moving to paradise and leaving us behind," Doug said, grinning. He shoved his hands into his pockets, making eye contact with both of us. "Congratulations, you guys."

Although Lisa loved her life in Boise with Sam, she was troubled that our move would take us so far away.

"You can come with us," I teased.

"Mom, you know I'd never leave Sam."

"Of course I know that, but never forget you will always have me as your mom." I would miss my sweet Lisa with every fiber of my being, but because she hadn't lived at home for almost a year, I'd grown accustomed to not having her near me. She and Sam had their jobs and their lives together, and that comforted me. I smiled, thinking back on their separate bedroom promise and wondered how they were doing with that.

When Mike heard the Ponderosa news, his joy was obvious— but when Hawaii entered the conversation, it turned to elation. "So in a year, when I'm discharged from the Army, you and Dad will be living in Kona, right?"

"That's the plan."

"Then I'll ship my belongings to Kona, and see you there," he said, planning ahead. "But don't move to Hawaii until after my leave in January! I'd like to see Banks II one more time."

I detected a slight sadness in Mike's tone and realized he had memories by the thousands at Lower Banks. Mike's attachment affirmed for me that I had made the right decision when I had disrupted his and Lisa's lives, separating them from their early childhood friendships in Rainier.

"Mike, our last day at the restaurant will be December 15. We have a short-term rental in Boise—can't wait to see you in January."

When Ol' Blue, overloaded with personal effects, pulled out of the Ponderosa parking lot, Bill hollered out the window, "Aloha! Color us gone!"

Driving away, I glanced back over my shoulder, and my eyes fixed on the Ponderosa. The reader board retreated behind us, but the block letters were still large enough for me to read: *8 oz. SIRLOIN STEAK SPECIAL $6.95.* I blinked back tears, closed my eyes, and said to myself, *"We did it, Dad, with your help!"*

Then we were around the first bend, and it was all behind us— the three-unit motel, the cabin where we'd slept, Woody's Rafting with the scary backroom, Alice's *im*-mobile home, the four-tier deck overlooking *KYBR*, and our wonderful friends and hardworking employees. And my sweet Myra was in a category all to herself. I still hadn't told her goodbye and never planned to.

"Now what do you want to do, Annie?" Bill asked lightheartedly.

"Relax and sleep!" We drove the next couple miles in silence. No Ponderosa, no teenagers, and no Sherm or Tuffy—what were we going to do? No sixteen-hour days, no dirty motel rooms, no catering, and no more chef salads. Suddenly, I started singing like Johnny Paycheck: *"Take this job and shove it. I ain't working here no more."*

Bill laughed so hard he almost drove into the river until I yelled at him to watch the road. "One thing I'm not going to miss is this damn highway!"

A motel room with a tiny kitchen, featuring a two-burner electric range, was our home for the next month and a half. It took time to get used to the sight of the measly two dinner plates and two coffee cups in the cupboard. The twenty pounds I'd lost over the last five years began to return.

In January, Mike disembarked the airplane looking content and healthy, revealing that army life was conducive in preparation for the next door to open in his life. Mike's mantle of maturity filled me with pride.

"Let's drive up to Lower Banks today," Mike suggested.

"Yeah, good idea. We'll have lunch at the Ponderosa and then go say hello to Doug and Adelle," Bill added.

Mike, Bill, and I slid into the booth overlooking the river. "So this is what it feels like to be a customer here," I said.

Archie moved toward us, holding an order book and pen. "May I take your order?" It had been five years since Lisa had spoken those exact words for her very first time on rehearsal night. Although Archie's simple words jarred me, they also ignited a new realism on how fast time moves us along. In just days, Mike would return to Germany, whereas, Bill and I would board a plane to Kona—the start of a different unforgettable.

We ordered coffee and the meatloaf special.

"I'm surprised Archie and Juanita hired an extra cook. Don't they realize it's winter and money doesn't flow in very fast?" worried Bill.

"Shhh, it's *their* baby now," I whispered.

Archie walked over to refill our coffee cups. "Did you hear about what happened last week?" he asked.

"No, we didn't," Bill answered politely.

Archie's wild eyes said it all. Of course he had a hummer of a story to tell us—it was life at Banks II. I hoped Archie didn't notice Mike kicking me under the table, Bill nudging my knee, or me pinching Bill's leg—probably a little harder and more painfully than needed to make my point.

Archie, his eyes as big as our coffee cups, excitedly pulled up a chair, sat down, and said, "You aren't going to believe this."

The End
(Aloha)

All changes, even the most longed for, have their melancholy;
for what we leave behind us is a part of ourselves.
We must die to one life before we can enter another.

—Anatole France

Epilogue

A SLOW VEHICLE TURNOUT

In July 1992, the cottonwood fire in West Central Idaho was started when sparks flew from the metal wheel rim of a car being pulled behind a motor home. The fire ravaged the forest covering the steep terrain of Lower Banks, and because the land wasn't replanted, soil-stabilizing roots had rotted away. Triggered by an extraordinarily wet Idaho winter, combined with warm temperatures, causing heavy snowmelt, on January 1, 1997, mud, truck-sized boulders, and old-growth timber tumbled down the hillside and into the canyon. Most of the homes in the small community of Lower Banks were damaged, making them unsafe, and the Trail's End (formerly the Ponderosa) Restaurant and Motel was buried in mud. With the danger of another slide, the community was condemned, and Lower Banks residents were ordered to vacate their property forever. This wide spot in the road is now a slow vehicle turnout and a part of history.

Author's Notes

Packing only our summer wardrobe, sunglasses, and one-way tickets, Bill and I moved to Kona, Hawaii, in early 1993. We hung loose, enjoyed the climate, and marveled at the warm Pacific Ocean for five years before returning to Oregon. After forty-eight years of marriage, we are now retired and live on a seven-acre farm. No surprise that we vacation every winter in Kona.

Mike joined us in Hawaii after being honorably discharged from the military in late 1993. Presently, Mike resides in Idaho with his son and daughter. He is a shop foreman, a driller, and a mechanic for a drilling company.

Lisa and Sam were married in 1994. They live on ten forested acres in a small rural community in Oregon with their two sons. Recently they purchased a shut-down/failed café in their neighborhood and are working long hours.

Ed and Myra also married in 1994. They live on the Main Payette River, in a home with a view. Ben is a senior chief in the US Coast Guard, stationed in Chatham, Massachusetts.

Flora passed away at the age of ninety-eight. Gentleman Joe phoned us a couple of times a year until he passed away at the age of seventy-eight. He never left Lewiston, Idaho.

My dear friend John Vander passed away at the age of fifty-eight. John didn't expect anything but appreciated everything. There's a quote that says, "Life is not a journey to the grave with the intention of arriving safely in a pretty and well-preserved body. Skid in broadside, thoroughly worn-out, totally used up, and loudly proclaiming, '*Wow!* What a ride!'" John Vander, loved by many, did exactly that.

All my siblings reside in Idaho, enduring the extreme weather and loving every moment. We visit often and treasure each other's stories.

About the Author

Unheralded author Anna Kirkpatrick was born in Portland, Oregon, and raised in Boise, Idaho, with her four brothers and three sisters. After graduating from Boise High in 1969, she attended Boise State University until her marriage to William Kirkpatrick in 1971. The following year, they moved to Oregon. At the age of twenty-four, Anna (along with her husband) owned and operated her first business, the Lindberg Grocery and Gas Station in Rainier, Oregon. Twelve years passed, and Anna relocated back to Idaho and became a successful restaurant and motel owner of the defunct Ponderosa Restaurant and Motel at Lower Banks, Idaho, about forty miles north of Boise on the unforgiving Highway 55.

While navigating through her adulthood as an entrepreneur and hopscotching from Idaho and Oregon, Anna raised a son and daughter and now dotes over her four grandchildren. She recently helped her daughter and son-in-law open a café in the rural community of Colton, Oregon, approximately thirty-five miles southeast of Portland, Oregon.

Over the years, Anna found pleasure in writing poems about family and enduring times. Anna is currently retired and residing in Beavercreek, Oregon (a ten-minute drive from the Colton Café), during the summer season and then soaking up the warmth of Kona, Hawaii, through the winter months. Anna continues to pursue her passion—writing about her real-life experiences.